Revolution and the 20th-Century Novel

Paul N. Siegel

MONAD PRESS, NEW YORK

DISTRIBUTED BY PATHFINDER PRESS, NEW YORK

For Christie Portia, Juliet, Jenny, and the Future

ACKNOWLEDGEMENTS

Portions of this book were first published in *Clio: An Interdisciplinary Journal of Literature, History and the Philosophy of History, Confrontation, International Socialist Review, Modern Fiction Studies, PMLA,* and *Twentieth Century Literature.* I thank the editors of these periodicals for permission to reprint them.

First edition 1979
Copyright © 1979 by the Anchor Foundation, Inc.
All rights reserved

Library of Congress Catalog Card Number 79-89424
ISBN: 0-913460-71-0 (cloth); 0-913460-72-9 (paper)
Manufactured in the United States of America

Published by Monad Press for the Anchor Foundation
Distributed by Pathfinder Press
410 West Street, New York, NY 10014

CONTENTS

III. Post-War Disillusionment with Revolution in the West

IV. Russian Reexamination of Revolution in the "Thaw"

Preface

The purpose of this book is to study in depth ten twentieth-century novels concerned with the concept of social revolution, analyzing them as works of art, probing their political ideas, examining their relation to their time and place, and observing their connections with each other. These novels—Arnold Bennett's *The Old Wives' Tale*, Jack London's *The Iron Heel*, André Malraux's *Man's Fate*, Ignazio Silone's *Fontamara*, Richard Wright's *Native Son*, Arthur Koestler's *Darkness at Noon*, Norman Mailer's *The Naked and the Dead*, George Orwell's *1984*, Boris Pasternak's *Doctor Zhivago*, and Alexander Solzhenitsyn's *Cancer Ward*—range in their attitudes towards the struggle for social revolution from wholehearted commitment to outright hostility.

Of all the forms of literature, the novel is best equipped for dealing with the idea of revolution. In its historical origin bound up, as Ian Watt and others have shown,[1] with the rise of the bourgeoisie and acting as a response to aristocratic romance, it has continued since the time of Cervantes to be a means of attack on archaic modes of thought. It has also been distinguished, especially since the French revolution, which Steven Marcus regards as the event that developed the nineteenth-century novel's distinctive subject,[2] by its concern with the relation between the individual and the social structure. The novel, says Lionel Trilling, differs "from all other highly developed literary forms" in that

it deals with reality and illusion in relation to questions of social class. . . . To these characteristics of the novel . . . we must add the unabashed interest in ideas. . . . Every great novel . . . is . . . a romance of culture. By culture we must mean not merely the general social condition to which the novel responds but also a particular congeries of formulated ideas. The great novels, far more often than we remember, deal explicitly with developed ideas, and although they vary greatly in

5

the degree of their explicitness they tend to be more explicit rather than less.[3]

Trilling was urging a return to the tradition of the novel, from which much of serious fiction had departed. The general trend since he wrote his essay has, however, been further in the direction which he deplored. Since World War II, as Gerald Graff points out, there has been in the novel an even greater increase in the "subjectivization and privatization of human experience." The fundamental cause for this phenomenon he finds to be "the obsolescence of the world-view of liberal bourgeois individualism, with its optimistic belief in progress and the rational intelligibility of experience,"[4] an obsolescence that had produced the fragmentation of culture which T. S. Eliot speculated in 1923 made realism no longer a suitable mode for fiction.

The ten novels I shall study do not conform to these developments in the novel, which Steven Marcus has summarized as "the movement toward poetic form, the inability to deal with society, the poverty of ideas."[5] They have instead an "unabashed interest" in the idea of revolution, although in the case of *The Old Wives' Tale* this has not been generally realized. It is an interesting fact, even though it does not mean all of them are outstanding as novels—I shall argue that *Darkness at Noon* and *Doctor Zhivago* are inferior works and that *Man's Fate*, despite some powerful pages, is overrated—that the eight of them published since World War I received both high critical acclaim and a mass readership (although I strongly suspect *Doctor Zhivago* was more widely bought than read), resembling in this respect such nineteenth-century novels as those of Scott and Dickens.

The Old Wives' Tale and *The Iron Heel*, written in the first decade of the century, furnish a kind of prologue to the subsequent novels. *The Old Wives' Tale* is deeply influenced by Herbert Spencer's theory of social evolution, from which the Webbs derived their theory of "the inevitability of gradualness," to which Bennett was also indebted. His conscious view of history, expressed in his attitude toward the Paris Commune, is, however, at variance with his implicit showing of "revolution" as part of evolution in the history of English commerce and in the development of character of his two heroines. *The Iron Heel*, the product of early American Marxism, contrasts with *The Old Wives' Tale* in that it is the conscious expression of the idea of revolutionary socialism as opposed to that of evolutionary socialism.

Man's Fate, Fontamara, and *Native Son* were written by active partisans of the revolution during the period of world capitalist crisis of the 1930s. Malraux was a prominent fellow traveler of the French Communist Party, Silone a leader of the Italian Communist Party, and Wright an outstanding cultural figure in the American Communist Party, but each had the independence of spirit needed for artistic integrity. Each saw the tremendous difficulties of revolution but also its necessity.

Darkness at Noon, The Naked and the Dead, and *1984* are the products of Western postwar disillusionment and reaction against the idea of revolution. The first was the work of a Hungarian ex-Stalinist rejecting Marxism; the second was the work of a young self-avowed American Marxist who had absorbed his Marxism in his prewar college days and did not realize that what he called a novel full of hope was permeated by pessimism about the possibility of revolution; the third was the work of a British independent socialist whose nightmare vision of the future partly swamped his continuing faith in the "proles," the working class.

Doctor Zhivago and *Cancer Ward* are the products of the Russian "thaw," when there began a reexamination of the revolution and its course in the Soviet Union. The author of each hoped to have his novel published in his own country, was refused, and saw it published abroad, to be hailed as an event of the highest moment. However, they are the works of men of different origins, temperaments, and views of the revolution, the view of Solzhenitsyn in *Cancer Ward* not to be identified, as we shall see, with that in his later political pronouncements.

Just as these novels go counter to the dominant trend in the writing of novels, so does my criticism of them go counter to the dominant trend of criticism. The criticism of the novel has undergone a development analogous to that of the novel itself. In the thirties, the era of "proletarian literature," which intruded upon the progress of modernism, literature was conceived of as a "weapon" in the political struggle, often in the narrowest and most immediately utilitarian sense. The frequent unvoiced assumption was that just about any stick would do to beat a dog (the right dog, according to the current party line). In the period that followed, that of the New Criticism, literature was regarded as totally autonomous, apart from society, uncontaminated by ideas. Criticism was an analysis of form; anything else was "extrinsic" to the work under examination.

The New Criticism, originally connected with the explanation and defense of modernist poetry, was mostly concerned with the close study of poems. Save for the more flexible of them, such as Cleanth Brooks, the New Critics, with their microscopes for the study of technique, have not succeeded so well, however, with the novel, which works with larger units and depends on cumulation rather than concentration for its effect—a fact, incidentally, which makes it much more translatable than poetry and amenable in translation to criticism. Nevertheless, the New Critics have influenced the criticism of the novel and indeed the novel itself.

In my studies of the ten novels I have chosen, I have sought to engage in what the New Critics call "close readings," using, however, what they call the "extrinsic" aids that the Marxist makes use of. One such aid will be brief introductions to each grouping of the novels that will trace the course of the revolution in these periods and the changes of attitude of the European and American intelligentsia toward that revolution and the social system against which it is directed—changes of attitude which affected these novels. In tracing the course of world revolution, I shall quote rather copiously from leading Marxist theoreticians, not because I regard them as infallible seers—as Trotsky said of Lenin with regard to the Stalinists making him a god in order to confer divinity on his successor, "he was 'only' a man of genius"[6]—but to illustrate the correctness of their general orientation and to profit from it. Such historical sketches, while perforce only very rough outlines, may serve as aids towards the understanding of the materials and the contexts of our novels, a study of which in turn will give solidity and depth to the sketches.

The criticism of novels dealing with the idea of social revolution by an adherent of social revolution such as myself raises in its sharpest form what Eliot called "the problem of belief": how does one respond to the literature of the past and other literature that expresses a set of beliefs with which one cannot agree, a problem that is especially present in our age of dissolving beliefs? Rosa Luxemburg's answer was that "with the true artist, the social formula that he recommends is a matter of secondary importance; the source of his art, its animating spirit, is decisive."[7] This is essentially what Trilling said in a broader generalization: "It is simply not possible for a work of literature that comes within the borders of greatness not to ask for more energy and fineness of life, and by its own communication of awareness, bring these qualities into being."[8]

The "animating spirit" must, however, find a proper form if it is to communicate itself. "A work of art," says Leon Trotsky, "should, in the first place, be judged by its own law, that is, by the law of art."[9] So far this might have been said by a New Critic, but Trotsky says in addition, "The effort to set art free from life, to declare it a craft self-sufficient unto itself, devitalizes and kills art."[10] Of the Russian formalists, the forerunners of the American New Critics, he says that their methods have a "subsidiary, serviceable and technical significance," but only "the social and psychologic approach . . . gives a meaning to the microscopic and statistical work done in connection with verbal material."[11] So much for the absolute autonomy of art and the "affective fallacy"! Art is not for art's sake; it is for life's sake. It does not merely contain patterns, symbols, and images which can be traced, counted, and classified; it makes us think and feel and "enriches the spiritual experience of the individual and the community."[12] Even the art which parades under the banner of "art for art's sake" serves a social purpose.

Because I believe that a novel is something more than a specimen mounted on a slide to be scrutinized under a microscope, I have not hesitated, although my focus has been on the work itself, to enter into discussions of the ideas contained in it or lying behind it. For I too have an "unabashed interest" in these ideas. But where I refute them, I am not "refuting" the novel itself. The laws governing the novel are not the same as the logic of the ideas in it—although the novelist's dominating ideas will affect the form of the novel and, in the case of a novel with a psychological thesis such as *Darkness at Noon*, the invalid thesis may force the novelist to violate consistency of character.

My discussions of the ideas present in the novels are contrary to the practice of the university establishment, where the scientism of conventional historical scholarship joins with the New Criticism's exclusive concern with technique to condemn the intrusion of the critic's own ideas in the examination of a literary work (although biases are often unconsciously revealed). For Matthew Arnold, however, literary criticism was a humanist discourse that included the criticism of society, since literature itself was a "criticism of life." And not Arnold alone. Steven Marcus notes:

> The novel and literary criticism exist in close and reciprocal relation. Historically both forms have been characterized by their discursiveness, their impulse to moralize, and their topicality. And through their complex and highly sophisticated development . . . both . . . continue to share an insistent concern with . . . the immediate social and cultural situation.[13]

In only one instance, however, that of my study of *The Iron Heel,* has my analysis of the work been primarily political rather than aesthetic. *The Iron Heel* is an example of the first of Raymond Williams's seven categories of the relation between fiction and ideas: the ideas are propagated rather than either embodied or argued or presented as conventions or expressed as characters or dissolved into a fictional world or contained as a superstructure at variance with what is implicit in the novelist's creation. As Williams points out, it is wrong to limit such "propaganda fiction" to "any particular sect or emphasis"— *Darkness at Noon* comes close to being such "propaganda fiction," for of course, as Williams indicates, the categories are not hard and fast—or "to suppose that this kind of fiction is always trivial."[14] Although some of its scenes will endure in literature as a vivid picture of man's inhumanity to man apart from the ideas being propagated, *The Iron Heel* is dependent on the validity of its ideas in a way that the other novels are not. It retains its value mainly because those ideas are still relevant, as my analysis of its remarkable anticipation of our own society will show, and also because they are presented with such vigor and dramatic flair.

Except for the unsuccessful *Darkness at Noon* and *Doctor Zhivago,* which are worth studying for their important part in the intellectual history of our time and to dispel the undeservedly high reputation they continue to have, the others, *Man's Fate* at least in part, have their own value, a value of a more complex literary order. They furnish us with the special kind of illumination literature has to offer. Literature, says F. R. Leavis in his anti-Marxist essay "Literature and Society," can furnish us with an "insight into the relations between abstract or generalizing thought and the concrete of human experience" that will give an "edge and force" to "social and political studies."[15] This is a statement to which Marxists can subscribe. One can learn more about the development of French society from Balzac despite his royalism, said Engels, than "from all the professional historians, economists and statisticians of the period together."[16]

One of the things with which I shall be concerned is the elucidation of the knowledge of contemporary society to be obtained from the novels I am discussing. But I shall be concerned with more than that. Irving Howe in his *Politics and the Novel* says that his chapters on nineteenth-century political novels "contain far heavier stress upon the literary side of things" than his chapters on twentieth-century political novels because "in a book like *1984* politics has achieved an almost total dominion."[17] It is my belief that the twentieth-century novels to which Howe refers are as susceptible to aesthetic analysis as any other. More than that, their aesthetic effect is related to the understanding of our society we can gain from them. We need not accept Orwell's political belief, derived from James Burnham—that in both the Soviet Union and the western capitalist states a "managerial" class is consolidating the power it has attained—to find that he has illuminated what it means to live in these two societies. That illumination is achieved through the way he has ordered and shaped his novel to convey Winston Smith's isolation and alienation, the isolation and alienation that are so prevalent today. I shall therefore analyze the "laws" governing these novels—or, where the novels have been unsuccessful, their failure to follow their own "laws"—in addition to demonstrating the sociological understanding to be gained from them.

I

EVOLUTION AND REVOLUTION
AT THE BEGINNING
OF THE CENTURY

Introduction to Section I

The twentieth century was greeted with joyous optimism as the century of peace and progress, of unprecedented triumphs to be attained by humanity. The theory of an uninterrupted advance within the existing social system was widely held. One expression of it had been voiced by the popular historian Thomas Henry Buckle, who found that the leading countries of Europe, especially England, had so shaken off previous shackles on intellectual freedom that "progress will continue with accelerated speed." The progress of civilization must mean, despite "aberrations," the eventual elimination of war: "That this barbarous pursuit [war] is, in the progress of society, steadily declining, must be evident, even to the most hasty reader of European history."[1]

Within the socialist movement the idea of capitalism peacefully and gradually growing into socialism, opposed by Rosa Luxemburg in *Reform or Revolution* (1899) and by Lenin in *Marxism and Revisionism* (1908), became dominant. Karl Kautsky, the leading figure in the Second International, who, after defending the Marxist concept of revolution, succumbed to this outlook, propounded the theory of "ultra-imperialism," which held that, as a result of the growth of international trusts, there would no longer be wars between nations.

Lenin, however, in *The Historical Destiny of the Teaching of Karl Marx* (March 1913), predicted an end to both domestic and international peace:

> The "peaceful" period of 1872-1904 [1872—the year after the defeat of the Paris Commune; 1904—the year before the Russian revolution of 1905] has gone completely, never to return. High cost of living and the pressure of the trusts is causing an unprecedented intensification of the economic struggle. . . . Owing to the feverish race of armaments, and the policy of imperialism, the "social peace" of modern Europe is more like a barrel of gunpowder.[2]

But the threatening signs of World War I were overlooked by liberal public opinion, which was ignorant of the secret treaties and of the diplomacy conducted behind the scenes. So little pressure was there from public opinion that the British House of Commons had only two debates on foreign policy in the three years before the war.[3] British intellectuals participated serenely in "the Edwardian garden party," unaware of the impending storm.

1. Arnold Bennett's 'The Old Wives' Tale': British Gradualism and the Dialectics of Revolution

Although many critics of the caliber of E. M. Forster have seen Arnold Bennett's *The Old Wives' Tale* as a fine novel falling just short of greatness,[1] it is now often regarded as merely a specimen of the dead literary past. Virginia Woolf's well-known criticism of Bennett as a novelist who overwhelmed his readers with facts about the externals of the society in which his characters lived but never really got inside them has taken hold.[2] V. S. Pritchett has applied this idea that Bennett merely presented a lot of facts without getting at the essence of things to his depiction of society itself: "Bennett's picture . . . is history. History presented . . . with the dilettante's and collector's indifference to any theory of what history may be about."[3] Actually, *The Old Wives' Tale*, Bennett's supreme artistic effort, is a masterpiece of characterization and is written in accordance with a theory of social evolution that deals with the idea of social revolution.

An account of middle-class life, which after a period of misunderstanding and initial neglect on its publication in 1908 has been selling steadily, it may be said to be the bourgeois novel par excellence. It is the story of two sisters, Constance and Sophia Baines, whose mother owns a drapery shop in the provincial city of Bursley in the 1860s. The gentle and placid Constance marries the shop assistant, with whom she runs the shop. The tempestuous and headstrong Sophia runs away to Paris with a commercial traveler, with whom she has fallen in love. Deserted by her husband, Sophia becomes wealthy in Paris as the owner and manager of a hotel. After thirty years, the sisters are reunited and live in Bursley until the death first of Sophia and then of Constance.

The theme of the novel, Arnold Bennett says in his preface, is the pathos of the fact that "every stout ageing woman was once a young girl with the unique charm of youth" and that "the change from the young girl to the stout ageing woman is made up of an infinite number of infinitesimal changes, each unperceived by her."[4] Personal evolution, not social revolution, the day-by-day lives of ordinary persons unconcerned with public affairs, not dramatic historic events—this is avowedly the stuff of *The Old Wives' Tale*.

These ordinary persons, however, are presented in a finely visualized world which changes as they change. *The Old Wives' Tale* is concerned with the development of English middle-class society from 1863, when the novel begins, until 1907, when it ends, as well as with the development of its characters. For his general view of the development of English society during this period, Bennett was indebted both to the Fabians and to Herbert Spencer—but, as we shall see, his artist's insight enabled him to transcend these interpretations and to adumbrate a view of evolution as containing within itself revolution, similar to the Marxist view. In dealing, however, with the Paris Commune, he reveals the deficiencies of his understanding of revolution.

A member of the lower middle class who was a lifetime friend of H. G. Wells, advancing like Wells to the point at which he hobnobbed with cabinet ministers and press lords, Bennett, says Walter Allen,

considered himself all his life a socialist, but at no time was he a militant propagandist for socialism; he was, in fact, a member of the Liberal Party, an advanced radical for whom the enemy was always the Tories. . . . As a socialist in the heyday of Fabianism and as an admirer of the Webbs, [he] may have been convinced of the inevitability of gradualness; he certainly did not construe gradualness as faster than a snail's pace.[5]

Bennett has nothing to say about socialism in *The Old Wives' Tale*; presumably, this ultimate goal lies too far in the distant future to be discerned in the social changes of the recent past. However, he no doubt regarded the progressive bettering of the working conditions of the maids of the Baines and Povey households as indicative of a trend that would eventuate in socialism. Moreover, he shows Bursley as entering the modern world when the Midland Clothiers Company, a chain-store business, takes over the Baines shop. This growth of large companies, with the "elimination of the purely personal element in business management," Sidney Webb saw as tending to socialism, for it meant, he thought, fewer capitalists and made it possible for the government to take over business with greater ease.[6] No doubt Bennett, while deprecating the depersonalization of modern big business, felt the same way.

A much greater influence on him than that of the Fabians, however, was the influence of Herbert Spencer. Bennett himself is witness to the effect of Spencer on him: "By filling me up with the sense of causation everywhere, it [Spencer's *First Principles*] has altered my whole view of life. . . . You can see [it] in nearly every line I write."[7] It may seem strange that Spencer, who reinvigorated the old doctrine of laissez faire by the theory of "the survival of the fittest," should have influenced Bennett, the admirer of the Webbs, who advocated the state ownership of the means of production. However, the Fabians themselves were influenced, if only in a general way, by Spencer. It was from him, said Beatrice Webb, that she got the idea of society as an organism which must evolve slowly and gradually.[8] So, too, Sidney Webb wrote:

Owing mainly to the efforts of Comte, Darwin, and Herbert Spencer, . . . the necessity of the constant growth and development of the social organism has become axiomatic. No philosopher now looks for anything but the gradual evolution of the new order from the old, without breach of continuity or abrupt change of the entire social tissue at any point of the process.[9]

In short, Spencer and the Fabians were in agreement that England was progressing slowly but surely to a higher form of society, but they disagreed on the nature of this higher form of society.

The tone of sympathetic pity governing *The Old Wives' Tale*, but a pity that is distanced by the pervasive irony in which it is written, is the expression of feeling of an author who saw his characters as unwitting participants in what he called "the great evolutionary procession," in which social evolution is only an aspect of cosmic evolution.[10] So Constance at the end of the novel goes forth in bad weather despite her sciatica to vote against the hated federation that would cause Bursley to lose its identity. "She was not a politician: she had no general ideas; she did not see the cosmic movement in large curves. She was incapable of perceiving the absurdity involved in perpetuating municipal divisions which the growth of the district had rendered artificial, vexatious, and harmful" (p. 604). Her opposition to federation, an opposition which she shared with the overwhelming majority of the inhabitants of Bursley, was absurd, but it was also a part of the great scheme of things. For, as was said by Spencer, the conservatism which holds on to the old is just as necessary as the liberalism which brings in the new (one is reminded of the Gilbert and Sullivan ditty in which it is said that every infant in England was born either a little Conservative or a little Liberal); the balance of forces is necessary if society is to progress but not "to destroy its old institutions before the new have become well-organized enough to take their places."[11]

But this view of things is granted only to the philosopher. Most people will continue to act out their roles without being aware of the drama. And so Constance does not see "the cosmic movement in large curves," as did her creator from his Olympian vantage point—the "large curves" probably referring to what Spencer called "the cycle of changes," in the earlier part of which integration predominates, in the middle part of which there is an oscillation from integration to disintegration and back to integration, and in the latter part of which disintegration predominates until death brings an end to the cycle.[12] For individuals on either the ascending or the descending portion of the curve, it seems as if society is moving on a straight line, their scales being inadequate to measure distances over such a stretch of time.

Spencer, despite his statement that patriotic bias is a hindrance in the study of societies, regarded England as possessing "in a degree never before paralleled" the ability to progress without giving up the stability that comes from retaining the old, an ability which operates through a "perpetual compromise" that is "an indispensable accompaniment of a normal development."[13] In times of social revolution the normal lag between existing social arrangements and current ideas is considerably greater than it ordinarily is, making impossible the "tolerable harmony" and the "successive compromises" between social institutions and new ideas such as take place in societies which are in the course of development and not in the course of dissolution.[14] In a revolution those things which hold a society together are destroyed; revolutions, therefore, occur when a society is disintegrating. Of the great achievements for their countries and all humanity which the English, American, and French revolutions brought, Spencer has nothing to say.

Bennett shows the Paris Commune as part of the disintegration of the Napoleonic Empire. In contrast to France is England, which, Bennett suggests, is not given to violent, sudden changes, to wars and Communes. The counterpart of the Paris Commune's fight against the outside force of the army of the French ruling class is the electoral battle to retain the independence of Bursley against the Federationists. The counterpart of the public execution in Auxerre, with its brutalized, corrupt, sophisticated audience, is the Bursley Wakes, which Bennett calls, with his usual amused irony in dealing with Bursley, "an orgiastic carnival" (p. 71). One of the "delights of the horrible" displayed in one of the booths is "the atrocities of the French Revolution" (p. 71). Revolution is at a far remove from this provincial city, a subject for delicious shudders.

Yet, in dealing with what he knew so well, Bursley's retail trade and the lives of those two products of Bursley, Constance and Sophia, Bennett does not present a gradual, uninterrupted evolution. Indeed his technique—the means by which he attains his supreme achievement, the reader's sense of having lived a lifetime with his two heroines—consists of the masterly manner in which he summarizes the passage of years and dramatizes the events which bring about new epochs, events that go beyond the accumulation of small changes. The slow pace of time is not uninterrupted but is punctuated by leaps forward.

In this, Bennett, while undoubtedly unaware of it, is much closer to the Marxist view of evolution than to the Spencerian and Fabian views. The leading Marxist theoretician of the time, Karl Kautsky, writing in 1902, pointed out that Darwin and the geologist Lyell are frequently cited by opponents of revolutionary socialism to show that, just as "nature knows no leaps," so social progress can "only proceed by way of accumulation of the smallest changes and improvements."[15] Kautsky does not specify who these opponents of revolutionary socialism are, but we have already seen how the Fabian socialist Sidney Webb referred to Darwin as well as to Spencer in arguing for a "gradual evolution of the new order from the old." To the reference to natural evolution as a model for social change, Kautsky replies that "many of the latest biological and geological theories recognize along with the slow accumulation of small and fractional changes, also sudden and far-reaching changes of form— catastrophic changes—which proceed from the former."[16] The most pertinent biological analogy, he suggests, is that between revolution and the act of birth: birth is the culmination of a gradual evolution of the fetus within the womb, but birth itself is a violent and sudden change. So gradual economic development brings the rise of a new social class, which by a revolution adopts a new political structure, establishes new institutions suitable for maintaining its rule, and builds a new culture expressing its world outlook.

In Marxist thought social revolution is in conformance with the laws that govern development in the universe. As Lenin stated it, writing in a compressed way for an encyclopedia article in 1914, the idea of evolution formulated by Marx and Engels is "much more comprehensive, much more abundant in content than the current theory of evolution." Their idea is characterized among other things by

> "breaks of gradualness"; transformation of quantity into quality; inner impulses for development, imparted by the contradiction, the conflict of different forces and tendencies reacting on a given body 'or inside a given phenomenon or within a given society . . . a connection that provides the one world-process of motion proceeding according to law.[17]

Or, as Trotsky put it in *In Defense of Marxism,* "Evolution proceeds through the struggle of antagonistic forces. . . . A slow accumulation of changes at a certain moment explodes the old shell and brings about a catastrophe, revolution."[18]

This view of evolution is in agreement with the current biological concept of evolution, the theories of which Kautsky spoke now being generally accepted. Thus George Gaylord Simpson, one of the foremost authorities on evolution, asserts in *The Meaning of Evolution* that two "interwoven patterns" of "constant occurrence and major importance" are present in evolution. "One of these is the pattern of trend, progressive, oriented change under the control of adaptation." This pattern is a gradual development in a given direction as the species of a group of organisms continue to adapt themselves to the conditions of a given environment. The other pattern is "the more rapid and sporadic, recurrent rather than continuous, pattern of change in adaptive type, adoption of a new and distinct way of life."[19] Here the lines of evolution among the species of the group diverge from each other because some of them develop other ways of life, expanding into new areas of adaptation which radiate from the older ones. Such an "adoption of a new and distinct way of life" occurred, for instance, when reptiles left water for the land, which had hitherto been devoid of vertebrate life. These times "of rapid expansion, high variability, and beginning adaptative radiation," says Simpson, "are the 'explosive phases' of evolution. . . . They are periods when enlarged opportunities are presented to groups able to pursue them."[20] Social revolutions may be compared to these "'explosive phases' of evolution" which provide "enlarged opportunities."

Although Bennett contrasts England, the mother of parliaments, to France, the mother of revolutions, he finds "revolutions" of a sort in Bursley. Three of the chapter titles in the first two books, which are concerned with Mrs. Baines and Constance, are "A Battle," "A Defeat," and "Revolution." As in Paris, a defeat, that of Mrs. Baines, is followed by a revolution, that within Constance and within the shop. For the truth is that there are battles and revolutions in Bursley, as there are in Paris. They are on a different scale; hence, the pervasive tone of amused and affectionate irony, akin to the mock heroic that describes trivial things in a grandiloquent manner, an irony which is, of course, present in these chapter titles. Yet Bennett is only partly ironic: to the persons concerned, the battles, defeats, and revolutions are very real. The changes in the retail trade of Bursley follow the same law as the much more infrequent but tremendously larger leaps of social revolution, of which Bennett lacked an understanding. In observing, as in slow motion, the process of social change in Bursley, Bennett was better able to apprehend that process and became an unconscious dialectician.

Describing Samuel Povey laboring with Constance over his original idea for shop tickets, which the "crass Toryism" of the wholesale stationer regards as outraging the "decency of trade" (p. 89), Bennett says: "Those two, without knowing or guessing it, were making history—the history of commerce. They had no suspicion that they were the forces of the future insidiously at work to destroy what the forces of the past had created, but such was the case" (p. 88). Mr. Povey, the shop assistant who marries into the little commercial oligarchy of the city, giving it new blood and new ideas, is indeed, ridiculous though he may be in some aspects, a force for change, a threat to Mrs. Baines's rule over her household and her shop. He wins both.

Constance's marriage is in fact a revolution in her life. However, she accommodates herself to Samuel, as he does to her. She is the force for stability; he is the force for innovation. Without consulting her, he gets a great signboard for the shop, an act which marks "the dawn of a new era." He upsets Mrs. Baines by showing her the proof of a poster announcing his first annual sale, but, we are told, "Constance, happily for Constance, was not present at this final defeat of the old order" (p. 177).

At the end of the novel, however, the shop, which Constance

had sold some time after Samuel's death to Charles Critchlow, the Methuselah of Bursley, deteriorates with the rest of the Square. For Bursley is robbed of most of its trade by the electric trams that take people to neighboring Hanbridge, which profits from being the geographical center of the Five Towns. Critchlow rents the Baines shop to the Midland Clothiers Company, which has branches in a number of counties. The Midland Clothiers Company combines the Baines shop and Mr. Critchlow's chemist shop into one great store, advertises gaudily, and sells large numbers of inferior goods at low prices.

Worst of all for members of the commercial oligarchy is the movement for federating the Five Towns, making them into the twelfth largest city in England. Old-timers such as Constance are violently opposed to Bursley's enforced demise and see the federation movement as a plot hatched by the grasping tradesmen of Hanbridge to benefit themselves. In a referendum, federation, to the surprise of everyone, is defeated, "the mere blind, deaf, inert forces of reaction, with faulty organization, and quite deprived of the aid of logic," proving "far stronger than the alert enthusiasm arrayed against them" (p. 635). The supporters of federation, however, find a way of circumventing the referendum, and in the penultimate paragraph of the book it is indicated that they will prevail.

And so large chain-store business and political centralization triumph over the commercial oligarchy of Bursley. Society evolves slowly through, in Trotsky's words, "the struggle of antagonistic forces," but after a point the many small quantitative changes bring about a qualitative change. There is then a sudden leap forward, a signboard which proclaims "the dawn of a new era," an annual sale which marks "the final defeat of the old order," the cut-rate sale of the Midland Clothiers Company. Bennett, in whimsically using the clichés of the historian—"the dawn of a new era," "the final defeat of the old order"—is pointing up the minuteness of these changes measured on the scale of the life of nations but also their momentousness measured on the scale of the commercial life of Bursley.

Bennett's presentation of the development of his two heroines is also dialectical: each of them develops not through the unperceived "infinitesimal changes" of which he speaks in his preface but through internal struggles which suddenly bring about a significant alteration after a gradual accumulation of changes. In this it is like, although the rate of progress is not so hectic, the analytical description of childhood, the most dynamic period of development in human life, by Arnold Gesell and Frances L. Ilg, who speak of inner growth as bringing about a period of disequilibrium—the "difficult" period known to parents—which, the child surmounting its difficulties, is succeeded by a period of equilibrium, of the consolidation of conquests.[21]

Sophia as a girl is aghast when Constance, whose sympathy has been aroused by Mr. Povey's toothache, snatches his tooth from Sophia's work-box, determined that he should not be a subject for ridicule. "It was the . . . astounding, inexplicable development in Constance's character, that staggered [Sophia] into silent acceptance of the inevitable" (p. 37). The kindly sympathy of the mild, placid Constance and her dawning interest in Samuel produces her sudden fierceness and her breaking of the rules of their existence, one element of her character emerging into being when the situation calls for it. The incident prefigures the time when, as a middle-aged woman, she, "quite unlike her usual self," crying and "behaving just like a child" (pp. 550, 549), wins the battle over the masterful Sophia as to whether they are to live in Bursley or stay abroad, breaking the rules in first making a painful scene and then piteously supplicating Sophia. The Marxist doctrine of evolution, says Lenin, provides for "development that repeats, as it were, the stages already passed but repeats them in a different way."[22] With individuals, as with nations, there are anticipations, reversions, and "astounding, inexplicable" developments, each of which is in reality an outburst of what has been maturing unseen, the birth of that which has been silently growing inside.

Interestingly enough, literal birth, the birth of Cyril, is seen by Bennett as a revolution. It is made ready for by "preparations, intricate, revolutionary," like the plans for an insurrection. The labor pains are a "shattering army, endless, increasing in terror as they thundered across her." Constance is "in the midst of a cataclysm" (p. 196).

However, if Bennett sees birth as a revolution, he paradoxically does not see revolution as a birth but as an aberration. The Paris Commune is for him a foolish episode in the life of a city. Sophia "was more vexed than frightened by the Commune; vexed that a city so in need of repose and industry should indulge in such antics" (p. 463). Although Sophia is presented as politically ignorant, Bennett shows that she, an Englishwoman, is essentially right in her impatience with the French. The French are represented as highly impractical, their romanticism contrasting with English common sense. They are easily carried away, emotionally hailing a French victory that is in reality a false rumor. For Sophia her admirer, Chirac, epitomizes the national character. Although a newspaper man with knowledge of the military facts, he joins in the transports of the crowd, "weeping like a child" (p. 414). "She felt towards the French nation as a mother might feel towards adorable, wilful children suffering through their own charming foolishness. . . . Her heart bled for France and Chirac on that morning of reaction and of the truth" (p. 419).

The establishment of the Commune, then, is presented as a childish antic on the part of a people given over to "Latin theatricality" (p. 448), to facile emotion and false heroics. Bennett's attitude of patronizing, amused tolerance leads him to use in his dialogue a literal translation of French idiom for those speaking in French for humorous effect. The suggestion is that the French are so elaborately mannered, so charmingly quaint, so un-English.

Writing more than thirty-five years after the event, Bennett continues to express the national self-congratulation at the time of the Commune that England was English and not French, but the interval has softened the expression of feeling from what it was. "The general attitude was represented by *The Times*, which," says Frank Jellinek, ". . . thanked Heaven in its editorial columns that such things do not happen in England. . . . Most Englishmen thought the Commune meant that the French, driven to desperation by the war, had quite simply gone mad."[23]

Moreover, although Sophia's view of the Paris Commune is presented by Bennett as essentially correct, the impression we gain from it is modified by other impressions. Just as she regards Chirac with scorn as well as with sympathy for his lack of human dignity in pining away for her, so does she regard with scorn Madame Foucault, the aging courtesan in financial straits who saved Sophia's life by nursing her through a severe illness. The "feeble theatricality" of Madame Foucault's bursting through the door and prostrating herself before Sophia with the cry "Save me!" (p. 417) offends Sophia's taste. However, Sophia herself is regarded by Bennett with some amusement for her self-righteousness: "Sophia coldly condemned Madame Foucault for having allowed herself to be brought into the world with such a weak and maudlin character, and for having allowed herself to grow old and ugly" (p. 417). Bennett has it both ways: he patronizes both the "Latin theatricality" of the French and the provincial self-righteousness of the English. The evolutionist philosopher is tolerant of the shortcomings of individuals and nations, for he knows that self-regard and patriotism cause people to be unable to stand back at some distance and to fail consequently to see the full picture.[24]

Sophia herself, it may be remembered, had behaved like a willful child in eloping with Gerald Scales, only to awaken to a "morning of reaction and truth." As, four years later, she follows Gerald to observe his last fatuous escapade, she muses over her own past folly in sacrificing her career as a schoolteacher for the chance of seeing Gerald every three months at the shop, scarcely observing in her reverie the sumptuous carriages bearing men in splendid uniforms and women with enchanting toilettes to what, unknown to them, was the last fete of the Napoleonic Empire. Echoing in the ears of the wearers of these uniforms are

the long phrases of Napoleon the Third about his gratitude to his people for their confidence in him as shown by the plebiscite, and about the ratification of constitutional reforms guaranteeing order, and about the empire having been strengthened at its base, and about showing force by moderation and envisaging the future without fear, and about the bosom of peace and liberty, and about the eternal continuance of his dynasty. [Pp. 371-72]

The mimicking of Napoleon's orotund rhetoric culminates in the dramatic irony of the last phrase. The juxtaposition of Sophia's thoughts about her blind folly and the comment about Napoleon's blindness amid the pomp and glitter that surrounds him suggests that the ruler of a country and his entourage, "the supreme pillars of imperialism," may be as ignorant of reality as an untutored girl. Here it is the government, not the people, which is at fault, but the implication would seem to be that this people, with its love of theatricality, is capable of having been taken in by the showiness and rhetoric of this government.

The basic Baines structure of Sophia's character enables her to recover from her suffering and disillusionment, but it is at a terrific price. Such times of crisis, it is implied, come to nations as well as to individuals. The chapter entitled "Fever," in which Sophia's feverish illness is described, also tells of the contagious effect of the false news of victory upon the Parisian crowd, which is seized by a "sudden fever" and becomes "thicker and more febrile" by the moment until every one in Paris is caught up in "the vast national delirium" (pp. 415, 413).

Sophia emerges from her illness a "different" woman. A revolution has been effected in her life. She, who had fought to take up a career as a teacher in order to get out of being shut up in the Baines shop, devotes the rest of her life until she joins Constance to running first her pension and then the Hotel Frensham. She, who had been attracted to Gerald Scales partly because of the glamour he radiated through his acquaintance with such places as Paris, the cultural capital of the world, shuts herself off from French culture, including the novels of which she had been an assiduous reader. The title of the chapter "Success," the concluding chapter of the book concerned with her stay in Paris, is partially ironic.

The revolution within Sophia, however, unlike the revolution of the Paris Commune, is shown as the climactic change that is the culmination of a development within her. We are prepared for Sophia's refusal of Chirac and her self-imprisonment in her pension by her earlier withdrawal from life when she had given up her teaching career only to find that Gerald was no longer the representative of the firm for which he had visited the shop periodically. Holding herself responsible for the death of her father (the invalid had died when she left him a few minutes unattended in order to see Gerald), she had left her studies and entered the shop. "In the splendour of her remorse for a fatal forgetfulness, she had renounced that which she loved and thrown herself into that which she loathed. It was her nature to do so" (p. 101). When she comes to realize, however, that a large part of the reason for her entering the shop was really the hope of seeing Gerald there again, she takes to a sternly practiced religion which her family has to endure for a year and a half. So too when she later awakes from her dream of marriage to Gerald to the reality of what he is, she accepts his caprices and does not permit herself to have desires of her own. "She was ready to pay the price of pride and of a moment's imbecility with a lifetime of self-repression. It was high, but it was the price" (p. 364).

In taking up the life of a hotel proprietress, she exercises the talents of organization, common sense, and determination which she had absorbed in her home in England, observing the bourgeois virtues against which she had once rebelled. She is also, however, manifesting the "haughty moral independence" which had always been "the foundation of her character" (p. 451), the haughty moral independence which she prizes in others as well as herself. It is this quality which prompts her to pay the price of her folly rather than to sacrifice her human dignity by accepting a man lacking it or by returning to England. This decision, which sets her off on a new course, is the culmination of what we might call the first stages of the revolution within her, the period just before Gerald leaves her. Sophia is acutely conscious at this time of a "fundamental change in herself" and believes that the old Sophia is dead, but the new Sophia is in reality "still the same Sophia more fully disclosed" (p. 363). The revolution within her, the victory of self-repression over spirited defiance, is the result of a dialectical development which has proceeded "through the struggle of antagonistic forces" within her.

Thus in the development of the character of Sophia, as of the character of Constance, we see, in the words of Lenin, "inner impulses for development" that are "imparted by the contradiction, the conflict of different forces and tendencies. . . ." We do not see, however, the class struggles in French society that brought about the Paris Commune. Social revolution for Bennett comes about not as a result of gradual economic development leading to a change in the relations between classes ("the transformation of quantity into quality"), but is the product of the fixed category of national character. As such it is alien to England. The county in which Bursley is located is, Bennett tells us in words reminiscent of the celebrations of "Middle America," "England in little, lost in the middle of England, unsung by searchers after the extreme." In its lack of excess the county is representative of England. Even the river Trent is "the calm and characteristic stream of Middle England" (p. 3).

In his finding the origin of the Paris Commune in qualities of the French national character lacking in the British national character, Bennett, it must be said, is highly superficial. No doubt we can speak of national traits, but only with sharp qualification: we must allow for individual variety and the complexity that goes beyond stereotypes; we must understand that class differences are much more important than national traits; we must realize that a change in social conditions brings changes in national character. England is said to be the country of moderation— but this is to forget the seventeenth-century civil war and Puritan revolution and the revolutionary Chartist movement of the early nineteenth century (to say nothing of the imperialist conquests of the British ruling class, scarcely by peaceful, evolutionary means). Russia was said to be the country of Slavic passivity and resignation, and China of Asiatic fatalism, but this did not prevent revolution from coming to them at the proper time.

The Paris Commune was not a game engaged in by play-acting Parisian workers. It was a new social order that was strangled in its infancy, as Winston Churchill said in the years of the Russian revolution that the baby must be strangled before it grows up to be a giant. The agents of the French ruling class, who, after their conquest of Paris, in one week killed between 20,000 and 25,000 persons, ten times as many as were killed during the year of revolutionary terror of the French revolution, did not regard the Commune as a theatrical production. Jellinek quotes Dufaure, "the merciless Minister for Justice," as saying to "some Liberals who pleaded that the Commune was merely a rash but not unpardonable outburst of patriotic municipal exasperation," "No, gentlemen, it was not a communalist, a municipal movement; it was in its ideals, its ideas and its actions the most radical revolution ever undertaken!"[25]

So it was deemed by Marx, who at the time of its occurrence hailed it in *The Civil War in France* as "the glorious harbinger of a new society." When Lenin fled to Finland just before the October revolution, one of the two books he took with him was this book. It was the basis of his *The State and Revolution*, the principles concerning proletarian revolution which guided him in gaining power and in building the proletarian state. That the revolution degenerated under Stalin does not invalidate the Marxist theory of revolution, for Lenin and Trotsky were vividly aware of the possibilities of such degeneration in Russia's isolation and backwardness.

And how does it stand with the evolutionary theories of Spencer and of the Fabians? The first is quite dead, and the second is, to use the Fabians' own favorite figure of speech, a fossilized relic of the past. A great war, major class battles culminating in a nationwide general strike, a devastating depression, another great war, the loss of an empire, the decline as a power relative to other powers, the present drift, stagnation, inflation, and labor unrest—these have done away with the notion of Great Britain as the country of continuous peaceful reform showing the way to the rest of the world. That *The Old Wives' Tale* has so well captured the self-assured England of the late nineteenth century, preeminent among the nations of the world, from whose soil both the social theory of Herbert Spencer and the Fabianism of the Webbs grew, that it traces its evolution in such an insightful fashion, transcending in some respects the Spencerianism and Fabianism of its author—this is what gives it its enduring power.

2. Jack London's 'The Iron Heel': The Vision of Revolutionary Socialism and Present-day American Capitalism

Outside of the United States, Jack London's *The Iron Heel* has had an enormous effect, educating large numbers in Marxism and inspiring generations of revolutionists. Disregarded at its appearance in 1908 by the Social Democratic journals, it was the one American work listed by Bukharin in his bibliography of communist literature, published shortly after the Russian revolution, and today it continues to sell throughout the world in the millions in many translations.

In the United States it was greeted with derision by most critics as dreary propaganda mixed with wild-eyed sensationalism, and with dismay by reformist socialists as a presentation, as John Spargo phrased it, of "the old and generally discarded cataclysmic theory"[1] that could only frighten away many potential supporters of socialism. It was hailed, however, by militant radicals such as Eugene Debs and Bill Haywood. After an extended period of neglect, it was reissued following World War II as an amazing prophecy of fascism. Today radicalized young intellectuals continue to come to it afresh.

The Iron Heel belongs to that genre of prose fiction which Northrop Frye calls the "anatomy," taking the word from Burton's *Anatomy of Melancholy*, where it means a dissection or analysis. The "anatomy," therefore, is an analysis of ideas in a loosely narrative form in which stylized characters act as expressions of intellectual viewpoints.[2] A branch of this genre is the utopian romance, known to London through Edward Bellamy's famous *Looking Backward*, of which he said that it had served a useful purpose in its time but that what was now wanted was an exposition of socialism rooted in the doctrine of class struggle.

Since *The Iron Heel* is an "anatomy," it would be a mistake to look to it for the subtle characterization, the realistic dialogue, or the closely knit plot we look for in a typical novel of merit. A sympathetic critic such as Philip Foner is, for instance, carried away by his sympathy when he finds that its hero, Ernest Everhard, "grows in reality until at the end we begin to get close to him in a personal and intimate way."[3] Ernest Everhard's very name indicates that he is not a three-dimensional human being but, as his wife says of him at one point, "the spirit of regnant labor,"[4] a powerful cartoon figure unbending in his iron determination to liberate his class and all humanity. He is also presented as the ideal lover upon whom his wife looks adoringly, but he is never a real person. If, however, *The Iron Heel* does not have the complexity of characterization of the realistic novel, it does succeed as an "anatomy" by its dramatic clash of ideas and its lucid exposition of them.

The Iron Heel purports to be an account by Avis Everhard of how she met her husband, Ernest, became converted by him to socialism, and worked with him when he was leader of the underground movement against the brutal oligarchic rule established by the American capitalists after the electoral victory of socialism. The account, which covers the years 1912 to 1932, is represented as having been discovered after seven centuries, four centuries after socialism finally triumphed over the oligarchy that had gained world domination, and published with a foreword and notes by an historian of the period.

The initial exposition proceeds through a series of colloquies. Ernest Everhard demolishes with his materialistic philosophy the metaphysical meanderings of the churchmen at the house of Avis's father. He shakes Avis and the saintly Bishop Morehead with his argument concerning the essential inhumanity of the rulers of society and the irreconcilability of their interests and the interests of the workers. He rouses to rage a club of plutocrats with intellectual interests when he lectures to its members on the revolution that will take away their power and build a new society. He demonstrates to a group of middle-class businessmen how monopoly will grow and swallow them up but how the capitalist system must break down and give way to socialism, leaving them frightened with the picture of their demise but mistrustful of socialism and determined to try to break the trusts despite everything.

Avis Everhard, referring to a pamphlet of Ernest's, says, "His written word was as his spoken word, clear and convincing. . . . He had the gift of lucidity. He was the perfect expositor" (p. 24). She is right, for London knew his own strength. Ernest's style, moreover, is not only clear; it is vigorous and dramatic. It is not subtle, but it has "swing and smash," as Avis says of it.

After the discussion with the middle-class businessmen, events come in a rush. The trusts beat labor in a number of strike battles and crush the middle class after using it against labor. The socialist party makes great gains as a result of this intensification of the class struggle, and the socialist leaders look forward to taking over the government through an electoral victory. Ernest alone foresees that the capitalists will not peacefully cede power. This is indeed what happens. On the pretext of an alleged plot to bomb Congress, in reality the work of an agent provocateur, they institute naked repression. Woven through this narrative are such stories of subsidiary characters as the martyrdom of Bishop Morehead, the victimization of Avis's father, and the winning over of young Wickson, the son of the plutocratic chief.

The novel ends with the smashing of the first of many revolts against the Iron Heel, the repressive regime that has been established. The bloody vision of the final chapters, in which are described the looting, marauding, and massacre of the "roaring abysmal beast" (p. 256), the masses brutalized by the Iron Heel, and the warfare in the streets of Chicago between the revolutionists and the mercenaries, is most powerfully drawn. It is a vision which cannot be expunged from the memory.

Looking Backward concludes with Julian West dreaming that he is back in the nineteenth century, only to awake and find that the reality is the fair twentieth century, not his own dark, oppressive time. William Morris's *News from Nowhere* concludes with the narrator awaking from his sojourn in the future, uncertain whether it was a dream and determined to tell others of it so that it will be a vision, not a dream. *The Iron Heel* concludes with the nightmare experience of Avis, made feverish by what she has seen, wandering through the streets of Chicago and observing the aftermath of the carnage. She sees a solitary tottering wretch leaving a bloody trail behind him as he seeks "some hole to crawl away in and hide like any animal"; a mound of dead bodies from which there is "lifted a head, gory with nameless horror, that gibbered at me and then lay down and moved no more"; a moving stream of "the very young and the very old, the feeble and the sick, the helpless and the hopeless, all the very wreckage of the [labor] ghetto," from which "arose groans and lamentations, cursings, babblings of senility, hysteria, and insanity" (pp. 295-97). These and other scenes register themselves on her brain with the vivid intensity of a horrible dream, interspersed with intervals of unconsciousness. This nightmare is reality under the Iron Heel.

But she wakes from it when the disguised Ernest, who has found her, commandeers an automobile from the authorities and drives them out of Chicago.

Soon we were in the green country, and I took one last glance back at the smoke-filled sky. Faint and far came the low thud of an explosion. Then I turned my face against Ernest's breast and wept softly for the Cause that was lost. . . . "For this time lost, dear heart," he said, "but not forever. We have learned. Tomorrow the Cause will rise again, strong with wisdom and discipline." [P. 300]

The last sentence of *The Iron Heel*, broken off abruptly in the middle when Avis was warned that the Mercenaries were coming, is "The magnitude of the task may be understood when it is taken into" (p. 303). The magnitude of the task of conquering capitalism, the power and ferocity of the ruling class, is the theme of *The Iron Heel*. But there is no doubt that the workers will finally perform their historic mission.

The scholarly framework surrounding the purported Everhard manuscript serves several purposes. In providing an editor of the socialist era, it gives assurance of the ultimate victory of socialism. Some footnotes, in the guise of explanations to inform an audience of a much later time, inform London's own audience, making use of the items of a socialist's notebook to provide facts that drive a point home. Other footnotes are elucidations of things familiar to London's readers that present them in a new perspective, as in the footnote explaining will-breaking, in which it is said that "will-making and will-breaking became complementary trades, like armor-making and gun-making" (p. 66n.). These sardonic notes may have been influenced by Ambrose Bierce's *The Cynic's Word Book*, from which London once quotes (p. 83 n.). Finally, the notes sometimes amusingly illustrate the difficulties of historians, even those living in the socialist era, in getting facts exactly right, as when the editor, telescoping the eras of the Roman Empire and of American capitalism, glosses "he took no quarter": "This figure arises from the customs of the times. When, among men fighting to the death in their wild-animal way, a beaten man threw down his weapons, it was at the option of the victor to slay him or spare him" (p. 18 and n.). The point is, however, that although the fact may be wrong the comment on the brutality of the times is essentially right.

Using the form of the utopian romance, Jack London wrote a remarkable Marxist prognostication of the capitalist society of the future. It is true that London knew little of Marx directly besides the *Communist Manifesto*. London, however, assimilated the insights of genius contained in this seminal work and made them a part of his own artist's vision. He learned from the brutal strikebreaking of the private armies of the American capitalists and from the savage repression that followed the attempted revolution of 1905 in Russia, to both of which he refers a number of times. His observation of his own historical period, the understanding he gained from the *Communist Manifesto*, and his own fighting spirit serve to make *The Iron Heel* what it is.

Before, however, we go on to discuss London's use of Marxist ideas in his utopian romance and their significance for us today, there is a lion in the path which we must first confront. This is the matter of his racist social Darwinism, the manifestation of the well-known deep-lying contradictions within London, contradictions that finally killed him. Brought up by an impoverished middle-class foster-father who failed at many enterprises, knowing grueling labor as a boy, and determined to rise out of the pit of poverty by his own efforts, he was all of his life obsessed by the notion of demonstrating his personal superiority by becoming rich despite the odds against him which the system imposed. In the writings of Benjamin Kidd, a popular expositor of social Darwinism of the day, and of Herbert Spencer, Friedrich Nietzsche, and Ernst Haeckel, he found a philosophy which answered to his needs. What appealed to him was not Spencer's concept of social evolution—which influenced Bennett—but his exaltation of capitalist competition. Such Spencerian and Nietzschean phrases as "the struggle for existence," "the survival of the fittest," "the Superman," the "blond beasts," and "the will to power" intoxicated him. They rationalized the racial prejudices he imbibed from his parents and his social environment, and they ministered to his narcissism.

These ideas and the ideas of Marxist socialism existed together in Jack London's mind. He was aware of the conflict within himself and of the dangers it held for him: Martin Eden, his autobiographical hero in the novel of that title, a Nietzschean individualist, is told by his friend, seeking to convert him to socialism, "socialism will save you in the time of disappointment that is coming to you."[5] But at the end Jack London died at the age of forty-one, sated, like Martin Eden, by a success that had become meaningless to him and probably, like him, a suicide.

The Iron Heel, however, is, with some lapses, true to the socialist ideals of proletarian fraternity, solidarity, and internationalism. It was written at one of those times, says London's daughter, Joan, in her Marxist biography of him, when

> race barriers went down before his enthusiasm for the Cause, and when, dazzled by the extent and militancy of the struggle, he lost his distrust of the working class and called all men Brothers and Comrades. . . . At such times he was completely sincere, forgetting his Anglo-Saxon superiority, his determination to beat the capitalists at their own game, . . . and his creed of the "survival of the fittest" in the "tooth-and-nail" struggle for existence.[6]

There are, to be sure, Nietzschean phrases in *The Iron Heel,* but they have been rendered almost entirely innocuous. Avis says of Ernest, "He was a natural aristocrat—and this in spite of the fact that he was in the camp of the non-aristocrats. He was a superman, a blond beast such as Nietzsche has described, and in addition he was aflame with democracy" (p. 7). He is like London's Nietzschean heroes, Wolf Larsen and Martin Eden— and like Jack London—in possessing a splendid body of average height, and a powerful mind; but he does not have their Nietzschean contempt for the masses, which was the projection of Nietzsche's bourgeois thinking. "He had been born in the working class," says Avis later, "though he was a descendant of Everhards that for over two hundred years had lived in America." Although London could not forbear giving this biographical detail in telling of the hero modeled on himself, he adds in a footnote: "The distinction between being native born and foreign born was sharp and invidious in those days" (p. 23 and n.). Proletarian fraternity and solidarity prevail over racism and vanity.

Revolutionary internationalism also prevails. Although it must be sadly said that London was to speak out for the Allies against "the Hun" when World War I actually came, in *The Iron Heel* on the day that Germany and the United States declare war on each other the working class of each country goes out on general strike with an ultimatum that it will be continued until the war is called off. And although, it must again be sadly said, London wrote about "the Yellow Peril" for Hearst, in *The Iron Heel* we are told that Japan, "ever urging and aiding the yellow and brown races against the white," "dreamed of continental empire and strove to realize the dream" but that "she suppressed her own proletarian revolution. . . . The coolie socialists were executed by tens of thousands" (p. 199). The crying up of color by the Japanese rulers is thus shown by their massacre of their own people to be a fraud and a cover for their own imperialism; it is the class war which is the real conflict, and the Japanese socialists are aligned with their brethren in other lands.

One bit of racism, however, does find its way into the novel. When the troop trains ahead of them show the riders of a train going to Chicago that the Iron Heel is preparing a great blood-letting there, "the very negroes that waited on us," we are told, "knew that something terrible was impending. . . . The lightness of their natures had ebbed out of them" (p. 269). Here London unthinkingly accepts the racist stereotype of the "happy darky," little knowing that Blacks, casting aside their mask of subservience and giving vent to their accumulated grievance, would fifty years later be in the very forefront of the struggle against the social status quo. It must be added, however, that he made the Black maid on the train a member of the underground—although the fact that he speaks of her as a "mulatto" (p. 268) may be another subtle indication of submerged racism.

With Jack London's belief in the biological inferiority of all races to the white race, especially the Anglo-Saxons, went a belief in the biological inferiority of women—although in his militant socialist periods he was an ardent advocate of women's suffrage and agreed with his brilliant Russian-Jewish friend, Anna Strunsky, on the equality of women. His second wife, Charmion, however, who could write complacently that Jack "held a reserved opinion as to the intellectuality of the average female brain,"[7] regarded him with self-abasing adulation. "I am forever enslaved to him for his love," she says in the preface to her gushy biography of him,[8] and later, telling of how he did not permit her to have a separate bank account or even an "allowance" although she had come to him independently wealthy, she says, "I found the bondage sweet."[9]

Avis, like Charmion, was the daughter of a professor who met her husband when he was taking courses at the university despite his lack of formal schooling. She regards him with the same kind of adulation that Charmion regarded Jack. "Such pride was mine," she says when he is facing the club of plutocrats, "that I felt I must rise up and cry out to the assembled company: 'He is mine! He has held me in his arms, and I, mere I, have filled that mind of his to the exclusion of all his multitudinous and kingly thoughts!'" (p. 66). Later she says of her role in life, "To bring forgetfulness, or the light of gladness, into those poor tired eyes of his—what greater joy could have blessed me than that?" (p. 156). But although Avis is capable of such exclamations she is also capable of participating in the underground struggle, and there are other women, undoubtedly inspired by the Russian women terrorists and by Jack's women friends in the Socialist Party, Anna Strunsky and Jane Roulston, who perform legendary feats as members of the Fighting Groups. The fact that the chief of these, Anna Roylston (Anna [Strunsky] + [Jane] Roylston), is called the "Red Virgin" (p. 243) perhaps suggests, however, that in doing so she abjures her femininity.

Avis's mawkishness is a defect in the novel. The socialist historian speaks in his foreword of the "vitiation" of her account "due to the bias of love" and adds, "Yet we smile, indeed, and forgive Avis Everhard for the heroic lines upon which she modelled her husband." Perhaps this remark expresses Jack's own perception of the extravagance of Avis's (and of Charmion's) adulation, or perhaps the historian's judicious statement that Ernest, although "exceptionally strong," was not as "colossal" (pp. vii-viii) as his wife represented him, is designed to indicate that the serene future will be unable to plumb the heroism aroused by a time of struggle. In any event, the indulgent smile which he suggests is elicited by Avis's worshipfulness comes closer to being an embarrassed grin.

The chief expression of London's social Darwinism and his Nietzscheism, however, is not his lapses into racism and sexism but his biological determinism, manifesting itself in references to the caveman and in the animal images with which the novel teems, a biological determinism, however, which differs, as we shall see, from that of such novels as *The Call of the Wild*. Thus Ernest, looking forward zestfully to arousing the assembled plutocrats, says: "I'll make them snarl like wolves. . . . I shall menace their money-bags. That will shake them up to the roots of their primitive natures. . . . You will see the cave-man, in evening dress, snarling and snapping over a bone" (pp. 64-65). His challenge to their power and wealth does indeed reveal their wolf-natures. The "low, throaty rumble" that emanates from Ernest's aroused audience is "the growl of the pack, mouthed by the pack, and mouthed in all unconsciousness," "the token of the brute in man, the earnest of his primitive passions" (p. 73).

The irony is that these men teach their children under the Iron Heel that they, as aristocrats, represent humanity as against the bestiality of the masses.

They looked upon themselves as wild-animal trainers, rulers of beasts. . . . If ever they weakened, the great beast would engulf them and everything of beauty and wonder and joy and good in its cavernous and slime-dripping maw. Without them, anarchy would reign and humanity would drop backward into the primitive night out of which it had so painfully emerged. [P. 256]

There is this much truth in their rationalizations: they themselves have brutalized the masses, arousing their animal natures. "There in the labor-ghettos is the roaring abysmal beast the oligarchs fear so dreadfully—but it is the beast of their own making. In it they will not let the ape and tiger die" (p. 259). At the conclusion, when Avis gazes in pity upon the mounds of dead of the people of the abyss, she uses a different kind of animal image. "Poor driven people of the abyss, hunted helots—they lay there as the rabbits in California after a drive"—and in a footnote the socialist historian describes the custom of rabbit-driving: "On a given day all the farmers in a locality would assemble and sweep across the country in converging lines, driving the rabbits by scores of thousands into a prepared closure, where they were clubbed to death by men and boys" (p. 296 and n.).

Ernest himself is more than once described in animal images. Avis often refers to him as her "eagle," and it is in this image that he is presented in his speech to the plutocrats:

"We want in our hands the reins of power and the destiny of mankind. Here are our hands. They are strong hands." . . . And as he spoke he extended from his splendid shoulders his two great arms, and the horse-shoer's hands [Ernest had been a blacksmith] were clutching the air like an eagle's talons. He was the spirit of regnant labor as he stood there, his hands outreaching to rend and crush his audience. [Pp. 4, 72-73]

When he addresses Congress, taunting its Republican and Democratic members with being "creatures of the Plutocracy," there is a great uproar. "He stood disdainfully till the din had somewhat subsided. He waved his hand to include all of them, turned to his own comrades, and said: 'Listen to the bellowing of the well-fed beasts.'" When pandemonium breaks out again, and there are cries of "Sedition!" and "Anarchist!", "Ernest was not pleasant to look at. Every fighting fibre of him was quivering, and his face was the face of a fighting animal, withal he was cool and collected" (p. 217). His composure is not only in sharp contrast to the raging members of the Congress; it is in sharp contrast to the raging plutocrats he had addressed, of whom Avis had ironically said, "These, then, were the cool captains of industry and lords of society, these snarling, growling savages in evening clothes" (p. 77). Ernest has the combative spirit of an aroused animal, but his command of his passions makes him representative of that humanity which is superior to its own animal nature.

Instead, then, of the romantic primitivism of many of Jack London's other works, in which the supposed physical courage and vigor of man's animal and primitive past are glorified and contrasted with the decadence of civilization, we have something else: an animal nature that is only in part glorified and that must be transcended by humanity. The capitalists "will not let the ape and tiger die." Under socialism, however, people will not be brutalized but will attain their full human height.

Instead of competitiveness and individualism being regarded as the law of evolution, in accordance with the tenets of social Darwinism, cooperation is presented as the law of human social evolution, and its final achievement will be the realization of a classless society.

> You are perishing [Ernest Everhard tells the small businessmen] and you are doomed to perish utterly from the face of society. This is the fiat of evolution. . . . Primitive man was a puny creature hiding in the crevices of the rocks. He combined and made war upon his carnivorous enemies. They were competitive beasts. Primitive man was a combinative beast, and because of it he rose to primacy over all the animals. And man has been achieving greater and greater combinations ever since. . . . Socialism [is] a greater combination than the trusts, a greater economic and social combination than any that has as yet appeared on the planet. It is in line with evolution. . . . It is the winning side. [Pp. 13-15]

London possibly got this idea of man as surviving through cooperation at second- or third-hand from Peter Kropotkin's *Mutual Aid as a Factor in Evolution*, which was published in 1902 but was not available in English at the time of the writing of *The Iron Heel*. The Russian anarchist and geographer, however, had found through personal observation in Siberia that not only man but many animals survived through cooperation. As the noted Dutch astronomer and Marxist theorist Anton Pannekoek, taking up this point, said in his pamphlet *Marxism and Darwinism*,

When a number of animals live in a group, herd, or flock, [the] combining of the animals' separate powers into one unit gives to the group a new and much stronger power than any one individual possessed, even the strongest. . . . These relations throw an entirely different light upon the views of the bourgeois [social] Darwinists.[10]

Pannekoek found that man "rose to primacy over all the animals" not, as London said, because he alone was a "combinative beast" but because he had a flexible thumb and developed a superior brain. It was these which made it possible for him, as breeder and cultivator, to intervene in the workings of the laws of biological development but made him subject to the laws of social development:

The use of tools marks the great departure that is ever more widening between man and animals. . . . Organs are natural, adnated (grown-on) tools of the animal. Tools are the artificial organs of men. . . . Owing to the construction of the hand to hold various tools, it becomes a general organ adapted to all kinds of work. . . . Man . . . by transferring his organic development upon external objects . . . has been able, within the short period of a few thousand years, to rise above the highest animal. . . . With the origin of tools, . . . human organs remain what they were, with the exception of the brain. The human brain had to develop together with tools. . . . The principle that struggle leads to the perfection of the weapons used in the strife . . . leads [in animals] to a continuous development of natural organs. . . . In men, it leads to a continuous development of tools, of the means of production. . . . When men freed themselves from the animal world, the development of tools and productive methods, the division of labor and knowledge became the propelling force in social development.[11]

Thus Darwinism and Marxism are really explanations of a fundamental law that manifests itself differently in the animal world and the world of humans.

The social instincts of the primates and other social animals, says Pannekoek, developed into moral feelings in humans, as they developed in consciousness. Whereas, however, among animals the social group remained the same, with little variation, among humans social groups change in accordance with economic development. Under primitive communism the social group was the tribe. Social groups expanded far beyond the tribe with the rise of civilization, but, says Engels, "exploitation of one class by another being the basis of civilization, its whole development involves a continual contradiction." Civilization made possible the advances of humanity by producing surpluses beyond immediate needs, "but these exploits were accomplished by playing on the most sordid passions and instincts of man."[12]

This insight of Engels, which is significant for London's biological determinism, is corroborated by twentieth-century anthropologists. "Nothing comparable to war exists at low levels of [human] development. This obviously implies that there is no biological determination of war," writes the distinguished student of primitive peoples, Bronislaw Malinowski.[13] The well-known anthropologist Ashley Montagu, drawing upon Malinowski and others, concludes in *Man and Aggression*, a volume he edited in which many scholars in allied fields take issue with the works of the new wave of social Darwinism (Robert Ardrey's *The Territorial Imperative*, Konrad Lorenz's *On Aggression*, Desmond Morris's *The Naked Ape*):

> Throughout the two million years of man's evolution the highest premium has been placed on cooperation. . . . Intra- or intergroup hostilities, in small populations, would have endangered the very existence of such populations. . . . There is not the slightest evidence nor is there the least reason to suppose that such conflicts ever occurred in human populations before the development of agricultural-pastoral communities. not much more than 12,000 years ago.[14]

Far from humans being biologically determined to aggressiveness and competitiveness by their animal and primitive past, it is only with "the development of agricultural-pastoral communities," that is, class society, that these drives have been generated in us. Jack London's picture of the capitalists as cavemen in evening clothes, "snarling and snapping over a bone" (p. 65), traduces the cavemen. It is class society, not primitive instincts, which is responsible for covetousness. However, Jack London's perception of the human being as a fundamentally cooperative animal capable of achieving a classless society—or, rather, of returning to it on a higher level—holds good.

The Iron Heel pictures the forces in capitalist society that work towards the revolution through which the classless society will be attained, and the forces that work against it. It is time to turn to this picture to see its significance for our time.

It has been frequently pointed out that the society of *The Iron Heel* remarkably resembles fascism, with its brutal repressiveness, its omnipresent secret police, its elitist ideology, its integration of controlled unions into the national government, its praetorian troops, its industrial and financial oligarchy at the top of the pyramid. Fascism, however, occurring at a time of the sharpest crisis of monopoly capitalism, is only its ultimate consummation.

The Iron Heel society has many features similar to our own monopoly capitalist society. For some of these Jack London is indebted to *Our Benevolent Feudalism*, published in 1903 by W. J. Ghent, a leading socialist of the day, in which an ironic picture is presented of monopoly capitalism growing in power, stabilizing itself, and reducing all classes to a contented subservience to itself in a society almost as stratified as that of feudalism. Much more, however, is he indebted to the *Communist Manifesto*, with its theses about the growth of big business, the concentration of wealth, the decline of the middle class, and the recurrence of economic crises.

Ernest, in speaking to the small businessmen, tells them that their efforts against the trusts are to no avail: big business will come to dominate the economy even more than it already does. How does the monopolization of business stand today, after the trust-busting legislation of Theodore Roosevelt, the New Freedom of Woodrow Wilson, and the fulminations against the "economic royalists" by Franklin D. Roosevelt? The then Attorney General John N. Mitchell, in a speech on June 6, 1969, said: "In 1948, the nation's 200 largest industrial corporations controlled 48 percent of the manufacturing assets. Today, these firms control 58 percent, while the top 500 firms control 75 percent of these assets."[15] Mitchell is not notable for his general veracity, but on this matter it can be assumed that he told the truth—or, at least, that he did not err in the direction of exaggeration. In fact, others have found that if we break down the figures concerning the 200 largest firms, big business becomes even more huge. Thus Willard F. Mueller, director of the Federal Trade Commission's Bureau of Economics, said, in testifying before a United States Senate subcommittee, that, while the 200 largest manufacturing corporations in 1962 held 56 percent of all assets, the 20 largest manufacturing corporations held 25 percent of all assets, the same amount as the 419,000 smallest companies.[16]

Ernest also tells the small businessmen that monopolization of industry will mean a greater concentration of wealth. Ferdinand Lundberg in 1968 said that "the share of top wealth-holders at this writing is easily the greatest in history" and estimated that the share of the top 0.5 percent was greater than one-third of the total wealth.[17] The significance of this is brought out more sharply by Richard Parker when he cites the *United States Treasury, Statistics of Income 1962*, the last date the government published these statistics, to the effect that "the total wealth of the richest 2% of Americans was greater than the *U.S. Gross National Product*" (his italics).[18]

Despite enormous tax loopholes that permitted some of the persons with the greatest incomes to escape paying taxes altogether and greatly reduced the taxes of others, Parker points out that the 4,000 persons with the highest reported incomes in 1968 claimed a total income of nearly 4 billion dollars, twice as much as the government was spending on its antipoverty program and enough to provide a poverty-level income for over one million families.[19] Paul Samuelson, the Nobel laureate in economics, visualizes for us what such figures mean: "If we made an income pyramid out of child's blocks, with each layer portraying $1,000 of income, the peak would be far higher than the Eiffel Tower, but almost all of us would be within a yard of the ground."[20]

Ernest also says that the small businessmen are doomed to be wiped out and to join the ranks of the working class. This has not happened on the scale envisaged in the *Communist Manifesto* and in *The Iron Heel*. To the old middle class has been added what has come to be known as the "new middle class"— technicians, foremen, engineers. This "new middle class," it should be noted, was actually foreseen in the *Communist Manifesto*. The petty bourgeois, it states, "see the moment approaching when they will completely disappear as an independent section of modern society, to be replaced in manufactures, agriculture, and commerce, by overlookers [i.e., supervisors, foremen], bailiffs [farm managers], and shopmen [sales executives]."[21] The members of this class are more obviously dependent on large capitalists and more obviously subject to the vagaries of the economy than those of the old middle class. Thus highly trained engineers may undergo long periods of unemployment. And the masses of white-collar workers, who have been regarded by some as members of the "new middle class," really belong with the working class, as the militant strikes of teachers and civil-service employees indicate.

As for the old middle class, it has declined in proportion to labor: the percentage of wage-earners in the gainfully employed population rose from 62% in 1880 to 84% in 1957; that of entrepreneurs fell from 37% to 14% in the same period.[22] The old middle class exists today only in the interstices of the economy and by sufferance of big business. The rate of bankruptcy of the average small business is very high, and its economic life is very short. It is typified by the gasoline filling-station operators, who are nominally running independent enterprises but are in reality dependent on the big oil companies. Of this middle class it may be said what Jack London said of it in describing the economic situation just before the socialists' electoral victory: "The sturdy skeleton of it remained; but it was without power. The small manufacturers and small business men who still survived were at the complete mercy of the Plutocracy" (p. 176).

A section of the middle class is the farmers. What happened to them is described by Avis as follows: "The hard times of 1912 had already caused a frightful slump in the farm markets. . . . Thus the farmers were compelled to borrow more and more, while they were prevented from paying back old loans. Then ensued the great foreclosing of mortgages and enforced collection of notes. The farmers simply surrendered the land to the farm trust" (p. 177). This process has been taking place since the appearance of *The Iron Heel*, greatly accelerated during the depression thirties, the story of which was told by John Steinbeck in *The Grapes of Wrath*. Today, writes the Marxist economist Ernest Mandel, a recipient of the highly prestigious Alfred Marshall Fellowship of Cambridge University, the number of farmers, their employees, and family help, is less than 5,500,000 (it had been 32 million in 1910, when the population was so much smaller), fewer than the number of college students.[23] The "farm trust" has indeed taken over. "Nineteen percent of the U.S. farmers," said Senator Abraham Ribicoff in a speech on April 2, 1973, "raise over 75 percent of all our agricultural products, and 7 percent of the Nation's ranchers raise 80 percent of the Nation's beef. What we have in our country today is large agribusinesses which dominate the industry."[24]

Explaining in simple terms the doctrine of surplus value, Ernest Everhard shows to the small businessmen how the production of surplus value must lead to crises of "over-production," resulting from the fact that labor cannot buy back what it has produced. He slyly tells them how the problem can be solved. "'I'll tell you a way to get rid of the surplus,' Ernest said. 'Throw every year hundreds of millions of dollars' worth of shoes and wheat and clothing and all the commodities of commerce into the sea. Won't that fix it?'" (pp. 128-29).

Ernest's proposal is not seriously intended; it is a feint preliminary to a satiric thrust at the desire of his listeners to go back to the primitive mode of production of small capitalism. Despite the absurdity of Ernest's ironic proposal, it was actually acted upon during the depression of the thirties, when farmers were paid to plough their crops under and to slaughter piglets, in a program of restricting agriculture that continued until 1974.

During the post–World War II boom capitalist economists believed that Keynesianism had repealed the laws of capitalism leading to periodic crises of "over-production," with recessions being limited and of short duration. Paul Samuelson, taking issue with Marxist economists such as Paul Sweezy, predicted that "the ancient scourge of intermittent-shortage-of-purchasing-power" would not recur in the next hundred years.[25] Less than two years later he was urging Gerald Ford to increase the amount of tax rebates in order to stimulate purchasing power sufficiently. Keynesian economics merely postponed the time of reckoning, made deficit spending addictive, and brought permanent inflation.

It is interesting to note that Keynesian economics was anticipated by Jack London. Under the Iron Heel are built great "wonder cities," with the employment of millions of laborers at starvation wages so that in them "the oligarchs [may] dwell and worship beauty"—and expend the surplus "in the same way that the ruling classes of Egypt . . . expended the surplus they robbed from the people by the building of temples and pyramids" (p. 194). The Mercenaries, the soldier caste which evolved out of the old regular army, living in cities of their own and receiving special privileges, also consumed, we are told, a large amount of the surplus. In our day it is the army, with its gigantic expenditures, which sustains the economy (Paul Sweezy and Harry Magdoff calculated that, directly and indirectly, it gave employment to 22.3 million people in 1970);[26] "wonder cities" there are not, and less ambitious public works expenditures are comparatively negligible.

London got one feature of American society under the Iron Heel not from the *Communist Manifesto* but from Daniel De Leon, the leader of the Socialist Labor Party. From De Leon, Jack London—and Lenin—got the phrase "aristocracy of labor" (p. 199) to refer to the specially privileged top stratum of the workers, who follow the lead of the conservative trade union bureaucrats whom De Leon called the "labor lieutenants" of the capitalists. Lenin in *Imperialism* pointed out that as a result of the superprofits the capitalists of imperialist countries exact from their colonies they are able to create labor aristocracies which are detached from the mass of proletarians. He added, however, that this division among workers can cause only a "temporary decay in the working class movement,"[27] for it is dependent on a prolonged period of prosperity such as England experienced during the heyday of its empire.

Avis describes the formation of the labor castes as rising from the membership of the favored powerful unions:

> "Give us more pay and charge it to the public," was the slogan of the strong unions. . . . In charging it to the public, it was charged to the great mass of unorganized labor and of weakly organized labor. . . . This idea . . . was merely carried to its logical conclusion, on a large scale, by the combination of the oligarchs and the favored unions. . . . Finding it impossible to dwell in safety in the midst of the betrayed proletariat, they [the members of the favored unions] moved into new localities inhabited by themselves alone. . . . The members of the favored unions became the aristocracy of labor. They were set apart from the rest of labor. They were better housed, better clothed, better fed, better treated. . . . And for the less fortunate brothers and sisters, the unfavored laborers, the driven people of the abyss, they cared nothing. [Pp. 197-99, 255]

Here London is misapplying the concept of a "labor aristocracy." He is no doubt reflecting the reality of trade unions in his day, when the norm was the craft union, which often made deals with employers that resulted in blocking the organizing of nonunion workers. Nevertheless, London's view that the higher-paid workers got their higher wages from the earnings of "the great mass of unorganized labor" is incorrect. All workers, whether they are paid highly or not, are paid out of the earnings they themselves produce out of their own labor. If a worker were not to produce enough to cover his or her own wages plus profit for the employer, that worker would be fired.

The labor aristocracy is "bought off" in the sense that these more privileged workers are made to feel superior, and to feel that their interests and those of the capitalists are the same. The lower-paid workers, on the other hand, are encouraged to feel that the higher-paid workers are living off them and don't have the same interests. Such feelings are most prevalent during periods of prolonged expansion, when capitalists have more flexibility to give higher wages to a few in order the better to perpetuate their system at the expense of all workers. During periods of contraction, when the wages of all workers are under assault, it is more readily seen that the bosses use the division between the higher-paid workers and the lower-paid or unemployed workers to drive down the wages and working conditions of all workers. Hence the support of the steelworkers union for affirmative action to end discrimination against Blacks and women in the *Weber* case.

If London, however, mistakenly accepts the view that the "labor aristocracy" benefits at the expense of the other workers, his description of the "people of the abyss" under the Iron Heel is prescient, containing features suggestive of the situation today in the ghetto slums:

> The rest of the working class was more harshly treated. . . . Its wages and its standard of living steadily sank down. . . . Its public schools deteriorated. . . . The increase in the younger generation of children who could not read or write was perilous. . . . [P. 199]

One is reminded of those living in the South Bronx, 35 percent Black and 65 percent Puerto Rican, 40 percent of whom are on welfare and 30 percent of whom are unemployed; where 20 percent of the apartments are without water (drinking water is obtained in bitter cold weather from open fire hydrants) and 50 percent lack heat half of the time during the winter; where packs of wild dogs scavenge the garbage and not infrequently attack people. To visit this area, as Martin Tolchin said in describing these conditions, is, "even for a native New Yorker, . . . a journey to a foreign country where fear is the overriding emotion in a landscape of despair."[28]

The "landscape of despair" is not confined to one section of New York City. In 1968 a CBS television documentary, "Hunger in America," shocked the nation in its portrayal of the deprivations suffered by an estimated thirty million Americans unable to afford an adequate diet.[29] Politicians vowed to wipe out this shame, but this was soon forgotten. Today inflation and unemployment have manifestly made things worse, not better. Kenneth Keniston, Mellon Professor of Human Development at Massachusetts Institute of Technology and chairman and executive director of the Carnegie Council on Children, writes:

> The one out of every three children who lives below the minimum adequate budget established by the Labor Department must face the multiple scars of poverty. . . . Approximately one-quarter of all American children do not receive anything approaching adequate health care, nor did their mothers before they were born—whence our disgraceful infant mortality rates.[30]

And this in a country which, although having only 6 percent of the world's population, has a ruling class that possesses a monstrously disproportionate amount of the world's wealth! In the words of the *Communist Manifesto*—echoed by Ernest's statement to the plutocrats, "You have failed in your management" (p. 25)—the bourgeoisie "is unfit to rule because it is incompetent to assure an existence to its slave within his slavery, because it cannot help letting him sink into such a state that it has to feed him instead of being fed by him."[31]

The processes at work in capitalism are, of course, exaggerated in *The Iron Heel* for artistic effect, both, on the one hand, in the rapidity of events that lead to the rule of the Iron Heel and, on the other hand, in the length of time in which it holds power. If, however, London shows the Iron Heel as enduring for four centuries, the existence of a classless society under which Avis's manuscript is edited vindicates Ernest's faith in the inevitability of socialism. The statement in the *Communist Manifesto* that the victory of the proletariat is inevitable has been caviled with on the ground that one cannot speak of inevitability, only possibility. Marx, however, did not mean, of course, that socialism would come without the will or action of the proletariat, but that the problems of capitalism could be solved only by socialism, that the new social organization can be achieved only through the working class, and that, since being determines consciousness, the working class will, sooner or later, come to this understanding and act accordingly.

It is true, however, that the *Communist Manifesto* says that previous class struggles "ended either in a revolutionary reconstitution of society at large or in the common ruin of the contending classes."[32] Today, with the natural resources of the world, upon which the entire human race of the future must depend, being depleted at an alarming rate by capitalist anarchy, and with the possibilities of nuclear destruction, the choice may well be that of socialism or common ruin.

Fortunately, the possibilities of an American proletarian revolution are not as remote as many might think, despite the low degree of socialist consciousness in the working class today compared to that of Jack London's time. In the 1920s, industry-wide unionization of the basic industries, which had been vainly striven for by nineteenth-century militant unionists like Debs, by DeLeonites, and then in the twentieth century by the IWW and the Communists, seemed equally unlikely, but it was achieved through great class battles when labor rose up after recovering from the first shock of the depression. With these class battles came a great rise of socialist consciousness. Today American capitalism, which has witnessed the steady worldwide advance of socialism during the past half-century but which profited at the expense of its capitalist rivals in the first phase of capitalism's decline, confronts a new world crisis, marked by unemployment, inflation, monetary instability, and sharpening interimperialist rivalry. To solve its problems, American business is seeking to cut labor costs; this is the meaning of the forecast of continued high unemployment. This is also the meaning of the attacks on wages and conditions of work and the cutting of environmental controls. The economic position of workers is becoming more and more insecure. The load of indebtedness on such things as housing and automobiles is very great. A prolonged serious illness or unemployment or a continued high inflation means great hardship for most people.

But labor will not indefinitely continue to give up what it has gained since the war. The radicalization which has proceeded unevenly in different sectors of American society will make its way to labor, with members of those sectors within the ranks of labor—the Blacks, the youth, the women, that is, labor's most oppressed elements—playing an important role in the radicalization. And labor has through its position in production the power that these sectors, standing by themselves, do not have.

We, who have seen the various revolutions of the twentieth century, can better understand the mechanics of proletarian revolution than did Jack London. As he envisaged it, at least in one portion of the narrative, the revolution was a military uprising by a highly disciplined organization of revolutionists, situated in key points, who sought for surprise in a carefully planned lightning blow. This is far from Trotsky's description of the masses in the Russian revolution as the steam power which propelled the engine of revolution but the disciplined revolutionary party as the piston-box which concentrated the power and prevented it from dissipating itself.

There is, in fact, significant confusion in London's mind as to how the revolution will triumph. Ernest, predicting the society of the Iron Heel, foretells the formation of the labor castes and the brutalization of the rest of labor and says,

Membership in the labor castes will become hereditary. . . . There will be no inflow of new strength from that eternal reservoir of strength, the common people. . . . And beneath will be the abyss, wherein will fester and starve and rot, and ever renew itself, the common people, the great bulk of the population. And in the end, who knows in what day, the common people will rise out of the abyss; the labor castes and the Oligarchy will crumble away; and then, at last, after the travail of the centuries, will it be the day of the common man. [Pp. 192-95]

However, in the description of the first revolt, largely planned by Ernest, we are told that the revolutionary organization—we are not told how it is recruited—has its agents by the thousands in the labor castes and in the Mercenaries and has even penetrated the secret police and the oligarchy itself, as well as having agents among the people of the abyss. The function of all of these agents is to create a maximum of disruption while the revolutionists are "gaining control of all the machinery of society." There is no question of the common people rising out of the abyss. They are "to be loosed on the palaces and cities of the masters," acting as a diversionary force by calling forth great numbers of police and Mercenaries to quell them. "It would merely mean that various dangers to us were harmlessly destroying one another" (p. 264).

The "unorganized people of the abyss," capable only of destructive rage, are, then, only a danger to the revolutionists despite what Ernest had said. Perhaps we are to think that this is because it is as yet too early a stage in their development and that eventually they will fulfill Ernest's prediction, but there is no hint as to how "the refuse and the scum of life" (p. 279) will be transformed into a revolutionary force. On the other hand, it seems that the labor castes and even the Mercenaries offer possibilities, after all, for the revolutionists to gain mass followings. In Chicago, with its traditions of militant class struggle, "even the labor castes . . . were alive with revolt," and their spirit "had infected the Mercenaries" (p. 265), three regiments of whom were ready to join the revolution. The Chicago revolutionists and their followers are, however, isolated and crushed by the Iron Heel, which precipitates a premature revolt by feeding them false news of "insubordination all over the land," defections of Mercenaries in California, and "an outbreak of the populace in New York City, in which the labor castes were joining" (pp. 270, 271). Why the Chicago revolutionists should have believed it reasonable that these things were occurring, what the grounds for this expected wide rebelliousness were, and how the revolutionists sought to mobilize it is not indicated.

The picture of the people of the abyss in *The Iron Heel* is derived from its author's personal observations in London's East

End slums during the coronation year of 1902, described in his book entitled *The People of the Abyss*. Here we find the same mixture of compassion, repulsion, and dread with regard to the slum inhabitants and the same outrage and indignation against the rulers of a society in which such a horrible state of affairs exists. The appalling description of "a mob, an awful river that filled the street, the people of the abyss, mad with drink and wrong, . . . in concrete waves of wrath, . . . withered hags and death's-heads bearded like patriarchs, . . . crooked, twisted, misshapen monsters . . . a raging, screaming, screeching demoniacal horde" (p. 279) is anticipated in this passage of London's sociological study, with the same image of the crowd as the waves of a fiercely flowing body of water:

> The streets were filled with a new and different race of people, short of stature, and of wretched or beer-sodden appearance. . . . Here and there lurched a drunken man or woman. . . . Tottery old men and women were searching in the garbage. . . . For the first time in my life the fear of the crowd smote me. It was like the fear of the sea; and the miserable multitudes, street upon street, seemed so many waves of a vast and malodorous sea, lapping about me and threatening to well up and over me.[33]

It is in this sea that Avis is indeed swept up and borne along.

The people of the abyss in *The Iron Heel* are, however, highly exploited workers, not members of the lumpen-proletariat, demoralized and disorganized, as the slum-dwellers of the East End were. Here London, who read the *Communist Manifesto* to such good effect, might have profited from a closer reading of it. "The 'dangerous class,'" say Marx and Engels of the lumpen-proletariat, "the social scum, that passively rotting mass thrown off by the lowest layers of old society, may, here and there, be swept into the movement by a proletarian revolution; its conditions of life, however, prepare it far more for the part of a bribed tool of reactionary intrigue."[34] The workers, however, far from being a "passively rotting mass," are constantly "recruited from all classes of the population."[35] "With the development of industry the proletariat not only increases in number; it becomes concentrated in greater masses, its strength grows, and it feels that strength more."[36]

And, finally, what of the Iron Heel itself? Is London's warning that the ruling class will not permit socialism to be instituted through an electoral victory applicable today? Lenin, writing in

The State and Revolution in 1917, pointed out that Marx in 1871 implied that it may not be necessary in England, as on the Continent, to smash the "ready-made state machinery" to effect a social revolution. But England, said Lenin, at that time had no militarist clique and was largely without a bureaucracy, while now "both England and America . . . have completely sunk into the all-European filthy, bloody morass of bureaucratic-military institutions which subordinate everything to themselves, trample everything underfoot."[37] How much more is this true today! As we think of the power of the Pentagon, the CIA, and the FBI, and how these have operated, we can see that the American machinery of state will not be able to be operated by a party determined to make a social revolution.

An expression of contemporary Army thinking reveals how remarkably prophetic Jack London was in this matter. The "apocalyptic" imagination of the creative artist anticipates the cold-blooded planning of the military technician. Describing the warfare under the skyscrapers of Chicago, London says, "Each building was a possible ambuscade. This was warfare in that modern jungle, a great city. Every street was a canyon, every building a mountain" (p. 276). In the January 1968 issue of *Army*, a magazine published by the Association of the U.S. Army that describes itself as "a professional journal . . . representing the interests of the U.S. Army," its associate editor, Colonel Robert B. Rigg, wrote as follows:

> During the next few years organized urban insurrection could explode to the extent that portions of large American cities could become scenes of destruction approaching those of Stalingrad in World War II. . . . Man has constructed out of steel and concrete a much better "jungle" than Nature created in Vietnam. . . . To prevent and to curb urban violence of any order we must establish an effective system of intelligence in the ghettos of urban America. . . . There will also be needed among the well established political-tactical-military informants those who can help guide troops and police through the maze of buildings, stair-wells, streets, alley-ways, tunnels and sewers. . . . The active Army . . . must train for the concrete jungle as well as for the other kind.[38]

The army commanders who loosed such horrors in Vietnam are ready to do the same in the United States. It can happen here.

II

REVOLUTIONARY CONSCIOUSNESS IN THE 1930s

Introduction to Section II

What Lenin called the powder barrel of imperialist rivalries exploded in 1914. After three years of war, the Bolsheviks triumphed in humanity's first successful proletarian revolution. The Bolsheviks regarded their revolution as one that would spread to other European countries, which would cooperate in the building of socialism. "We have always proclaimed and repeated this elementary truth of Marxism," stated Lenin in 1922, "that the victory of socialism requires the joint efforts of workers in a number of advanced countries."[1] In the last article he ever wrote, "Better Less but Better" (April 1923), he said: "We are not civilized enough to pass directly to Socialism though we have the political premises for it."[2]

However, the German, Austrian, and Hungarian revolutions were crushed in blood. The Russian revolution itself was not crushed because, as Trotsky said in *Europe and America* (a collection of two speeches, one delivered in 1924 and the other in 1926), "our backwardness proved temporarily to be also to our advantage."[3] The revolution survived despite years of blockade, civil war, and foreign military intervention by relying on its vast underdeveloped hinterland. Trotsky proposed a program of industrialization and of inducements for voluntary collectivization of agriculture to strengthen the Soviet Union until the resurgence of European revolution. Stalin opposed the Left Opposition's program of planned industrialization and collectivization until Trotsky had been exiled to Central Asia and the economy had begun to collapse; then he frantically plunged into a distorted version of it, a breakneck industrialization without regard to the harmonious development of the different branches of industry and a forced rather than voluntary collectivization without material and educational preparation, arousing great peasant resistance and bringing the country to the verge of ruin. As Isaac

Deutscher said, barbarism was scourged out of the Soviet Union by barbaric means—which meant that barbarism survived in other forms.[4] The unprecedented advance in production, education, and science attested to the inherent superiority of the new economic system, beset though it was by the problems arising from the existence of a parasitic bureaucracy that grew up because Russia was "not civilized enough to pass directly to Socialism." The despotic and reactionary features of the Soviet regime—a betrayal of the ideas of socialism—were world capitalism's revenge upon it, a reaction rising from the pressure of the rival system.

In the capitalist world the intelligentsia's faith in rationality and intellectual progress was shattered by the First World War. But in the United States, where economists, politicians, and business leaders vied with each other in proclaiming the unlimited continuance of postwar prosperity (an anthology of their statements was published as bitter commentary during the depression), there were new illusions about capitalism overcoming its periodic economic crises. Trotsky, while entirely free of these illusions, grasped the implications of America's new economic ascendancy better than did its own leaders, predicting a course of expansionism and counterrevolution which they, still caught up in the tradition of isolationism, were only hesitantly groping for—a course which became fully apparent only after World War II. He foresaw that the United States would become the world's leading imperialist power, replacing "the colonial rule of England by the economic domination of America," with England having to be content with the modest role of a junior partner. If America did not have the bases of the far-flung British Empire, which had enabled England to maintain its sway over countries in all the continents, "America will find allies and helpers all over the world—the strongest power always finds them—and together with these allies will find the necessary bases."[5] The Wilsonian "toga of pacificism" would be replaced by the armor of a militarized America.[6]

With the accumulation of capital in the United States, Trotsky continued, that country would have to invest its surplus all over the world. But "the more the United States puts the whole world under its dependence, all the more does it become dependent upon the whole world, with all its contradictions and threatening upheavals."[7] Consequently, "there is no enemy of Bolshevism more principled and more savage than American capitalism."[8] But the world domination of America would itself sow the seeds of revolution. "Even where American capitalism penetrates into China with its slogan of the 'Open Door' . . . it finds there among the popular masses not the religion of Americanism but the political program of Bolshevism translated into the Chinese language."[9]

America, moreover, is not itself exempt from the economic laws of capitalism and is, in fact, aggravating them. Its insistence on putting Europe "on rations" by demanding the payment of war debts from its allies and forcing them to collect reparations from Germany was bound to deepen the coming economic crisis, ruin Europe, and, unless there was a successful revolution, lay "the groundwork for new wars on an unprecedented scale and of unimaginable monstrosity."[10]

Precisely this happened. Over-production—the paradox of too many goods producing mass deprivation and unemployment—and the menacing rise of fascism in the capitalist countries contrasted with the advances of the Soviet Union. Western intellectuals looked in great numbers to the Kremlin as the source of hope. In accepting the tutelage of the Kremlin, most of them gave up their critical independence. Trotsky spoke ironically of the vast international literature of "Socialism for Radical Tourists," inspired by the genuine accomplishments of the Soviet Union but blind to the harsh repression and inequalities that accompanied them, written for those who liked to feel that they were in step with the times but who were incapable of making a revolution in their own countries or of distinguishing the revolution in a country where it had succeeded from the leaden rump of the bureaucracy sitting heavily upon it.[11]

3. André Malraux's 'Man's Fate': The Chinese Revolution and 'The Human Condition'

Alfred Kazin, looking back upon his youth in *Starting Out in the Thirties,* describes the effect of André Malraux's *Man's Fate* upon the radicalized young intellectuals of the day: "Malraux, himself still inflamed with the power of Communism to give creative energy to the heroic will, was read by intellectuals as the ideal revolutionary novelist. Although *Man's Fate* was politically a bitter criticism of Stalin's policy in China, which in 1927 had ordered collaboration with Chiang Kai-shek against the better instinct of the Communists who were soon to be massacred by him, this political heresy was not really taken in by those eager to show what Communism could do for intellectuals. . . . He was the novelist of the intellectuals' revolutionary *grandeur.* To those for whom society was a metaphor and the instrument of their newly exalted revolutionary will, Malraux was intoxicating, a breath of power."[1]

The existentialist movement that came into being in France after the Second World War, the Occupation, and the Resistance, when, Sartre said, young intellectuals were "tossed by the cruelty of the time into the forlornness from where one can see our condition as man to the limit, to the absurd, to the night of unknowingness,"[2] found new meaning in *Man's Fate* and Malraux's other novels.

Man's irremediable solitude [says Joseph Frank], his absurd but unquenchable longing to triumph over time; his obligation to assume the burden of freedom by staking his life for his values; his defiance of death as an ultimate affirmation of "authentic" existence—all these Existential themes were given unforgettable artistic expression by Malraux long before they became fashionable intellectual catchwords or tedious artistic platitudes. Indeed, the genesis of French Existentialism as a full-fledged cultural movement probably owes more to Malraux than to Heidegger or Jaspers, Berdyaev or Chestov. For it was Malraux, through his novels, who shaped the sensibilities which then seized on doctrinal Existentialism as an ideological prop.[3]

Malraux himself voiced his characteristic themes from his earliest youthful efforts, which were written in the manner of surrealism, the cult of irrationalism that was the product of the disillusionment with the belief in reason and progress of the Europe which had engaged in the carnage of World War I. In his first work, "Paper Moons," a surrealistic fantasy published in 1921 when he was twenty, says David Wilkinson,

a party of strange little men journey to the Bizarre Kingdom to kill its ruler, Death, so that they can seize power from Satan, who has dethroned God. The disappearance of God from human experience, the dominion of a "demonic" within man himself, the journey into unfamiliar lands to seek power and to struggle against the very real presence of death, all subsequently became elaborate themes for Malraux.[4]

Malraux was obsessed by the idea of death throughout his artistic career. Robert Payne tells a story about him as a thirteen-year-old schoolboy which is significant:

At the battle of the Marne the army of General von Kluck was thrown back near Paris, and soon the schoolchildren from Bondy were being taken to see the battlefield. There had been no time to bury the dead: the bodies were piled up, soaked in gasoline and burned. The children had just arrived on the battlefield when lunch, consisting of bread, was given to them, and at that moment the wind turned and covered the bread with a light sprinkling of ashes from the white funeral pyres. André remembered the children dropping the bread in terror.[5]

Even though he was a pacifist, Malraux, defiant of the death which had horrified the children, volunteered for service during the war at the age of seventeen, but was rejected as underage. It was a defiance which he continued to parade during his entire life.

Although Malraux, prior to the publication of *Man's Fate* in 1933, was well known in literary circles in Paris, where his intelligence, erudition, great verbal facility, and reputation as an adventurer, as well as his earlier literary work, made an impression, it was *Man's Fate* that won him the acclaim of France and the whole world. *Man's Fate* was the product of Malraux's stay in Asia, where he was for two years an editor of a newspaper in Saigon that was often in trouble with the authorities but was not suppressed. There are many stories about Malraux's involvement in the events narrated in the novel—the workers' insurrection in Shanghai on March 21, 1927, and the coup of Chiang Kai-shek three weeks later on April 11, in which he turned against and massacred his Communist associates in the Kuomintang, a coalition organization of the "national" bourgeoisie and revolutionary workers and peasants which sought a unified, independent China free of foreign influence. Malraux himself, after years of silence, told his biographer Galante that he had not taken part in these events.[6] Whatever was Malraux's role, if any, it is clear that he was intimately acquainted with what went on at this time.

Malraux shows that Kyo, one of the chief Communist organizers of the insurrection, is aware that workers, peasants, and soldiers are aggrieved by the Communist Party's holding them back from seeking to consummate the revolution, subordinating them instead to the bourgeois wing of the Kuomintang, and that Chiang Kai-shek, in response to the revolutionary upsurge, must turn against Communists. When Kyo receives orders from Hankow, the headquarters of the Communist leadership, to acquiesce to Chiang's demand that the Shanghai Communists give up their arms to him, he goes to Hankow to plead against it. Vologin, the representative of the Communist International, tells him that neither Moscow nor the Chinese Communist leadership will tolerate the Shanghai Communists refusing to submit to Chiang. As Kyo ruminates back in Shanghai, "the Central Committee, knowing that the Trotskyist theses were attacking the union with the Kuomintang, was terrified by any attitude which might, rightly or wrongly, seem to be linked to that of the Russian Opposition."[7] Disarmed physically and psychologically, the Shanghai Communists and Workers' Guards are crushed when Chiang attacks.

Malraux's account of the Shanghai insurrection, of the upsurge of the mass movement, of the decision of foreign capital and the Shanghai bankers and merchants to support Chiang financially, and of the various preliminary indications of Chiang's treachery is corroborated by Harold R. Isaacs's _The Tragedy of the Chinese Revolution_, which, despite the author's political change of heart marked by the changes in successive editions, remains the best-documented history of what took place. Isaacs also gives the international background, which Malraux only hints at in the sentence just quoted. In the political struggle going on within the Russian Communist Party, which involved both domestic and foreign policy, the dominant Stalinist faction and the Opposition took different positions on China.

Stalin was gambling the whole international position of Russia on the successful emergence in China of a strong Chinese nationalist ally against Britain. Trotsky, with astonishing clarity considering the paucity of information at his disposal, saw that Stalin was actually leading the whole Chinese revolution toward incalculable disaster. Although hardly a speech or an article by any Stalinist spokesman in this period failed to belabor Trotsky for his demand that the Chinese Communists be allowed to free themselves from their Kuomintang strait jacket, Trotsky was never allowed to express his views publicly.[8]

In an article submitted on April 3, the very eve of the coup, but not permitted publication, Trotsky warned of a "Chinese Pilsudski" (the formerly Socialist Polish dictator), and wrote:

The policy of a shackled Communist Party serving as a recruiting agent to bring the workers into the Kuomintang is preparation for the successful establishment of a Fascist dictatorship in China at that not very distant moment when the proletariat, despite everything, will be compelled to jump back from the Kuomintang.[9]

The international Communist press, however, insisted until the very time of the coup that "far from dividing, as the imperialists say, the Kuomintang has only tightened its ranks" and that "a revolutionist like Chiang Kai-shek" would not "struggle against the emancipation movement."[10] Stalin himself, addressing three thousand functionaries in Moscow on April 5, said, "Chiang Kaishek is submitting to discipline. . . . Why drive away the Right when we have the majority and when the Right listens to us?"[11] We can, then, understand the terror of the Chinese Communist Central Committee at being linked to the Russian Opposition.

But while *Man's Fate* is accurate political reportage, the Chinese revolution in itself is not its real concern. The Chinese revolution is only a stage on which Kyo and Katov, a Russian organizer of the insurrection, can act their roles as exemplary heroes in the face of death and the human condition. The title of Malraux's novel on its publication in France was *La Condition Humaine.* The phrase is used by Old Gisors, the wise, philosophical, opium-smoking French father of Kyo who is the confidant of the diverse characters of the novel, in a key passage: "It is very rare for a man to be able to endure—how shall I say it?—his condition, his fate as a man" (p. 241). The "human condition" is man's awareness of being trapped in a universe incomprehensible and indifferent to him, with only one lifetime to live, a lifetime which is rendered meaningless by the certainty of death. As Old

Gisors is quoted by his son, "the essence of man is anguish, the consciousness of his own fatality, from which all fears are born, even the fear of death" (p. 159).

The phrase "the human condition" had been used by Pascal, the tormented, doubting seventeenth-century seeker of religious faith, in a passage referred to by Berger, an autobiographical character in Malraux's post-World War II novel *The Walnut Trees of Altenburg:* "Imagine a large number of men in chains, and all condemned to death, every day some of them being butchered before the others' eyes, the remainder realising their own plight from the plight of their fellows . . . This is the picture of man's estate."[12] Ordinarily, we forget the human condition, which is hidden from us by the film of familiarity that comes from the day-to-day routine of living. In the extremity of suffering, however, one becomes acutely aware of it.

In the very first pages—in which Ch'en, having fulfilled his mission of killing a sleeping man in order to get from him a paper enabling the insurrectionists to acquire a shipment of arms, feels cut off from the world of men—we have this consciousness. Ch'en chases an alley cat that has come in through the window, feeling that "nothing living must venture into the wild region where he was thrown," and finds himself on the balcony, suddenly facing nighttime Shanghai.

In his anguish the night seemed to whirl like an enormous smoke-cloud shot with sparks; slowly it settled into immobility, as his breathing grew less violent in the cooler outside air. Between the tattered clouds, the stars resumed their endless course. A siren moaned, and then became lost in the poignant serenity. . . . All that expanse of darkness, now motionless, now quivering with sparks, was life. [P. 13]

This darkness is "the night of unknowingness" of which Sartre spoke, the vast calm of an incomprehensible universe indifferent to human anguish, perceived by us in our anguish and mocking our anguish. When Ch'en escapes from the hotel, he sees the puddles from the afternoon showers reflecting the glowing sky. "Without knowing why, Ch'en looked up: how much nearer the sky had been a while back, when he had discovered the stars! He was getting farther away from it and his anguish subsided, as he returned to the world of men" (p. 16).

The darkness of night returns each time a character is plunged into suffering. Old Gisors, seized with the consciousness that he does not really know the son whom he loves dearly, looks out through the window at "the motionless and indifferent night" (pp. 70-71). Kyo and Ch'en walk in the "calm and almost silent night" (p. 155) as Ch'en, now become a terrorist, relates to Kyo his nightmares and longing for death. "As Kyo tried to make out through the darkness that angular face with its kindly lips, he felt in himself the shudder of the primordial anguish, the same as that which threw Ch'en into the arms of the octopuses of sleep and into those of death" (p. 159). When Kyo leaves the office of the Communist functionary in Hankow, he emerges into the night. "The peace of night once more. . . . On this very night, in all China, and throughout the West, including half of Europe, men were hesitating as he was, torn by the same torment between their discipline and the massacre of their own kind" (p. 167).

Not only is the universe incomprehensible; humanity is incomprehensible. "There is no knowledge of beings" is a favorite saying of Old Gisors (p. 67), the truth of which he comes to realize even more fully when he becomes aware of how little he knows Kyo. Kyo himself is strangely disturbed when he cannot recognize his own voice on a phonograph record. His father explains to him that ordinarily we hear our own voices through the vibrations in our throats but we do not hear these vibrations in a recording of our voice. Kyo ruminates when he feels estranged from his wife after she has told him that, out of pity for a friend during this time of trouble and uncertainty of life, she has had intercourse with him:

"We hear the voices of others with our ears, our own voices with our throats." Yes. One hears his own life, too, with his throat, and those of others? . . . First of all there was solitude, the inescapable aloneness behind the living multitude like the great primitive night behind the dense, low night under which this city of deserted streets was expectantly waiting, full of hope and hatred. "But I, to myself, to my throat, what am I? A kind of absolute, the affirmation of an idiot: an intensity greater than that of all the rest." [P. 59]

We know ourselves as little as we know others. We can only feel.

The darkness of the universe, then, is continued on into people's souls. Each is imprisoned in the solitary confinement of his or her own consciousness. Whatever contact we make with our fellow-prisoners is only fleeting. Kyo, listening to Ch'en's description of his anguish as they walk in the darkness of the night, feels towards him a "prisoner's fellowship" in the realization that "they were all condemned" (p. 156) by the inevitable repression of Chiang, to which the International has consigned them. For the moment, separated as they are by the darkness, they share the same prison cell: "In spite of the vast reaches of the night, Kyo felt near to him as in a closed room" (p. 157). But this is only the feeling of a moment. Ch'en says that he would not want to leave the assassination of Chiang to others because he doesn't like the women he loves to be kissed by others. "The words opened the flood-gates to all the suffering Kyo had forgotten: he suddenly felt himself separated from Ch'en" (p. 160). For suffering, while it brings us more closely in touch with our human condition, separates us from other individuals.

Malraux's vision of life dictates the form of the novel. Since neither the universe nor human beings are finally comprehensible, we do not have either a highly integrated plot which tells a well-ordered story or full-bodied characters whom we fully understand; instead, we have a montage as the scene jumps from one character to another without the author telling a connected story. The movement from place to place and person to person, with the moments of action and turmoil being described in fiery detail, renders life as Ch'en had perceived it on the hotel balcony looking out upon Shanghai, an "expanse of darkness, now motionless, now quivering with sparks" (p. 13), a blackness relieved by moments of intensity. Nor do we have a highly visualized physical setting that gives us the comforting sense of a solid background; instead, we have the metaphysical setting which the characters perceive in flashes of insight. At the moments of anguish of each of the characters, the point of view is that character's so that the reader may identify with him and perceive his anguish as the lot of every person; at other times the point of view may be that of other characters or the omniscient author. The style is clipped, telegraphic, often cryptic, and even monotonous, but often having the dramatic urgency of a telegram at a crucial moment and often attaining a poetic intensity.

Instead of the logical development of the well-told story, *Man's Fate* has a time scheme. Parts 1 and 2, which present the Shanghai insurrection, take place on March 21 and 22, with each of the three subsections in part 1 and the four subsections in part 2 being given an exact hour within this two-day period. Part 3, which presents Kyo's conversations with the Communist leaders and with Ch'en in Hankow and is something of an extended interlude, is merely dated March 27. Parts 4, 5, and 6, which present Chiang's coup, take place on April 11 and 12, with each of the six subsections in part 4, the three subsections in part 5, and three of the four subsections in part 6, as in the presentation of the Shanghai insurrection, being given an exact hour within the two-day period (the last subsection of part 6, after the completion of the coup and the deaths of Kyo and Katov, is merely labeled "next day"). The last part, part 7, which is something of an epilogue, presenting the aftermath of the coup for Ferral, the French head of the Franco-Asiatic Consortium that financed Chiang, for May, Kyo's wife, and for Old Gisors, merely has two subsections without definite times, "Paris, July" and "Kobe." The effect is to give the sense of the inexorableness of the passage of time. During the fateful hours each character is engaged in his own concern. Ch'en dies in his attempt to assassinate Chiang, which is really a form of suicide. An hour later Clappique, the declassed French aristocrat who lives in a world of fantasy, acting out various roles in order not to face himself, becomes absorbed at a roulette table, "discovering that gambling is a suicide without death" (p. 259), a form of intoxication like the suicidal intoxication of Ch'en. He therefore fails to keep his appointment with Kyo, whom he had thought to warn that he has advance knowledge that the midnight meeting at the Military Committee headquarters which Kyo is going to attend will be raided. As Clappique watches the roulette ball in fascination, he resolutely does not look at his wristwatch, abandoning Kyo to his fate and losing the money which he himself needs to escape from Shanghai, his own life being endangered as a result of his having played a part in the Communists having obtained arms. Leaving the nightclub at one o'clock in the morning, he hears the sound of the gunfire and smells the odor of the corpses which already permeates Shanghai. He goes to the nearest brothel, where he tells the woman, before going upstairs with her, that he is going to kill himself immediately afterwards, knowing that he is not going to do so, but "drunk . . . with the fictive world he was creating" (p. 263). His imaginary suicide, even though losing his escape-money is a kind of suicide, is in ironic juxtaposition to Ch'en's real suicide.

Clappique's refusal to look at his watch, to face the reality of the passage of time as his entire being is absorbed by the roulette ball, which assumes for him "the living reality of conjunctions of planets, of chronic diseases, of everything by which men believe their destinies to be governed" (pp. 257-58), recalls Ch'en in the clockmaker's shop that acts as an observation post during the insurrection. At least thirty clocks point to different hours. While bullets are flying outside, Ch'en becomes momentarily absorbed by the multitude of clocks, which take on for him the aspect of the indifferent universe, a "universe of clock-movements, impassive in the midst of the Revolution" (p. 130), proceeding in accordance with its own unfathomably complex movements, just as the roulette ball moves from compartment to compartment, carrying with it Clappique's destiny. Ch'en, however, unlike Clappique, tears himself from his absorption to look at his watch for the business at hand.

The montage contrasts the ways in which the various characters face up to the human condition. Clappique and Old Gisors seek to escape it, the one through alcohol and fantasy, the other through opium. Ferral and König, the chief of Chiang's police, seek to free themselves of it by the humiliation of others, Ferral by his financial power and his erotic domination over women, König by his physical torture of his victims. Katov and Kyo transcend man's fate in accordance with Kyo's idea that "all that men are willing to die for, beyond self-interest, tends more or less obscurely to justify that fate by giving it a foundation in dignity" (p. 241).

The contrasts and similarities, which have been worked out in detail by many commentators, are, however, rather schematic. There is a good deal of validity in the statement of H. A. Mason: "Malraux is fond of using the word *absurde* and his characters often declaim against middle-class society and the nullity of life in general. These attitudes are very often mere verbal exercises because the feelings, etc., referred to are not embodied in an adequate situation."[13] It is not, however, the situations which are at fault: they are such that the characters certainly have every reason for their anguish and feelings of alienation. The fault is that the characters are not drawn in any depth. A phrase of physical description, two or three sentences about their past lives, and their participation in philosophical dialogue and violent action do not suffice to give them body. They remain mere shadows in the night that dominates *Man's Fate*.

Nevertheless *Man's Fate* has, as we have seen, its moments of vividness and intensity. In the climax, in which Kyo and Katov reach heroic heights, Malraux successfully dramatizes the underlying idea of the novel derived from the passage in Pascal which states that all men live together in a prison cell awaiting their execution. This climax is foreshadowed not only by the prison images in the dialogue between Kyo and Ch'en we have already noted but by a conversation early in the novel between Kyo and

May. People go to prison, he tells her, not for love but to remain true to the idea they have of themselves. "Katov would go, even if he did not love deeply. He would go for the idea he has of life, of himself. . . . It's not for someone else that one goes to prison" (p. 54).

In the climactic scene Kyo and Katov are in the darkness of a great hall, formerly a schoolyard, with two hundred other wounded Communists waiting to be put to death by being thrown alive into the boiler of a locomotive, whose whistle is sounded immediately after each such execution.[14] As they wait, Kyo experiences the solitude of suffering. Katov is lying next to Kyo, "right beside him, separated from him by the vast expanse of suffering" (p. 319).

But, lying among the crowded forms, hearing their hushed chorus of lamentation, Kyo transcends his suffering and experiences an exaltation and a sense of fraternity before he bites into the cyanide which, unknown to the guards, he has hidden in his belt.

The fatality which they had accepted rose with the murmur of these wounded men like the peace of evening, spread over Kyo . . . with the majesty of a funeral chant. He had fought for what in his time was charged with the deepest meaning and the greatest hope; he was dying among those with whom he would have wanted to live; he was dying, like each of these men, because he had given a meaning to his life. What would have been the value of a life for which he would not have been willing to die? . . . No, dying could be an exalted act, the supreme expression of a life which this death so much resembled . . . He crushed the poison between his teeth as he would have given a command. [Pp. 322-23]

He dies displaying his existentialist "authenticity," his truth to his idea of himself.

Katov too experiences solitude and transcends it, but his heroism is even greater. "Katov, since the death of Kyo—who had panted at least a minute—felt himself thrown back into a solitude which was all the stronger and more painful as he was surrounded by his own people" (p. 324). But, listening to the sobbing of the two young fellow-prisoners beside him, who are terrified by their imminent awful death, Katov rises above this solitude. "'Human dignity,' Katov murmured . . . A man could be stronger than this solitude and even, perhaps, than that atrocious whistle: fear struggled in him against the most terrible temptation in his life" (pp. 325-26). The temptation is not to carry out his decision to give the terrified young men his cyanide to divide between the two of them. He offers it to them, but, as it is passed from one to the other, his fellow-prisoner, who is wounded in the hand, drops it in the darkness. The three men frantically grope for it. As they do so, their hands brushing, one of the hands takes his, presses it, holds it. " 'Even if we don't find it . . . ' said one of the voices" (p. 327). The cyanide is recovered, but the hand continues to hold his until it twists in the convulsion of death. The moment epitomizes Malraux's vision of life—the darkness, the prison cell crowded with humanity, the common sentence of death, the possibility of facing one's fate with dignity, the disembodied whispering voices of one's fellow-prisoners, whom one can barely distinguish from each other, the brief communication and expression of fraternity through the handclasp of a fellow-prisoner whom one cannot see.

The revolution to which Kyo and Katov had dedicated their lives, it is implied in part 7, has not been finally defeated. "The Revolution had just passed through a terrible malady," thinks May at the end, "but it was not dead. And it was Kyo and his men, living or not, vanquished or not, who had brought it into the world" (p. 353). The words are prophetic, for the Chinese revolution did indeed recover and triumph, but Malraux is really more interested in the victory in defeat of Kyo—a victory in defeat that he contrasts with the defeat in victory of Ferral, who at the end is humiliated by the refusal of the representatives of the great French banks to come to the aid of the Franco-Asiatic Consortium—than in the fate of the Chinese revolution. Kyo does not have the Nietzschean individualism of Garine, the French leader in the Canton general strike of 1925 in Malraux's previous novel *The Conquerors*. Garine, a Martin Eden who has joined the revolution, whom more than one commentator has identified with Malraux himself, hates the established order but is cynical about the revolutionary ideal and contemptuous of the "rubbish" of revolutionary doctrine. "I utterly detest the middle class into which I was born," he says. "But, as for the others, I am well aware that as soon as we have triumphed together, they will become contemptible."[15] Kyo, however, fights for the human dignity of the masses, but this is an abstraction that is not given reality (we do not see the awakening of the masses): what is real is the heroic dignity of Kyo. Malraux's lack of identification with the revolution and his Nietzschean admiration for "supermen" standing above the masses was to lead him to De Gaulle.

For Kyo revolution does not occur as the result of social law; it is the result solely of the will of man. "In Kyo's eyes," says Old

Gisors at the conclusion, Marxism "was a will," not "a fatality" (p. 355). Kyo resisted the argument of the Comintern functionary Vologin because he was not, as Vologin was, merely a machine man and because the signs of an imminent coup had become so evident for one on the scene. He had, however, no general theory by which he could have foreseen Chiang's reactionary turn. "Don't you think—really—" he asked Vologin, "that the obsession with economic fatality is preventing the Chinese Communist Party, and perhaps Moscow, from seeing the elementary necessity which is under our very noses?" (p. 153). Kyo's "Marxism" was the exaltation of will as against what he called "fatality."

True Marxism, however, recognizes both the importance of "will"—human action—and of "fatality," which is really the perception of social forces at work. Revolutionary will is necessary to overthrow a social order, but that will must act in conformance with historical possibility. The "fatalism" of the Comintern line did not spring from a Marxist perception of a historical process but from a mechanistic thinking that decreed that the revolution must proceed by stages, with the bourgeois-democratic revolution preceding the proletarian revolution. The "Trotskyist theses," which the Chinese Communist leadership so feared to be identified with and which anticipated Kyo's conclusion, sprang, however, from Trotsky's theory of the permanent revolution, which held that the bourgeoisie of a backward country in the epoch of imperialism was too dependent on foreign capital and too fearful of the masses to carry through a bourgeois-democratic revolution, whose tasks must be assumed by the proletariat through a socialist revolution. This theory was validated both by the Bolshevik revolution in Russia and the reactionary turn of the bourgeois wing of the Kuomintang in China.

That Kyo, Malraux's "Bolshevik hero," is not actually a Marxist is not surprising, for Marxism cannot be grafted upon Malraux's existentialist philosophy: the two are incompatible. "For Existentialism," says George Novack, "the universe is irrational; for Marxism it is lawful."[16]

The rationality, determinism and causality of the universal process of material development [he continues] do not exclude but embrace the objective existence and significance of absurdity, indeterminism and accident. However, these features are not more fundamental to reality than their contrary categories. They are not immutable and irremovable aspects of nature and history but relative phenomena which in the course of development can change to the extent of becoming their own opposites. Chance, for example, is the antithesis of necessity. Yet chance has its own laws which are lodged in the occurrence of statistical regularities. Statistical laws which derive regularities from a sufficient accumulation of random happenings, as in quantum mechanics or the life-insurance business, exemplify how individual accidents are convertible into aggregate necessities.[17]

The roulette ball which Clappique watched in fascination may be symbolic of his unknown future and therefore of the uncertainty of human existence, but there is enough certainty in that existence so that the gambling-hall owner could count on making his profit from the roulette table.

With Malraux's recurrent themes of the indifferent universe, the eternal stars, and the relentlessness of time, which dwarfs man and renders him absurd, we may compare the way of looking at the universe in Trotsky's essay greeting the twentieth century when he was twenty-one, an essay which, like Malraux's youthful "Paper Moons," expressed the philosophy that would govern his life:

> If I were one of the celestial bodies, I would look with complete detachment upon this miserable ball of dust and dirt. . . . But I am a *man*. World history which to you, dispassionate gobbler of science, to you, book-keeper of eternity, seems only a negligible moment in the balance of time, is to me everything! As long as I breathe, I shall fight for the future.[18]

Malraux says, "God is dead. Man is alone"; Trotsky says, "God is dead. Long live man!"

For Marxism, Malraux's isolated individual is an abstraction. "Take away from the person," says Novack, "all the socially conditioned and historically acquired attributes derived from the culture of the collectivity and little would be left but the biological animal."[19] Marxism finds the source of alienation in man's helplessness, his inability to master the world about him. Under capitalism, says Ernest Mandel in *The Marxist Theory of Alienation,* this alienation is of a special kind and a special force. Selling one's labor power means giving up control over a large part of one's life: the employer in the most advanced time-and-motion studies tells the workers how to spend literally every second of their working hours. It also means that workers give up totally the products of their labor, unlike the craftsmen of previous periods or even the medieval peasants, who retained part of their produce. Work is no longer a way of expressing oneself. Even leisure is conditioned by capitalist society. It is commercialized, and leisure activity is governed by the need of capitalism to stimulate artificial desires. The ability to communicate, moreover, is inhibited by the overspecialization characteristic of a social division of labor carried to an extreme in an economy of commodity production, by the tendency in such an economy to look at people as objects, things with which one has economic relations, and by the deep divisions between people as a result of opposing class interests.

> [A] terrible expression of this alienation [says Mandel] is the tremendous loneliness which a society based on commodity production and division of labor inevitably induces in many human beings. Ours is a society based on the principle, every man for himself. Individualism pushed to the extreme also means loneliness pushed to the extreme. It is simply not true, as certain existentialist philosophers contend, that man has always been an essentially lonely human being. There have been forms of integrated collective life in primitive society where the very notion of loneliness could not arise.[20]

Malraux is representative of bourgeois individualism pushed to an extreme. Mandel tells of the observations of psychologists who have recorded overheard conversations in which

> two people have talked along on parallel lines without once meeting with each other. Each talks because he welcomes the occasion to unburden himself, to get out of his loneliness, but he is incapable of listening to what the other person is saying. The only meeting place is at the end of the dialogue when they say goodbye.[21]

This is the loneliness of Malraux's characters, who only fleetingly establish communication, with the supreme example of such communication being a handclasp in death, the final farewell. Mandel, however, adds about the dialogues of which he has been speaking: "Happily, the majority of members of our society are not yet in that situation or otherwise we would be on the brink of a complete breakdown of social relations. Nonetheless, capitalism tends to extend the zone of this extreme loneliness with all its terrible implications."[22] The world, even under capitalism, is not yet made up of Malraux characters.

In attempting to graft Marxism upon existentialism, Malraux in part 7 has Hemmelrich, the German phonograph dealer who has led a miserable existence for thirty-seven years as a worker, soldier, and poor shopkeeper, write to May from the Soviet Union, to which he has escaped from Shanghai: "Before, I began to live when I left the factory; now, I begin to live when I enter it. It's the first time in my life that I work and know why I work, not merely waiting patiently to die" (p. 352). Apparently, the worker is to find comfort through meaningful work, though the intellectual will never finally escape the human condition but will maintain a proud and lonely eminence, for, as Old Gisors said, to think is to suffer. It is, however a simplistic Marxism which expects a revolution, especially one in a backward country, to do away with the alienation of the working class at a stroke.

The prerequisites for the disappearance of human alienation [says Mandel] . . . can only be created precisely through . . . the withering away of commodity production, the disappearance of economic scarcity, the withering away of social division of labor . . . and the elimination of the difference between manual and intellectual labor, between producers and administrators.[23]

In fact, "the bureaucratic distortion or degeneration of a society in transition" may add "specific factors of alienation," "the hypertrophy of bureaucracy, the lack of socialist democracy on the political level, the lack of workers' self-management on the economic plane, the lack of freedom to create on the cultural plane."[24] The Hemmelrichs of the Soviet Union have not, alas, become self-fulfilled.

Finally, Marxism denies Malraux's concept of anguish derived from the consciousness of mortality, as being the essence of humanity:

The dread of death [says Novack] is not the primal and central fact of human existence, an eternal attendant of man's condition, as the Existential metaphysicians contend. It is a historically conditioned psychological reaction. Many primitive peoples do not experience it. . . . The Existentialist displacement of the seat of value from life to death reflects both the ordeals of our age and a loss of vitality among sensitive souls who despair of triumphing over the dark and destructive forces of a sick social order.[25]

The "human condition" is in reality the condition of many in a given time. It is to that condition that André Malraux has given artistic expression in *Man's Fate*.

4. Ignazio Silone's 'Fontamara': The Peasants and Social Revolution

In 1930 Ignazio Silone, in exile in Switzerland, ill, and believing that he was dying, wrote *Fontamara* to convey to the world his bitterness and indignation at what had happened under Mussolini's fascism to the southern Italy in which he had grown up. A leader of the Socialist youth at the age of eighteen, a founding member of the Italian Communist Party at the age of twenty-one, and a member of its Central Committee in charge of its underground activity from that time on, he was while on sick leave undergoing an internal struggle over what he had seen at first hand of the bureaucratic degeneration of the Communist International. An incident that had made a particularly strong impression on him was the suppression by the Russian Communist Party Political Bureau of Trotsky's communication to it in 1927 on Stalin's China policy, and the subsequent condemnation of this communication by the Executive Committee of the Communist International without having read it. Malraux, although telling the truth about the Chinese events in *Man's Fate*, cynically accepted the bureaucratized Comintern apparatus as the necessary means by which the "Bolshevik hero" realized his heroism, and he continued to collaborate with the Stalinists, eventually justifying the staged trials of the Old Bolsheviks; but Silone was unable to accept the actions of the Comintern. In 1931 he finally broke with it.

Fontamara was, therefore, published without the support of the international Communist movement. It first appeared in 1933, three years after its completion, in a German-language edition in Zurich paid for by the author and 700 private subscribers. Copies of this edition and of the Italian manuscript, however, were carried all over the world by emigrants who pressed for its publication. The difficulties of publication were more than made up for by the swiftness of its readers' response. By the time it was published in the United States in 1934 after many publishers' rejections it was a best-seller in fourteen countries. As Silone himself said thirty-five years later,

I invented a village, using my bitter memories and my imagination, until I myself began to live in it. The result was a story which was rather simple, some of whose pages were frankly coarse, but because of its intense feeling and the love which animated it, it moved readers in various countries far beyond anything I had expected.[1]

Silone had come to Communism through the tradition of millennial Christianity, which had persisted through the ages in the unchanging countryside of southern Italy. "Under the ashes of skepticism," he says of the region in his essay "Emergency Exit," his account in 1949, of his spiritual pilgrimage, "the ancient hope for the Kingdom, the ancient expectation that love will take the place of law, the ancient dreams of Gioacchino da Fiore, the Spirituals and the Celestines have never died out among those who suffer most."[2] This spirit remained strong within him even when he gave up his Christian faith to become a Communist. For a period after he wrote *Fontamara*, he continued to regard himself as an independent Marxist, but by 1949 he could write that, although remaining a socialist because of the sense of social injustice and the desire for equality and fraternity that had originally brought him to Marxism, he had become skeptical of Marxism itself.

This credo, which continued to guide Silone until his death, was the one which he held when, in preparing *Fontamara* after the war for its first Italian printing, he revised it. The reason that he revised it, he says in his note for the new American edition, was that his book had continued to grow within him. The changes, however, as Malcolm Cowley noted in his foreword to the new edition, are less extensive than Silone suggests: "The novel begins and ends as before. Chiefly his revisions consist in omitting several passages—among them one long episode—and in telling us more about the life of Berardo Viola."[3] Cowley find nevertheless that the effect of the changes is decisive:

In the new version . . . the community recedes into the back-ground. . . . It is no longer a *fabliau* about peasants and the Devil ["incarnated as a Fascist official, the Promoter"]. Instead it becomes a golden legend about Christ reborn, tempted in the wilderness, and crucified in Jerusalem—or is Berardo rather John Baptist, who prophesies the coming of the Solitary Stranger? . . . Because of this changed emphasis, the question asked by a peasant at the end of the book—"What can we do?"— . . . has now become moral rather than political.[4]

But just because Silone's subsequent development had its origin in what was so much a part of him when he wrote *Fontamara* and because he had remained a socialist who believed that it was necessary to construct a new kind of society the revision is not the drastic alteration that Cowley states. Every reference to Berardo as a Christ figure in the revision was present in the original, and the presentation as the Devil of the Promoter (called "the Trader" in the new translation) remains the same in the revision as in the original. The community remains very much in the foreground, the center of the novel being its struggle for existence in the new conditions of its being. The additional material about the life of Berardo consists of only a few sentences introduced in the early part of the story to foreshadow what will happen: it is his destiny, it is frequently said, to die in prison like his grandfather the bandit. Moreover, Berardo himself is not the intellectual revolutionist of Silone's later novels but, although the most intelligent and strong of the peasants, their supreme representative. His internal struggle in prison does not rise from the philosophical uncertainties of the intellectual but from the "two souls" of the peasant of which Isaac Deutscher speaks in his essay on Maoism: "Of the peasants' 'two souls'—the expression is Lenin's—one is craving property, while the other dreams of equality and has visions of a rural community, the members of which own and till their land in common."[5]

It is true that the final words of Berardo to the young peasant in prison with him, the message he is to take back to Fontamara—"Unity. No more hatred among farmers. No more hatred between farmers and workmen. We need just one thing: Unity. All the rest will come of itself"—have been omitted in the revision, no doubt because Silone felt that exemplary action was more effective than an exhortatory statement. Yet this omission cannot alter the entire thrust of the novel, which brings the peasants from concern only with their own families to collective action, culminating in their putting out their newspaper together after they learn about Berardo's death, an action which is both moral and political. It is this element of collective action, its author's close identification with his peasants, and his Marxist insights which make *Fontamara* different from Silone's subsequent novels about revolutionary saints and their self-questionings and temptations. In revising his novel, he maintained its integrity.

Since the two versions of *Fontamara* are, therefore, not two different novels, I shall use for my discussion Silone's revision of the novel he had hastily and desperately written. It retains the unique quality of the original but has some structural improvements, notably the omission of the long story of the pimp and political mercenary who became a Fascist hero, which takes us away from the village that is the focus of the novel.

The story of Fontamara is told to the narrator in exile, nostalgic for his native village and troubled by rumors of what had happened there, by three peasants—an old man, his wife, and their son—who had managed to escape from it. The narrator relates it as it was told to him by the three, the story passing back and forth between them, each one giving the portion that was his or her experience. At times, says the narrator, he fell asleep in the course of the recital of events by the woman but without losing the gist of what she was saying, "almost as if her voice rose from the depths of my being" (p. 21).

The narrator, then, is the inspired spokesman of the peasantry, the means by which their collective voice is heard. He writes in standard Italian, not the native dialect that is the true language of the people, in order that he may be understood, but, he tells us,

the way the story is told seems to me to be ours. It is an art of Fontamara. I learned it as a boy, seated on the threshold of my house or at the hearth during the long evenings or near the weaver, following the rhythm of the pedal, listening to the age-old tales. There is no difference between this art of story telling, this art of making words, lines, sentences and images follow one another, of explaining something once without allusions or subtleties, calling wine, wine, and bread, bread, and this ancient art of weaving, this art of making threads and colors follow one another in a neat, clear and orderly fashion. First you see the stalk of the rose, then the petal, then the crown; but we all know it's going to be a rose from the beginning. [P. 23]

This is the art of *Fontamara,* unpretentious, seemingly artless, its rhythm that of the weaver's loom, proceeding by repetition, with one act of trickery and oppression being described after another, the culmination at the conclusion of the novel being the assault on the village by the Fascist police that kills most of its inhabitants and disperses the rest, the debacle we have sensed from the beginning. But his apparent artlessness is in reality art of a high order.

A distinctive characteristic of *Fontamara* is its bitter humor (the word *fontamara* means "bitter fountain"). In one of his essays in *Emergency Exit* Silone tells of a childhood experience that made a deep impression on him. He saw a "barefoot ragged little man, handcuffed between two policemen, . . . proceeding by fits and starts . . . as if to the rhythm of a painful dance."[6] The "pitiful, farcical sight" made the boy laugh, but his father sternly told him never to make fun of a man who has been arrested, for he can't defend himself, he may be innocent, and in any case he is unhappy. The peasants in *Fontamara* constitute such a "pitiful, farcical sight." They are derided for their poverty, ignorance, and gullibility by government officials and petty bureaucrats time after time, and the town loafers play jokes on them. We cannot join in the laughter, but we are aware of the grotesquery of the peasants' painful dance.

The painfulness of the peasants' ordeal is underscored with grim irony. When the Fascist militia invades the village, the women, terrified in the absence of the men and not knowing what to expect, recite a list of the traditional exorcisms of sin, concluding, "A spiritu fornicationis, libera nos, Domine" (p. 128). Immediately afterwards, the Fascists, searching the houses for nonexistent arms, engage in mass rapes. At the conclusion of the novel, when Raffaele Scarpone, who has succeeded Barardo as the leader after Berardo's death, suggests as the title of their newspaper *What Can We Do?*, the shoemaker Baldissera objects: "But it will be a ridiculous title. If a copy of our paper gets to Rome, anyone who sees it will burst out laughing" (p. 220). The authorities in Rome do not laugh; they wipe out the village.

The chief perpetrator of what amounts to a series of cruel practical jokes on the peasants is the Trader, the Roman capitalist who had got the entire countryside under his thumb, squeezing the peasants and making the old-time landowners and other members of the preceding order bow to him. First, a government functionary pressures the peasants into signing a petition whose contents they do not know, assuring them that it will not mean they will have to pay anything. It later turns out that the petition is for the diversion of the miserable, dirty little stream that waters their barren lands. When a peasant sees the road-workers altering the course of the stream, which to his simple mind seems a blasphemous violation of God's law, he runs to the village, exclaiming, "Run! Do something about it! We'll have to tell the police and warn the mayor as soon as possible!" The men being out in the fields, the women make their long, hot, dusty way to the town, where they find, after having been bureaucratically shunted about by derisive clerks, that the mayor, now called the "podestà" and appointed by the national government, is the Trader, to whose fields the water is being diverted. It is all a trick similar to that played upon them when the water in the public fountain in town mysteriously stops each time they rush to slake their unbearable thirst, resumes when they walk away in despair, and stops once more when they rush to it again.

When the excited women threaten to burn down the Trader's villa, the local lawyer, don Circostanza, the People's Friend, as he likes to be called, comes forward with a compromise that the women accept: three-quarters of the water will go to the Trader and three-quarters to the peasants, fair and even. When the time comes to divide the water and the peasants find that, with a hundred policemen assembled, every drop is drawn into the new bed dug by the town, their fury knows no bounds, but again don Circostanza proposes a compromise: the town has spent money for the new ditch, and moreover the transfer of the water is legal, but it should be only for a specified time. The Trader proposes fifty years, and, while the crowd of peasants screams imprecations and is pushed back by the police, don Circostanza and the other town notable appointed to represent the peasants by the Trader in his capacity as head of the town agree that the period should be ten lustra. It is only later that the peasants learn that a lustrum is five years.

The peasants know their ignorance and are mortified by it, but they are not the stupid children their deriders consider them to be. Far from being gullible, they are suspicious through long experience. The minute they see any legal form or are told anything is free they know it is a swindle—and they are right. But what can they do? They will have to pay one way or other. The old people remember the days when there were only three or four proprietors in the region, who governed by the law of custom, and when every village was under the protection of a "gentleman," to whom every villager would go for help in disagreements with inhabitants of other villages or for other favors. "We weren't well off," says the old peasant. "As a matter of fact, we were very badly off. But everything was simple" (p. 171). But this changed in the course of time. Now "protectors" of the people like don Circostanza cheat on behalf of "foreigners" like the Trader, and old-type proprietors and priests have degenerated into imitators and dependents of the Trader. The peasants find their whole existence has been shaken up. If they permit themselves to be tricked, it is out of their old habit of dependence and out of weakness and despair. Don Circostanza's "voice reassured us not a little," says the old peasant's wife of the time when he addressed them from the Trader's balcony. "We didn't feel alone any more. We were so tired and discouraged that we could confuse that old rascal with an angel sent by God" (pp. 67-68).

The peasants have their own wry humor, slyly ironic and straightfaced, which is in fact a pithy comment on the realities of their existence. Michele Zompa answers the angry government functionary who asks him if he doesn't know who is giving orders nowadays, by patiently explaining the order of the universe: God is at the head of everything; then comes Prince Torlonia, the great landowner of the region; then come his guards; then come his guards' dogs; then nothing; then more nothing; then still more nothing; then come the peasants. When the still more infuriated functionary asks him where he puts the authorities, he is gravely answered by another peasant that they are divided between the third and fourth classes in accordance with their salaries, with those in the class of the dogs being most numerous.

The peasants may not know of the new Fascist regime and they have to learn of its significance and of the significance of the capitalist expansion into the countryside in the person of the Trader, but they do know of their eternal exploitation, whatever the regime. The nakedness of this exploitation is such that they see through the sham of democracy of the previous regime and soon enough perceive the demagogy of the Fascist regime in a way that sophisticated members of a more complex society are often not able to do. They have a simple folk wisdom of their own. When the clerks and secretaries howl and shriek with laughter at the joke of the peasant women filling the city hall with their lice, the old peasant woman addresses one of the secretaries: "'Shame on anyone who laughs at the misery of others.' I tried to explain it to her. 'It's shameful to laugh at misfortune.' But she didn't understand me" (p. 46). So too the peasants look with amazement at the city of Avezzano, to which they had been trucked for a Fascist rally—at its blazing lights, its hectic gaiety, its drunken young dandies oblivious to the man without arms or legs begging from them: "Avezzano looked as if it were going mad. The way the people worked at their singing and dancing, it was hard for me to believe . . . Had they all gone crazy without knowing it?" (p. 188).

Their religion expresses their sense of injustice but at the same time teaches them resignation. This is epitomized in the story of the peasant saint who, on ascending to heaven after a life of dire privation, was welcomed by God and told that he could have whatever he wanted. The saint, abashed by his immodest desire, finally admitted timidly that he would like a nice big piece of white bread, whereat God embraced him, wept with him, and ordered that he have white bread for all eternity.[7] For, as the old peasant comments, when Christ said, "The bread here is My body," he must have meant the fine white bread that comes from the peasants' grain but that the peasants themselves cannot afford to eat: "If you have no white bread, if you have only corn bread, it is as if Christ had never been, as if there had never been a Redemption, as if Christ were yet to come" (p. 156). For the priest who tells this ever-popular story in his sermon—he has announced in advance that he will do so in order to bring to the services the men as well as the women and children—the white bread is the "pie in the sky" reward of humility: he goes on to scold the peasants for not paying their taxes, causing the men to walk out. For the peasants it is a reminder of the promise of Christ's second coming, when justice will prevail. "Aren't we Christians too?" (p. 117)—this cry of indignation, which they voice more than once in the face of mistreatment, is a protest against social inequality.

The peasants bear their burden with the resignation of centuries, but they also have within them the bitterness which has throughout history erupted sporadically in the great peasant outbreaks—the jacqueries in France, the uprising of Wat Tyler in England, whose cry "When Adam delved and Eve span, Who was then the gentleman?" was revived by the seventeenth-century Levellers, the Peasants' War in Germany, with its communistic Anabaptists, the Pugachev rebellion in Russia—only to pass without lasting consequences. The peasant may go for great stretches of time without outbreaks of any kind, but then his wrath bursts forth terrifyingly—and the memory of these outbreaks remains.

In *Fontamara*, when the outraged women start throwing stones at the Trader's villa, the communal secretary cries out, "It's the revolution! Call the police!" (p. 69). So too when, their grim faces whitened by the road dust, they had arrived in the main square of the town, there was general terror: merchants shut up their shops, windows and balconies were filled with anxious faces, and frightened clerks showed up on the steps of the town hall, as if expecting the women, who had come expecting the mayor to help them, to attack it. The extreme fright caused by a bunch of women has its comic aspect, as had the anger of the government functionary when he had found a louse on the table beside the petitions, which he took as a personal affront, demanding to know from which of the peasants it had come. Suspecting that they were making fun of him, he reported to the government that the village was a nest of subversives, the beginning of Fontamara's troubles. Yet there is more than comic misunderstanding in these responses to the peasants. There is the vague realization that beneath the peasants' passive acceptance of their lot there is a suppressed rage that can some time spring forth. "By Christ, we'll burn your villa!" exclaim the women (p. 70), ordinarily so submissive, who had formed their expedition only with the greatest difficulty and after internal bickering, in their frustration and their indignation at the Trader. It is an echo of all the religious slogans of the peasants of the past.

But their wrath is diverted because they lack leadership and have not learned to trust themselves and to maintain their unity. Although all of the families in Fontamara are kinfolk, the peasants think only of their own individual families and of gaining a little bit more water for their own land. The exception is Berardo Viola. Berardo is a landless peasant who has to hire himself out as a farm laborer. "He had no land, either with or without water," says the old peasant, "and he thus had no interests in conflict with the other peasants" (p. 79). But Berardo is above such selfish striving not merely because he has no land but because of his character. In fact, he lost his land as a result of his feeling for a friend with whom he had often shared his last crust of bread. Once he cracked a number of heads defending his friend, but his friend in order to save his own skin betrayed him to the police. Although Berardo was a violent man, he did not beat up his betrayer but resolved not to see him again and sold his land to go to America, unfortunately just before the enactment of a law suspending emigration.

Berardo has a great following among the youth of the village, for whom there is less work as a result of the elimination of the safety-valve of emigration, but the older peasants regard him and the other young men as stupidly rash. His teaching is that there is no sense in talking to the authorities or the landlords, who will always swindle the peasant. Sabotage is the only way to respond to oppression. Each trick of the Trader is answered by a "trick" of Berardo's. The Trader had the town build a wooden fence around the common pasture land he had appropriated. One night the fence burned up. "The wood was too dry," explained Berardo with unsmiling peasant humor. "The sun burned it" (p. 123). The Trader had another fence built at the town's expense and put an armed street cleaner on guard over it. But the fence burned up again anyway, the street cleaner swearing that a burst of fire had miraculously come out of the ground. The Trader, not being able to arrest the Devil, whose work the priest said the fire was, jailed the street cleaner. "'Who will win?' we asked ourselves. 'The Devil or the Trader?' (We were all against the Trader, but the only open partisan of the Devil was Berardo.)" (p. 124). The answer comes with the raid of the Fascist militia.

Earlier the women, awed by the Trader's energy and unscrupulousness, had regarded him as the Devil himself. So, for that matter, had donna Clorinda, the wife of the large landowner of the region, who had sold to the Trader the land that later greatly increased in value as a result of the diversion to it of the water. Then the priest came to the village to tell the older peasants not to oppose the Trader, who is "a terrible man, a demon the like of which has never been seen around here" (p. 77), perhaps even Satan himself. "The priest's words made a strong impression on us," says the old peasant, "especially when Baldovino told us that he had found out from the coachman that the surrey don Abbacchio had used to come to Fontamara belonged to the Trader. Truly, a demon with the priests on his side had never been heard of before" (p. 78).

The Trader, the spirit of capitalism, is subversive of the old order, and Berardo, the spirit of peasant revolt, is subversive of the new order superseding it. As destructors of order, they are both devils. Later, when Berardo speaks to a revolutionist in Rome, "a young man in clothes halfway between a worker's and a student's" (p. 120), the young man, whom he had first met in Avezzano and by whom he had been warned against an agent provocateur, tells him of the mysterious Solitary Stranger, who is accused of endangering the public order everywhere and is present wherever peasants revolt. "'But who is this fellow? Is he the Devil?' asked Berardo. 'Maybe he is,' answered the man from Avezzano. 'But he's a good devil'" (p. 201). This good devil suggests the Christ who is yet to come, and in following him Berardo's behavior becomes imitative of Christ's.

But first Berardo has to undergo his temptation. He had long loved Elvira, the most beautiful girl of the village, but because he had no land he felt that he could not marry her, especially since she had a good dowery. Then one night through force of circumstance he slept with her. After that, he became obsessed with the idea that he had to marry her but first had somehow to acquire land. He decides to go to Rome and to work harder there than anyone else and live more frugally so that he may save enough money to buy land, even though his devoted follower

Scarpone begs him to stay, for, ironically, now that he has changed, the entire village has come around to his former way of thinking and needs him as a leader.

In Rome, Berardo worships a new god. The peasants had thought there was only one bank, the bank from which the Trader got his money. In Rome, however, Berardo and the old peasant's son, who has accompanied him, find countless banks.

> In the center of Rome where we thought Saint Peter was, there were nothing but banks. "Look! Look!" said Berardo to me every time we came to a new bank. . . . Berardo never got tired of admiring things. "But they have cupolas!" I objected. "Maybe they're churches!" "Yes, but to another God," answered Berardo, laughing. "The God who really rules on earth is Money. And it rules everyone, even priests like don Abbacchio who talk about the God in Heaven. Maybe we were ruined by believing in the old God while the new one rules the earth." [P. 188]

He now argues that "the Trader just acted correctly for his own interests" (p. 190) and meditates that without water the price of land will go down, thinking of the land he himself wants to buy. He even acquires the enormous drive, determination, and unscrupulous trickery of the Trader. In the inn where he and the young peasant are staying is an impoverished lawyer, "a poor little old man with a cold" (p. 192), whom they engage to use his knowledge of how to cut through bureaucratic red tape to gain the work permits they now find they need. The lawyer, who is starving, makes them pay out all of their little sum of money in advance and wire to Fontamara for additional money, cheese, honey, hens, and peaches, some to bribe the official in charge of the permits and the rest for himself. Berardo, who knows that none of these things are obtainable (he has never eaten honey in his life), directs the lawyer to send the telegram to his father, who had died when Berardo was a child.

Then ensues a grimly comic spectacle. Both Berardo and the lawyer lie on their beds all day without money to buy food. Every time the postman comes, they dash downstairs, Berardo hoping that the work permits have arrived and the lawyer hoping that the money and the provisions have arrived. Each bitterly reproaches the other when the postman brings neither. "On the afternoon of the fourth day of hunger," says the old peasant's son, "we received good news" (p. 197), a telegram from Fontamara which the lawyer joyfully announces as the arrival of the money. The "good news" is, however, another of the ironic touches of the novel. Berardo reads the telegram, his face takes on a frightful expression, and he puts the telegram in his pocket without uttering a word. The young peasant infers that someone has died, and the reader realizes that it is Elvira. Later in the novel we learn that Elvira, who had told Berardo when he was refusing to listen to the urgings of Scarpone, "If you're acting that way for my sake, remember that I began to love you when they told me that you thought the other way" (p. 180), had gone on a pilgrimage to beg the Virgin Mary for Berardo's salvation, offering her life in exchange and being immediately afterward stricken with a fever from which she died. The evening after Berardo received the telegram he is informed by the lawyer that the head of the employment office had that day, in response to his request for the necessary certificate of morality from the podestà of Berardo's village, received one with the notation "Extremely unpatriotic conduct" (p. 198). Berardo will now never be able to get work, and he and the young peasant are evicted from the inn.

It is at this point that Berardo meets again the man from Avezzano, of whom he at first is mistrustful as a city person, especially now when all of life seems a cheat to him, but who becomes his salvation. Berardo, the young peasant, and the man from Avezzano are arrested in a restaurant in which the police find a package of revolutionary newspapers that they infer belongs to one of the three. In the prison cell which they share, Berardo and the revolutionist talk all night while the young peasant sleeps fitfully, hearing only snatches of their conversation. Berardo in his cynicism is resistant to the revolutionist's idea of an organization of city workers and peasants, membership in which could only entail privation and danger. But by morning Berardo's objections, which were really objections he was making to one side of himself, are overcome. "He was his old self again" (p. 206).

"From the way the two of them were talking and smiling," says the young peasant, "I realized that Berardo had formed a friendship with the stranger, and since I knew what friendship meant to him, I had the vague impression that Berardo was lost." But Berardo says, half to himself, "I thought my life had no more sense for me, but perhaps now it will have some meaning. . . . Maybe it will begin to make sense only now" (p. 206).

The young peasant is right in believing that Berardo is lost as a result of his friendship, for Berardo informs the police that he is the Solitary Stranger and that the package is his, causing the release of the revolutionist and sealing Berardo's own doom. But of course in losing his life he achieves the salvation for which Elvira had prayed. He is beaten time after time to make him reveal information. The last time "they led him back to the cell, holding him by the arms and legs, like Christ when He was taken off the Cross" (p. 211). He begins to have doubts again about the revolutionist, who is, after all, a city man and who is now free while Berardo is being tortured. When he informs the inspector that he is ready to tell all, the inspector shows him an underground newspaper published since Berardo has been jailed that tells of the series of events in Fontamara and asks him how he smuggled this information out. The headline of the newspaper is "Viva Berardo Viola." Berardo shuts his lips once more. "If I turn traitor," he agonizes aloud in his cell, "Fontamara will be eternally damned. . . . And if I die? It will be the first time a peasant dies not for himself but for someone else. . . . It will be something new. A new example. The beginning of something entirely new" (p. 213). The headline proclaiming that Berardo Viola will continue to live; the statements that he is dying so that Fontamara may not be eternally damned, that he is furnishing an example for others, that his death will be the beginning of something new; and the death which occurs next day under torture—all of these make him reminiscent of Christ.

The peasants of Fontamara, in dying as a result of their publication of a newspaper, are imitating the example of Berardo, who died not for himself but for others. They too will be examples in the irrepressible struggle that will be continued elsewhere. "Sometimes the government thought," the man from Avezzano tells Berardo, "it had the Solitary Stranger among those arrested. But after a short interruption the clandestine press took up its work again" (p. 201). The first peasant newspaper, which was printed by the people of Fontamara, will not be the last, even though it will be printed elsewhere. "When the newfangled things start up," says the old peasant's wife, speaking of the newspaper, "nobody can stop them" (p. 222). Although she is speaking with peasant mistrust and caution, she is right in her statement. In fact, we are told by the narrator at the beginning of the novel that "the strange events so faithfully recorded in this book have occurred in several places, although not in the same order nor at the same time" (p. 13).

For the Solitary Stranger is not an individual, whose capture means the end of the movement, but the spirit of revolution, which haunts the ruling class and which is suppressed in one place only to appear in several other places. "On the same day," as the man from Avezzano said, "he is discovered in several different provinces and even at the frontier" (p. 201). Although it is never stated, the man from Avezzano is evidently himself the Solitary Stranger. So, however, does Berardo become the Solitary Stranger when he affirms he is. The Solitary Stranger is whoever becomes the vessel for the spirit of revolution.

Silone, who was well aware when he wrote *Fontamara* how atomized the communist movement had become under fascist repression, holds forth no glowing prospects for the victory of the revolution, but he shows that the revolutionary road, exceedingly hard as it is, is the only one that can lead to the peasants' salvation. *What Can We Do?*, Scarpone's title for the peasant newspaper, repeated in despair by the old peasant at the end, echoes both Lenin's *What Is To Be Done?*, which is concerned with how the socialist revolution is to be achieved in tsarist Russia, and Tolstoy's *What Is To Be Done?*, which is concerned with how individual salvation is to be achieved. *Fontamara's* answer to the question of the two Russians is the same: selfless struggle in collective action for a new social order.

After World War II, when Mussolini was overthrown in the wake of Italy's military defeat, the Italian Communist Party, to the surprise of many who thought that the idea of socialism had been so obliterated by a generation of fascism that it would take a considerable period of reeducation for it to be revived, emerged as a great mass movement. However, thanks to its own class-collaborationist policy, by which it entered the government as a meek junior partner, and the might of American imperialism, the revolution was aborted. The Marshall Plan infused new vigor into Italian capitalism. But despite the "economic miracle" of postwar Italy, which furnished a new safety-valve to the southern villages in the form of jobs in the automobile factories of Milan and Turin, social commentators continue to speak to this very day of the "eternal backwardness" of southern Italy.

The picture of Montegrano, a village in southern Italy, we get from Edward C. Banfield's sociological study, *The Moral Basis of a Backward Society* (1958), is essentially the same as that of *Fontamara*: the peasants complain in the interviews of "La Miseria," the cloud of melancholy that hangs over them, and their sense of constant humiliation. Banfield makes the same comment about the peasants' concern only with their immediate families and their own little plots of land as the old peasant in *Fontamara* does, although he uses the sociological term "amoral familism" and makes it, not the social system, the principal cause of their plight: "The extreme poverty and backwardness . . . is to be explained largely (but not entirely) by the inability of the villagers to act together for their common good or, indeed, for any end transcending the immediate, material interest of the nuclear family."[8] With academic impartiality he suggests three external forces that may change the peasants' life: "The possibility of planned change depends upon the presence of an 'outside' group with the desire and ability to bring it about. . . . The political left, the church, and the industry of the north all contain elements which might inspire and support reform in the south."[9]

Fontamara shows, however, that the church and capitalism repress the peasants; these forces cannot liberate them. This simple tale written forty-five years ago contains profound insights applicable today: the innate conservatism of the village, in which a hundred peasant families try to join the ranks of the ten small landowner families; the deadening effect of tradition, personified in the old shoemaker Baldissera, who remembers the old ways and the old times, including the ceremonial service he performed as a boy for a baron; the dynamic effect of the transformation of the region by the capitalist market, which finally unites the villagers, including Baldissera; the role of the landless peasant, represented by Berardo (the members of the Fascist militia are of a different kind of landless peasants, not farm laborers but rural lumpen-proletarians—vagabonds, thieves, traders in thieves' markets, always ready to perform lackey services for the landowners, "poor yet the enemies of the poor"); the quasi-proletarianization of the peasants, who hire themselves out as laborers during their spare time; the limitations even of the Berardos, who can think only of sporadic unity for the purpose of sabotage, not political organization for the struggle to build a new society; the possibility of a revolutionary party originating among intellectuals and workers taking root among the peasants.

These insights go far beyond the situation in southern Italy. "All poor farmers," says the narrator at the beginning of *Fontamara*, "are alike in every country. They are men who cause the earth to bear fruit; they suffer from hunger; and whether they are called fellahs, coolies, peons, muzhiks or *cafoni*, they form their own nation, their own race and their own church all over the world, even though no two are exactly alike" (p. 14). Again, the artist has anticipated the academician. In many respects, Silone's presentation of his peasants foreshadows the 1974 scholarly study of the Third World peasant movement by Joel S. Migdal. "Peasant farmers in Coyotopec," says Migdal in his introductory comments, "feel the changes of the century. The electric light bulb hanging in their one-room houses does not always bring light because of the difficulty of keeping up with the costs, but it is as important a part of the house as the altar on the wall or the rolled-up straw mats used for sleeping."[10] So too, it may be recalled, the old peasant's account of the series of events that took place in Fontamara begins with the shutting off of the village's electricity because the peasants had not been paying the bills.

Migdal shows the same forces at work in the Third World that we have seen in Fontamara. "Capitalism's new forces of production," introduced in the Third World primarily by imperialism rather than, as in southern Italy, by the native capitalism of the north, have transformed social relations. "Lords' private domains were challenged by enterprising businessmen and political leaders, and the lords themselves were drawn into the profit-making techniques of the outside." "Increased market participation by peasants" has brought them new "economic crises." "This market participation" is "fraught with the dangers and unprofitability associated with corruption, monopoly, and structural incompleteness."[11] Where these conditions obtain, revolutionary movements have had the potentiality of drawing in the peasantry, but these movements have had to come from the outside.

> Revolutionary movements are created by the impetus of those from outside the peasant class. . . . [Peasants] are still relatively weak in organizational ability compared to other classes in the society. Also, they generally possess relatively little of the resources, such as expertise and education, associated with organization building. As a result, the participation of peasants in revolutionary organizations is preceded by the development of an organizational superstructure by students, intellectuals, and disaffected members of the middle class.[12]

In China, where the revolution triumphed, bringing one-fourth of humanity under its sway, it was led by a Stalinist party which had originally been based on a highly dynamic proletariat but which had found its way to the peasantry after the crushing and dispersion of that proletariat. The young men "in clothes halfway between a worker's and a student's" assumed peasant garb. Deutscher says:

It may indeed be that if this revolution had depended solely on the social alignments within China, Mao's partisans would have become, during their Yenan period, so closely assimilated to the peasantry that, despite their communist origin, they would have been unable to bridge the gulf between jacquerie and proletarian revolution. But . . . amid the cold war and in the face of hostile American intervention, Mao's party secured its rule by attaching itself to the Soviet Union and transforming the social structure of China accordingly.[13]

Thus the very unlikely but theoretical possibility which Trotsky would not rule out, in which, "under the influence of completely exceptional circumstances (war, defeat, financial crash, mass revolutionary pressure, etc.), the petty-bourgeois parties including the Stalinists, may go further than they themselves wish along the road to a break with the bourgeoisie," culminating in "the actual dictatorship of the proletariat,"[14] was realized.

The Chinese revolution was a great victory for world socialism. It has demonstrated the revolutionary possibilities under proper conditions of the "nation" of peasants all over the world. What would be decisive for the success of world socialist revolution would be victory in the advanced capitalist countries, most particularly the United States. World socialist revolution would make possible international planning, the solution of the peasants' problems, and the elimination of world hunger.

In a searching article, "The Great World Crisis I" (*New York Review of Books*, January 23, 1975), whose conclusions are buttressed by the technical reports of various institutions, the eminent British historian Geoffrey Barraclough says:

Properly used, according to Roger Revelle's calculations [in *Scientific American*, September 1974] the world area of potential arable land . . . could support . . . between ten and thirteen times the present population of the earth. "The limiting factors," he concludes, "are not natural resources but economic, institutional and socio-political restraints." This is a polite way of saying that what is at fault is the economic system and the political system it underpins. . . . Among the more notorious ["consequences resulting from colonialism and from lopsided development subordinated to the purposes of the industrial world"] are the stranglehold established by foreign financial institutions—American, British, French, and now Japanese—which, by granting or withholding loans and credit, largely determine the economic climate of most underdeveloped countries; the power wielded by the so-called multinational agribusiness corporations; and the role in all developing countries of the sector of wealthy hangers-on of foreign business, usually not more than 5 percent of the population, who have done exceedingly well out of the existing disparities and have no intention of surrendering their privileges.[15]

Only through world revolution will the tillers of the world be finally freed from the machinations of the international Trader, his banks, and his don Circostanzas, and be able to enjoy the fruits of the earth.

5. Richard Wright's 'Native Son': The Black Nationalist Revolution in America

Richard Wright's *Native Son,* published in 1940, made a tremendous impact when it appeared. In its first month it sold 250,000 copies. Many reviewers deplored the violence and hatred which they found in it, but all acknowledged its immense power. After some neglect in the war and postwar period, it has come into its own again, with the appearance of a number of books on Wright within a few years. For the ghetto uprisings in the 1960s demonstrated the validity of Wright's nightmare vision, the president's Kerner Commission itself affirming that the ghetto youth is "a time-bomb ticking in the heart of the richest nation in the history of the world."[1] This warning was forgotten—such is the fate of presidential commission reports—by the Ford administration spokesman who fatuously announced that the urban problem has been solved, but, with the extraordinarily high degree of ghetto youth unemployment, it is more timely than ever. The specter haunting white America is the specter of Bigger Thomas, Wright's young Black protagonist.

Wright was born in Mississippi. His life was a constant battle against assaults on his dignity. That he survived was a miracle made possible by his remarkable will and considerable luck. He met violence wherever he went during a migratory childhood in the South. When he was a nine-year-old in Memphis, a Black was lynched just outside of the city. The mob burned him alive, cut out his heart, and chopped him to pieces, which were exhibited on the main street of the city. The violence in Wright's fiction came from his experience in life.

Like Bigger Thomas, Wright was brought up in the South, was without a father, got only as far as the eighth grade (at the age of seventeen), and came with his family to Chicago. An omnivorous reader possessed from early childhood with the idea of becoming a writer, Wright found the Communist Party through being introduced to a branch of the John Reed Club, the literary organization of the party, by a fellow literary aspirant. He was a member of the party from 1932 to 1944.

The Communist Party gave Wright a coherent life outlook and a sense of belonging. It enabled him to see the Black struggle as one of the components of a worldwide struggle between oppressors and oppressed. On the other hand, Wright felt that the party was sectarian, not knowing how to talk to the masses, and that he could help it to learn how to do so. In his own writing, he came increasingly to feel that he was subject to bureaucratic pressure that would have him alter his personal vision to make his fiction fit the party leadership's blueprints. This pressure and his perception that the war had caused the party to sabotage the Black struggle (it denounced a proposed march on Washington to demand the hiring of Black workers in the war industries; it refused to participate in the fight against the racism of the draft laws; it called upon Blacks to give their blood to the Jim Crow blood banks) made him finally quit, although he remained a radical.

Native Son was written when the Communist Party adhered to the thesis that Blacks constitute an oppressed nation within the United States. This acceptance of Black nationalism was, however, vitiated by the party's sectarianism and bureaucratic authoritarianism. Instead of a policy of self-determination that would permit the Blacks themselves to decide whether they wished to establish an independent Black state, it undertook to make the decision for them, advocating that a separate territory be carved out for them in the Black Belt, the area in the South where Blacks were a majority of the population. It did not seek to encourage an independent Black political movement. Although it never had a real mass base among the Blacks, it made significant gains among them in the depression years, but it was unable to keep for any length of time the members it recruited.

Native Son is concerned with a ghetto Black who, alienated as he is from human beings, is untouched by any political movement. It is a novel with Black nationalist implications that go deeper than the party doctrine of the time. Jan, the white Communist, and Mary, the rich Communist sympathizer, in talking to Bigger reveal the gulf between them. Every word they utter, regardless of the friendliness of their intent, arouses his shame, hate, and fear, for they do not understand the complex of feeling that his life has given to him. Benjamin Davis, Jr., a Black Communist leader, expressing the uneasiness of the

Communist leaders with the novel (his review in the *Sunday Worker*, the official organ of the party,[2] appeared more than a month after the publication of *Native Son*, indicating their indecision), criticized its presentation of Jan and Mary. They are, said Davis, patronizing dilettantes not at all typical of party members and sympathizers. Jan is, however, neither patronizing nor a dilettante. He is the organizer for the local International Labor Defense, the legal defense organization of the party, and is completely taken up in his work. He and Mary simply do not understand the antagonism, hostility, and suspicion that Blacks like Bigger have against whites. The party leaders were right to be uneasy, for what is implied is the need for an independent Black political organization if the ghetto millions are to be drawn into the struggle against their oppressors, a struggle that must develop into a struggle for socialism in alliance with the white working class.

This is what Bigger at times dreams of:

> There were rare moments when a feeling and longing for solidarity with other black people would take hold of him. He would dream of making a stand against that white force, but that dream would fade when he looked at the other black people near him. . . . He felt that some day there would be a black man who would whip the black people into a tight band and together they would act and end fear and shame. He never thought of this in precise mental images; he felt it; he would feel it for a while and then forget. But hope was always waiting somewhere deep down in him.[3]

In this passage is indicated the basis for a Black nationalist movement: the realization of the necessity of collective Black action and of the necessity for instilling racial pride so that a determined defiance may take the place of the sense of hopelessness of the uprooted, disoriented ghetto masses. Wright knew better than anyone else the immense difficulty of uniting this colonized people, living a semi-lumpen proletarian existence in its own, fetid squalor. But he also knew better than anyone else the dynamite packed in the ghettoes. The use of Black soldiers in a war ostensibly fought against racism, the rise of Black nations in Africa, the obtaining of a foothold in industry by the Blacks, the concessions granted to them as a consequence of the cold war— these have drawn Blacks together in a new self-awareness. But the problem of a united leadership remains.

Native Son does not deal with the Black nationalist revolution directly. On its face it is a sensational murder story. With an amazing audacity Wright chose as his central character one who fits the stereotype of the murderous "bad nigger" who expresses the guilty fear of racist whites and serves as a rationalization for repression. Bigger ("b[ad n]igger"?), having put the drunken Mary to bed, unwittingly smothers her to death when he fears that her blind mother will, attracted to her mumbling, discover his presence in the room and leap to the conclusion that he has committed rape. Although the murder was accidental, we see that Bigger carries rape and murder in his heart and that he might well have raped this forbidden object of his hate if Mrs. Dalton had not come along. Bigger burns Mary's body, first chopping off her head so that he can force her into the furnace. Later, he kills his girl Bessie immediately after he had made love to her, knowing that she will impede him in his flight if he takes her with him and that she will tell on him if he doesn't. There can scarcely be murders more gruesome.

What Wright did was to take the bogeyman of the racists and show him to be frighteningly real, but created by white America itself and possessing a humanity that calls to ours. It is an achievement comparable to Shakespeare's in making Macbeth perform the most heinous of crimes and yet causing us to retain a horrified sympathy with him as he seeks to emerge from his nightmare existence by committing one murder after another.

The method which Wright uses is to restrict the point of view to Bigger, to show everything as it is seen through Bigger's eyes. At the same time that he renders Bigger's consciousness in vivid, dramatic detail, making us feel his fear and his shame, Wright comments upon it, relating it to his past experience. Some have objected to Wright's "editorializing," and others have charged that he has given Bigger ideas that are too complex for his character. Wright's comments, however, do not jar upon the tone and rhythm of Bigger's thoughts and feelings and never get in the way between Bigger's consciousness and the reader's. His commentary works, as it has worked in the hands of the masters from Fielding to Thackeray, the rigid exclusion of authorial comment being a point of craftsmanship only in the contemporary technique of fiction. As for the charge that Wright has given Bigger ideas that are too complex for his character, perhaps there are some few lapses, but usually Wright conveys the sense of having articulated for Bigger what he is actually feeling, as in the description of Bigger's longing for Black solidarity, quoted above.

It has also been said that the white characters have little reality, being, in the words of Irving Howe, "either 'agit-prop' villains or heroic Communists whom Wright finds it easier to admire from a distance than establish from the inside."[4] There are, however, no heroic Communists in the novel, and Wright is not seeking to establish his characters other than Bigger from the inside: they are all to be seen through Bigger's consciousness. In the case of Jan and Mary, we perceive them with a double vision: what they appear to Bigger and what we infer they are. They, and the other characters, are not seen in the round; they are, however, credible flat characters, which is all they need to be. Perhaps in one scene, the scene in which Jan visits Bigger in jail and expresses his sympathy and understanding, knowing that Bigger had killed Mary and sought to implicate him, credibility wears thin, the crisis within Jan not having been dramatized, only fumblingly articulated to Bigger.

Another charge that has often been made against *Native Son* is that it is luridly melodramatic. But nightmare horror is central to the effect of *Native Son,* and often what seems incredibly exaggerated is not exaggerated at all. The racism of the newspapers may seem too crude and blatant, for instance, to be credible. These newspaper stories are, however, as a matter of fact a rewrite of what was contained in the *Chicago Tribune,* the self-proclaimed "world's greatest newspaper," concerning an alleged Black rapist-murderer, Robert Nixon, whose case happened to break while Wright was in the middle of writing *Native Son,* a chance that indicates how deeply rooted in life the novel is. Today, as a result of the Black struggle, it is no longer "respectable" to voice racist feelings so openly. Perhaps, even for that earlier period, the prosecuting attorney's speech is not plausible. It too obviously exposes the fiction of equal justice for Blacks and whites, and it would, therefore, not have been permitted by the judge.

However, whatever the objections of critics, all agree, as I have said, concerning *Native Son*'s immense power. Its remarkable opening, in which Bigger kills a huge black rat and then dangles its body in front of his sister to enjoy her terror, is electrifying. It establishes the conditions in which his family lives, the terror of their existence, and Bigger's need for the release of violence. Above all, the cornered rat in its fear and defiance symbolizes Bigger, trapped in his ghetto. Later, when Bigger is in flight, looking for a place to hide, a big black rat, leaping over the snow, shoots past him and slides through a hole, and Bigger looks wistfully at that hole through which the rat had darted to safety. From the beginning, the novel proceeds with a drive that is unremitting. It is divided into three books—"Fear," "Flight," and "Fate"—but it contains no chapters. Nothing is to impede the rapid flow of the narrative. Yet so much does Bigger experience in the few days of the action that his progress to the death cell seems excruciatingly long as well as dizzyingly swift.

The conclusion towards which the novel drives has perhaps caused more critics, distinguished and obscure, to go astray, reading into it their own preconceptions instead of perceiving the author's purpose, than any other significant portion of a major work of modern American literature. Both Max's lengthy speech in the courtroom and his final scene with Bigger have been grievously misunderstood.

Irving Howe, for instance, finds that the "endlessly-repeated criticism" that Max's speech is a "party-line oration" "tends to oversimplify the novel" not because this criticism is incorrect but because it does not go beyond the speech to perceive that the union of Bigger's "raw revolt" and Max's "political conscious-ness" has not been effected.[5] So too Alfred Kazin declares that Wright's method is "to astonish the reader by torrential scenes of cruelty, hunger, rape, murder and flight, and then enlighten him by crude Stalinist homilies."[6] By "crude Stalinist homilies" Kazin undoubtedly means Max's speech and his conversations with Bigger.

Howe, Kazin, and the numerous other critics who have written on the matter have responded to the courtroom speech with a conditioned reflex: Richard Wright was a Communist; Boris Max is called a Communist (only, to be sure, by the red-baiting prosecuting attorney and newspapers, but that is overlooked); therefore, the speech must be a "party-line oration," a "crude Stalinist" homily. Before we examine the speech, let us see what Ben Davis, Jr., had to say about it.

Although Davis concedes that "certain passages in Max's speech show an understanding of the responsibility of capitalism for Bigger's plight," he checks off the following points against Max: "he accepts the idea that Negroes have a criminal psychol-ogy"; "he does not challenge the false charge of rape against Bigger"; "he does not deal with the heinous murder of Bessie, tending to accept the bourbon policy that crimes of Negroes against each other don't matter"; "he argues that Bigger, and by implication the whole Negro mass, should be held in jail to protect 'white daughters'"; he "should have argued for Bigger's acquittal in the case, and should have helped stir the political pressure of the Negro and white masses to get that acquittal." "His speech," Davis concludes, " . . . expresses the point of view held . . . by . . . reformist betrayers. . . . The first business of the Communist Party or of the I.L.D. would have been to chuck him out of the case."[7]

Davis's remarks distort the text badly. Max's statement that Bigger's existence is "a crime against the state" is, insofar as it is an indictment at all, far more of an indictment of the state than it is of Bigger. Max does deal with the murder of Bessie, making the point that Bigger knew that the white world would be concerned only with the murder of Mary, not of Bessie. He nowhere argues that Bigger, let alone "the whole Negro mass," should be held in jail to protect white daughters. However, whatever the distortions in the pronouncement of this party bureaucrat turned literary critic, he is, it must be acknowledged, a more authoritative interpreter of the party line of the time than either Howe or Kazin. Davis obviously wants the simplified propaganda that *Native Son* does not give: a hero who is a completely innocent victim and a lawyer who thunders his client's innocence, who brilliantly exposes a frame-up rooted in a corrupt society, and who calls for giant demonstrations against this frame-up. The fact that Max is not a party-line expounder is one of the points which made the party leaders uneasy about *Native Son*.

If, then, Max is not the novel's Communist spokesman who delivers a "party-line oration," what are his politics and what does he say in his speech? An old, wise, weary Jew, deeply aware of the radical defects of the society of which he is a member, Max, as we shall see that his courtroom speech makes clear, envisions a cataclysmic end to this society and seeks desperately to avert it by striving to have wrongs redressed. Neither a revolutionist nor a Stalinist, he does not look forward hopefully to a revolution; he fears it.

His speech is not an address to a jury, as Edwin Berry Burgum, James Baldwin, Dan McCall, and Edward Margolies affirm.[8] Max clearly states that, not daring to put Bigger's fate in the hands of a white jury whose minds have been inflamed by the press, he has entered a plea of guilty, which by the laws of Illinois permits him to reject a trial by jury and to have the sentence rendered by the presiding judge. "Dare I," he asks the judge, " . . . put his fate in the hands of a jury . . . whose minds are already conditioned by the press of the nation . . . ? No! I could not! So today I come to face this Court, rejecting a trial by jury, willingly entering a plea of guilty, asking in the light of the laws of this state that this boy's life be spared . . . " (p. 325).

It is to this judge that Max is speaking. Beyond the judge he is speaking to "men of wealth and property," who, if they misread "the consciousness of the submerged millions today" (p. 338), will bring about a civil war in the future. It is amazing that James Baldwin can say that Max's speech

is addressed to those among us of good will and it seems to say that, though there are whites and blacks among us who hate each other, we will not; there are those who are betrayed by greed, by guilt, by blood lust, but not we; we will set our faces against them and join hands and walk together into that dazzling future when there will be no white or black.[9]

Baldwin is here carried away by his own rhetoric. There is not a sentence in the speech stating or implying a dazzling future to which Black and white will walk hand in hand!

Nor is the speech a savage attack on capitalism or, as Robert Bone says, a statement of a "guilt-of-the-nation thesis,"[10] a plea for sympathy for one whose guilt we must all share. Max says,

Allow me, Your Honor, to state emphatically that I do *not* claim that this boy is a victim of injustice, nor do I ask that this Court be sympathetic with him. . . . If I should say that he is a victim of injustice, then I would be asking by implication for sympathy; and if one insists upon looking at this boy in the light of sympathy, he will be swamped by a feeling of guilt so strong as to be indistinguishable from hate. [Pp. 327-28]

The mob of would-be lynchers, he says, knowing in its heart of the oppression of Negroes, is as possessed of guilt, fear, and hate as Bigger is. In order to understand the full significance of Bigger's case, he urges the judge, one must rise above such emotion. To do so, he summons him to look upon it from a historical height. The "first wrong," the enslavement of the Negroes, was "understandable and inevitable" (p. 327), for in subduing this "harsh and wild country" (p. 328) men had to use other men as tools and weapons. "Men do what they must do" (p. 329). From that first wrong came a sense of guilt, in the attempted stifling of which came hate and fear, a hate and fear which matched that of the Negroes. Injustice practiced on this scale and over that length of time "is injustice no longer; it is an accomplished fact of life" (p. 330). This fact of life is a system of oppression squeezing down upon millions of people. These millions can be stunted, but they cannot be stamped out. And as oppression grows tighter, guilt, fear, and hatred grow stronger on both sides. Killing Bigger will only "swell the tide of pent-up lava that will some day break loose, not in a single, blundering, accidental, individual crime, but in a wild cataract of emotion that will brook no control" (p. 330). Sentencing him to life imprisonment, on the other hand, will give him an opportunity to "build a meaning for his life."

Max's speech is, in short, an agonized plea to the judge to understand the significance of Bigger and, understanding, to break through the pattern of hatred and repression that "makes our future seem a looming image of violence" (p. 337). It has frequently been pointed out that in book 3, which is entitled "Fate," we see realized the doom of Bigger that has been foreshadowed from the beginning. This is entirely true, of course, but "Fate" also refers to the doom of the United States, towards which Max sees us, "like sleep-walkers" (p. 324), proceeding. "If we can understand how subtly and yet strongly his life and fate are linked to ours,—if we can do this, perhaps we shall find the key to our future" (p. 324). Bigger killed "accidentally"—that is, he was not aware of killing as he killed—but this does not matter. What matters is that "every thought he thinks is potential murder" (p. 335). "Who knows when another 'accident' involving millions of men will happen, an 'accident' that will be the dreadful day of our doom?" (pp. 337-38).

Max's speech, far from being, as Howe says, "ill-related to the book," not a part of "a unified vision of things,"[11] grows out of the rest of the novel. It has, to be sure, a number of weaknesses. It and the prosecuting attorney's speech are not seen and heard from Bigger's point of view, which is otherwise rigidly adhered to in the novel, the vivid presentation of Bigger's visceral reactions, as events are registered on his consciousness, contributing to the novel's force and drive. Max's speech, which takes sixteen pages, is not, however, summarized and presented through Bigger's consciousness, and at its end we are told that Bigger "had not understood the speech, but he had felt the meaning of some of it from the tone of Max's voice" (p. 370). Moreover, the speech, far from being superimposed on what had gone on before and at variance with it, repeats too obviously what has already been said. Wright's awareness of this repetition and his desire to achieve a heightened effect in the final summing up may explain a rhetoric that is occasionally too highly wrought and too highly pitched.

That the speech, however, is not an obtrusion is indicated by the number of recurring themes and images in the novel which are brought together in it. The first theme that we might consider is that of blindness. Bigger, eating his breakfast the morning after he has killed Mary and looking upon his family and the world with new eyes, realizes that his mother, sister, and brother exclude from their vision of the world that which they do not wish to see. He also realizes that Mrs. Dalton is blind figuratively as well as literally, that Mr. Dalton and Jan are blind, and that Mary had been blind in not realizing that which was in him, the propensity to kill. When he joins Bessie, he feels the same about her being blind as he does about the family. She knows nothing but hard work in white folks' kitchens and the liquor she drinks to make up for her starved life. In flight, despite the danger of death, Bigger feels a "queer sense of power" at having set the chase into motion, at being engaged in purposeful activity for the first time in his life, and tells himself, "He was living, truly and deeply, no matter what others might think, looking at him with their blind eyes" (p. 203). When Jan visits him in prison, he tells Bigger, "I was kind of blind. . . . I didn't know we were so far apart until that night" (p. 244). Bigger, understanding that Jan is expressing his belief in him, for the first time looks upon a white man as a human being. "He saw Jan as though someone had performed an operation upon his eyes" (p. 246).

Max, in his image of the American people proceeding to their doom like sleep-walkers, catches up these images of darkness present on all sides. It is this blindness which he emphasizes throughout his speech. If the judge reacts only to what he has to say about the sufferings of Negroes, he states, he will be "blinded" by a feeling that will prevent him from perceiving reality and acting accordingly. "Rather, I plead with you to see . . . an existence of men growing out of the soil prepared by the collective but blind will of a hundred million people" (p. 328). "Your Honor," he exclaims, "in our blindness we have so contrived and ordered the lives of men" (p. 336) that their every human aspiration constitutes a threat to the state.

Related to the theme of blindness is the theme of Bigger's mistaken view of whites as constituting an overpowering natural force, a part of the structure of the universe. "To Bigger and his kind," says Wright early in the novel, "white people were not really people; they were a sort of great natural force, like a stormy sky looming overhead, or like a deep swirling river stretching suddenly at one's feet in the dark" (p. 97). The snowstorm that covers Chicago after Bigger's murders is symbolic of the hostile white world. When Bigger slips in running, "the white world tilted at a sharp angle and the icy wind shot past his face" (p. 205). The snow separates Jan and Bigger from each other, as Jan accosts Bigger in the street after Mary's disappearance and tries to speak to him, only to be driven away by Bigger's gun: "In the pale yellow sheen of the street lamp they faced each other; huge wet flakes of snow floated down slowly, forming a delicate screen between them" (p. 146). When Jan gets through to Bigger in prison, an image of the white world as a great natural force is used again, this time a force subject to erosion: "Jan had spoken a declaration of friendship that would make other white men hate him: a particle of white rock had detached itself from that looming mountain of white hate and had rolled down the slope, stopping still at his feet" (p. 246; see also p. 253).

With his fine sensitivity, Max understands Bigger's feeling about whites, which Bigger had conveyed to him in the prison interview, and tries to make the judge understand it, using the same image of the white world as a natural force, not made up of human beings: "When situations like this arise, instead of men feeling that they are facing other men, they feel that they are facing mountains, floods, seas . . ." (p. 327). But the judge blindly does not understand.

Another recurring image is that of the wall or curtain or veil behind which Bigger withdraws and hides rather than face reality.

> He knew that the moment he allowed himself to feel to its fullness how [his family] lived, the shame and misery of their lives, he would be swept out of himself with fear and despair. So he held toward them an attitude of iron reserve; he lived with them, but behind a wall, a curtain. And toward himself he was even more exacting. He knew that the moment he allowed what his life meant to enter fully into his consciousness, he would either kill himself or someone else. [P. 19]

So, Max says, the killing of Mary was "a sudden and violent rent in the veil behind which he lived" (pp. 330-31), tearing aside his alienated numbness and enabling him for the first time really to live.

The theme that Bigger's killing has given him a freedom he never before had is sounded frequently. "He had murdered and created a new life for himself. It was something that was all his own, and it was the first time in his life he had had anything that others could not take from him" (p. 90). And again: "He felt that he had his destiny in his grasp. He was more alive than he could ever remember having been; his mind and attention were pointed, focussed toward a goal" (p. 127). And still again: "There remained to him a queer sense of power. *He* had done this. *He* had brought all this about. In all of his life these two murders were the most meaningful things that had ever happened to him" (p. 203).

This is what Max tells the judge. In order to seek to reach him, he dares to speak of the killing as "an act of *creation*" (p. 325). He is not only concerned with conveying to the judge the bondage in which Bigger had lived so that it took this killing to give him "the possibility of choice, of action, the opportunity to act and to feel that his actions carried weight" (p. 333). He is concerned with conveying to him the sense of an impending awful catastrophe in which millions of others learn to be free through killing: "How soon will someone speak the word that resentful millions will understand: the word to be, to act, to live?"[12]

The sense of freedom that Bigger received was only transitory. Caught and imprisoned, Bigger wonders concerning the meaning of his life. Were the intimations of freedom, of "a possible order and meaning in his relations with the people about him" (p. 234) real? Or would freedom and meaning elude him and would he "have to go to his end just as he was, dumb, driven, with the shadow of emptiness in his eyes" (p. 235)? "Maybe they were right when they said that a black man was bad . . . Maybe he was just unlucky, a man born for dark doom, an obscene joke. . . ."

The big question of book 3 is whether Bigger will find himself. It is not answered until the very end of the novel, the farewell scene with Max. "At the end," says Howe, "Bigger remains at the mercy of his hatred and fear." It is hard to make men hear who will not listen. Seven times in the last page and a half of the novel Bigger cries out to Max, "I'm all right," the last time adding, "For real, I am" (p. 359). The repeated assurance "I'm all right" obviously means that Bigger is not at the mercy of fear, that he is sure that he will not, as he had dreaded, have to be dragged to the electric chair kicking and screaming, filled with animal terror because he had not been able to find human dignity. He has found what he sought, an understanding of himself that "could lift him up and make him live so intensely that the dread of being black and unequal would be forgotten; that even death would not matter, that it would be a victory" (p.

234). The meaning for his life which Max thought to gain him the opportunity to build during life imprisonment he grasped from his recent experience under the duress of death.

What was the understanding of himself which he had acquired? Bone believes that Bigger casts out fear by giving himself completely to hatred, thereby in reality suffering a defeat: "What terrifies Max is that Bigger, repossessed by hate, ends by accepting what life has made him: a killer. Bigger's real tragedy is not that he dies, but that he dies in hatred. A tragic figure, he struggles for love and trust against a hostile environment which defeats him in the end."[13] Since the conclusion has been so misunderstood, it will be necessary to quote at some length from it in order to examine it closely.

Max does not wish to talk to Bigger about the significance of his life, but he is forced to do so by Bigger's insistence. He tells Bigger:

It's too late now for you to . . . work with . . . others who are t-trying to . . . believe [in life, which is thwarted by capitalism] and make the world live again. . . . But it's not too late to believe what you felt, to understand what you felt. . . . The job in getting people to fight and have faith is in making them believe in what life has made them feel, making them feel that their feelings are as good as those of others. . . . That's why . . . y-you've got to b-believe in yourself, Bigger . . . [Pp. 357-58]

These words work upon Bigger. They give him what he wants. Ironically, however, they cause him to go further than Max intended. "Bigger, you killed," says Max. "That was wrong. That was not the way to do it." Bigger, however, accepts himself completely, including his overwhelming impulse to kill:

Sounds funny, Mr. Max, but when I think about what you say I kind of feel what I wanted. It makes me feel I was kind of right. . . . They wouldn't let me live and I killed. Maybe it ain't fair to kill, and I reckon I really didn't want to kill. But when I think of why all the killing was, I begin to feel what I wanted, what I am. . . . I didn't want to kill! . . . But what I killed for, I *am*! It must've been pretty deep in me to make me kill! . . . What I killed for must've been good! . . . When a man kills, it's for something . . . [P. 358]

Max's shock on hearing these words seems excessive for one who had shown such an understanding of Bigger and had said, "We are dealing here with an impulse stemming from deep down"

(p. 333). Perhaps this is a flaw in the scene. However, we must remember that this is the third great blow he has received. The first was when the judge, the representative of the establishment, had disregarded his desperate plea. The second was when the governor had refused to exercise clemency. These blows make it all the more difficult for him to sustain the blow inflicted by Bigger, the representative of Black millions. The catastrophe he foresees seems to him more than ever inescapable.

Is Bigger's acceptance of his feelings of hate a victory or a defeat? If Bone is, like Max, shocked by Bigger's words, and in his shock can see only that Bigger is defeated by his hostile environment, he should consider how Bigger's killing was presented as a means of liberation and so described by Max himself. Wright, of course, is not advocating murder. Murder gave Bigger a sense of freedom, but it also gave him a sense of guilt, and, not giving him a sense of relatedness to others, it finally left him empty. But hatred of the oppressor is a natural, human emotion; it is only unhealthy when it is kept stifled. Used as the motor power of an idea driving toward a goal, it can transform both the individual and society.

So Max in his courtroom speech said of the American revolutionary war: "Your Honor, remember that men can starve from a lack of self-realization as much as they can from a lack of bread! And they can *murder* for it, too! Did we not build a nation, did we not wage war and conquer in the name of a dream to realize our personalities and to make those realized personalities secure!" (p. 366). So too Sartre, in summarizing Fanon, echoes the statement that killing can be a creative act (the French existentialists, we may recall, acclaimed Wright and accepted him as one of their own):

In the period of their helplessness, their mad impulse to murder is the expression of the [colonial] natives' collective unconscious. If this suppressed fury fails to find an outlet, it turns in a vacuum and devastates the oppressed creatures themselves. In order to free themselves they even massacre each other. . . . [Compare with Bigger's violence in Doc's poolroom, when his fear of the hated white man forces him to attack Gus rather than to rob Blum's delicatessen.] This irrepressible violence [in a war of national liberation] is . . . man re-creating himself. . . . The native cures himself of colonial neurosis by thrusting out the settler through force of arms. When his rage boils over, he rediscovers his lost innocence and he comes to know himself in that he creates himself.[14]

Bone, moreover, overlooks completely—as does Howe—Bigger's last words before his final "goodbye": "Tell. . . . Tell Mister. . . . Tell Jan hello. . . ." (P. 359, Wright's dots.) Bigger does not go to death hating all white men. He accepts the comradeship of Jan, for the first time in his life dropping the "mister" in front of a white man's name. But this comradeship he will extend only to those who have earned it in action, not to superficial sympathizers, patronizing philanthropists, or bureaucratically arrogant radical sectarians. His pride in himself would not permit it otherwise.

Bigger realized in his death cell that "if there were any sure and firm knowledge for him, it would have to come from himself" (p. 350). And so it was. And just so, Wright indicates, the inner liberation of the Blacks will have to come from within themselves. Bigger in prison and in the face of death acquires the faith in himself and in his people that could propel the ghetto millions toward a goal that would catch "the mind and body in certainty and faith" (p. 98). Only between such Blacks and such whites as Jan, the conclusion of *Native Son* implies, can there be genuine unity in a common struggle for a different and better form of society. This struggle for the third American revolution promises, in view of the adamant position of the ruling class that had rejected Max's plea and caused him to despair, to become, like the Revolutionary War and the Civil War, a bloody conflict before it is victorious.

III

POSTWAR DISILLUSIONMENT
WITH REVOLUTION IN THE WEST

Introduction to Section III

The Communist parties of Europe and America were so tied to the conservative Kremlin bureaucracy that revolutionary opportunities in Spain, France, and Germany were lost in the 1930s, as they had been in China in 1927. In Germany the Nazis put down the threat of proletarian revolution by physically destroying, terrorizing, and atomizing the mass Communist and Socialist parties, and solved the problem of depression by preparing on a gigantic scale for the war it needed as a "have-not" capitalist power. The vastly richer United States could afford the luxury of various meliorative measures under Roosevelt. However, although it climbed part way out of the depression, it never really emerged from it until it converted itself into a vast armaments-making plant for the Allies. The Keynesian remedy of deficit spending was then applied on a scale it had never been before: the greatest deficit during the depression was 4.4 billion dollars in 1936, but the armaments-spending deficit in 1943 was 57.4 billion dollars.[1]

After the war, as Isaac Deutscher says, "the international balance of power swamped the class struggle."[2]

It is probable that had there been no Teheran and Yalta compacts, western rather than eastern Europe would have become the theatre of revolution—especially France and Italy, where the authority of the old ruling classes was in ruins, the working classes were in revolt, and the Communist parties led the bulk of the armed Resistance. Stalin, acting on his diplomatic commitments, prevailed upon the French and Italian Communists to resign themselves to the restoration of capitalism in their countries from the virtual collapse and even to co-operate in the restoration.[3]

In Greece, revolution was, with the aid of the United States and the connivance of Stalin, bloodily suppressed; but in Yugoslavia, where, as we know from the revelations of Djilas, Stalin wished to make a deal with England,[4] the revolution was successful despite him. In Eastern Europe, on the other hand, Stalin found that he had to consolidate by a "revolution from above" his hold over the coalition governments that were to act as buffer states, building in all of the instabilities resulting from a revolution imposed primarily by foreign arms rather than coming from a popular insurrection.

The great victory of the revolution was in China. Again, as Lenin had phrased it, the chain of world capitalism broke at its weakest link. Mao Tse-tung and his party had followed Stalin in attempting to form a coalition with Chiang, but Chiang had broken their agreement. "On February 23, 1946," writes General Albert C. Wedemeyer, "under the tutelage of General Marshall, who had come to China as a mediator, the Kuomintang and the Chinese CP concluded an agreement for the unification of their armed forces [, an agreement in which 'there was no question of a radical reform']. The road for 'social peace' seemed open."[5] But Chiang had thought himself strong enough to defeat the Red Army and had attacked it. As the Maoist leader Chu Teh said, "If the Kuomintang had put into effect the decisions of the Popular Consultative Conference [the meetings mediated by Marshall], there would have been no civil war."[6] Chiang was defeated by the revolutionary mobilization of the poor peasants which the Maoist leadership, after months of hesitation about breaking its alliance with the national bourgeoisie, undertook as a measure of self-defense.[7] Even after the victory of the Red Army, the Maoist leadership, which as Deutscher said, "had long and stubbornly dwelt on the limited bourgeois character of the Chinese revolution,"[8] did not carry out its nationalizations until it was directly threatened by American imperialist forces in Korea. Thus the logic of permanent revolution was triumphant despite all of the opposition to it of the Maoists.

The Chinese Communists began even further back than the Russians, but they had many advantages the Russians had lacked: once they came to power, they did not have to contend with civil war and foreign armies on their soil, and could give their undivided attention to economic reconstruction, in which they initially had the aid, niggardly as it was, of the Soviet Union. They were, furthermore, buoyed by the tide of anti-imperialist struggle in Asia, Africa, and Latin America, not disheartened, as the Russians had been, by the revolutionary defeats in Europe after World War I.

The Chinese revolution has remarkable achievements to its

credit. We may contrast its defeat of the age-old scourge of famine, its development of a system of health care reaching throughout the country, and its extension of education to the masses, with the beggary and starvation in India—as, incidentally, we may contrast such comparable countries as Cuba with Chile and Yugoslavia with Turkey. It is nevertheless a revolution deformed from its birth under Stalinist auspices in its monolithism, its leader-worship, its narrow bureaucratic nationalism and consequent opportunism in the field of foreign policy. The consequence of the regime's foreign policy was most vividly exhibited in the massacre of the Indonesian Communist Party, which on the advice of Peking had subordinated itself to Sukarno and the Front of National Unity as, ironically, the Chinese Communist Party had subordinated itself in 1925-27 to Chiang Kai-shek and the Kuomintang, with a resulting similar massacre. Following this debacle, the Chinese Communist Party, deprived of its main bargaining counter in its attempt to make a deal with American imperialism, cravenly subordinated itself to the foreign policy of the United States, supporting NATO and the Shah of Iran while denouncing revolutionary Cuba. As Deutscher says, "The impossibility of disentangling progress from backwardness is the price that not only Russia and China but mankind as a whole is paying for the confinement of the revolution to the underdeveloped countries."[9]

For American capitalism the rejection by the Chinese people of the "religion of Americanism"[10]—whose espousal by Chiang Kai-shek had brought them nothing but calamity—was a great blow. Everything was attributed to an "international Communist conspiracy" whose agents infiltrated the world. That revolutions rise from indigenous social conditions and come about only if a political party presents a program which answers the needs of the masses and engages them in action was a fact to which reaction was blind. At the same time the CIA began its own genuine conspiracy—thoroughly documented in various governmental admissions and in the books by Victor Marchetti and Philip Agee—of seeking to sustain the status quo throughout the world by secretly financing political parties, engaging in wholesale bribery, conducting assassinations, organizing coups, employing counterrevolutionary armies, and waging air warfare on its own.

Western intellectuals, especially those in the United States, by and large accepted the picture of the world conjured up by the proponents of the cold war. The "radical tourist" fellow-travelers of Stalinism found that their god had failed. The consolidation of a murderous police state after the great show trials which they had taken at face value, the Hitler-Stalin pact, and the Red Army intervention in Eastern Europe produced a reaction similar to the reaction after the Napoleonic conquests on the part of the English romanticists who had welcomed the French revolution.

In the years that followed, as a result of the boom brought about first by postwar reconstruction and then by continued deficit spending for military expenditures—Rosa Luxemburg had proved right in saying early in the century that militarism might become the driving force of capitalist economy[11]—the idea of revolution in the West receded. The sociologist Daniel Bell proclaimed "the end of ideology"—that is, the triumph of technology over the class struggle. It was felt that revolution could come in Europe only through conquest by the Red Army, which was held in check by NATO. As for the United States, the prevalent feeling in the 1950s was that this country had virtually solved all its social problems, only a few pockets of poverty in the Black ghettos and elsewhere remaining to be cleared out. The extent and depth of the country's poverty revealed in Michael Harrington's *The Other America* (1962) came as a genuine suprise to many middle-class intellectuals who thought that the improvement in their own economic circumstances was true for everyone.

7. Arthur Koestler's 'Darkness at Noon': The 'Logic of Revolution'?

Arthur Koestler's *Darkness at Noon* was one of the big guns whose fusillade marked the inception of the cold war. When it was published in England in 1941, it did not create much stir, but published in France after the war, at a time when the Communist Party was so powerful that its leader, Maurice Thorez, boasted that he could make a revolution by lifting up a telephone, it broke all sales records, and Koestler became one of the international prophets of anticommunism. His essay describing his experience with Stalinism appeared in the British Laborite Richard Crossman's book *The God that Failed* together with similar essays by Silone and Wright, the three being categorized as "The Initiates," with other essays by André Gide, Louis Fischer, and Stephen Spender, who were categorized as "Worshippers from Afar." The book made a significant impact on intellectuals disillusioned with communism. However, of the three "initiates" only Koestler in giving up Stalinism also gave up socialism.

A novelistic depiction of how an Old Bolshevik was made to confess at a Moscow show trial, *Darkness at Noon* was an indictment not only of Stalinism but of Bolshevism, in which it found the genesis of the trials. During the time of the trials intelligent observers in the West found it extremely difficult to believe that all of the surviving central leaders of the Russian revolution except Stalin had not only turned against it, become agents of foreign powers, and worked for the restoration of capitalism, but had even been foreign agents and plotted the assassination of Lenin at the time of the revolution itself. Yet why did they charge themselves with these things in open court in front of the world press? Koestler showed how his protagonist, Rubashov, was subjected to continuous interrogation, night and day, without being allowed a wink of sleep, under the glare of a very strong lamp in his eyes, until he was broken down and made amenable to the persuasion of his interrogator. Koestler indicated also that physical torture and threats of killing wives and children were used against many.

As an exposure of the methods of the GPU, *Darkness at Noon* is entirely accurate and was a good deal of a revelation in its day. Koestler, an ex-Stalinist, knew of these methods through Eva Weissberg, who with her husband Alex was a friend of Koestler's. An Austrian Stalinist living in the Soviet Union, she was imprisoned by the GPU, which sought to use her in the Bukharin trial. She was released and expelled from the Soviet Union as a result of the extraordinary efforts in her behalf of the Austrian consul, who was a friend of her mother's.

Since the time *Darkness at Noon* was published, the methods of the GPU have become universally known, thanks primarily to the revelations of Khrushchev but also to the accounts of former prisoners such as F. Beck and W. Godin, Alex Weissberg, and Arthur London (whose book, *The Confession*, was the basis of the excellent film of the same title by Costa-Gavras), to the disclosures of the defected high-ranking GPU men Walter G. Krivitsky and Alexander Orlov (who have, however, to be read with some caution), and to the research of such men as Roy Medvedev, the Russian Marxist who had to smuggle his remarkable *Let History Judge* out of the Soviet Union because its anti-Stalinism went beyond what the regime would permit. We need not accept the political conclusions of these men, including Medvedev, to make use of their data and their analyses.

The mystery of the confessions is no longer a mystery: the defendants were made to confess that they plotted with Trotsky to restore capitalism to the Soviet Union and to give portions of the country to Germany and Japan, in the same way that thousands of persons in the era of witchcraft trials were made to confess that they had entered into a pact with the devil—through physical and psychological torture and through mental suggestion practiced on them after they had been broken. Also, some of them were promised, according to the statement, cited by Medvedev, of the wife of one of the executed defendants whose husband had managed to communicate with her, that they would be permitted to live and do party or government work in the Soviet Far East and that they would be rehabilitated after the threat of Hitler had passed. In the Soviet Union itself the charges against the defendants are now no longer mentioned and they are not stigmatized as "enemies of the people," but they have not been officially rehabilitated with the exception of Ikramov, the Uzbeck codefendant of Bukharin, who was cleared of all guilt in the press of his native region but not in the central press.[1]

Darkness at Noon, however, is not a mere exposure of the

methods of the GPU but a purported psychological study of the character of an Old Bolshevik that demonstrates how Stalinism evolved from the Bolshevik idea that "the end justifies the means," an idea which resulted in actions that filled Rubashov with a repressed feeling of guilt but to which he adheres in presenting his false confession. Exhausted as he is, he has been persuaded that the party to which he has devoted his life needs his confession to rally the masses behind it in order to fend off danger within and without. His lifelong habit of serving the party no matter by what means and his sense of guilt, not about the fictitious crimes of which he accuses himself, but about the real crimes he has committed in the name of the party, make him deliver what seems to the world a self-abasing confession but is to him his last party duty and a settling of his account with history.

Rubashov's dialogues with the GPU men Ivanov and Gletkin are really dialogues he has with himself, for they echo his own ideas. As Ivanov says, their positions might well have been reversed, with Rubashov doing the questioning and Ivanov being the prisoner. In fact, Rubashov had in effect acted toward two deviationists—Richard, the young German Communist whom he betrayed to the Gestapo, and Little Loewy, the loyal proletarian party worker, whom he had denounced as an *agent provocateur*, causing him to commit suicide—as the judge passing sentence on the basis of oppositional ideas, just as Ivanov does upon him. And although Gletkin—crude and insensitive, of the generation after the revolution—has a different kind of mentality than Rubashov and Ivanov, he is their spiritual heir and quotes Rubashov's diary to convince him finally that he must continue to serve the party through his false confession.

The *Times Literary Supplement* said of *Darkness at Noon* that it is "a remarkable book, a grimly fascinating interpretation of the logic of the Russian revolution, indeed of all revolutionary dictatorships, and at the same time a tensely and subtly intellectualized drama."[2] Koestler's drama of ideas, however, the dialogue within Rubashov that mirrors his dialogue with Ivanov and Gletkin and proceeds to the inevitable conclusion that he must falsely confess, is, as we shall see, as much of a sham as the trial of Rubashov itself. *Darkness at Noon* is a novel with a thesis, but the thesis is false and the data from which it is derived are fraudulent. We shall have to examine these data in some detail to demonstrate this.

Before looking at the ideas which govern Rubashov, however, it will be useful to look at his personality. Koestler says in *The*

Invisible Writing, his autobiographical account of his seven
years as a Stalinist, that Rubashov's "manner of thinking" is
"modelled on Nikolai Bukharin's" and "his personality and
physical appearance" is "a synthesis of Leon Trotsky and Karl
Radek."[3] Earlier in the book, however, he says of his acquaintance with Bukharin and Radek, "Bukharin and Radek both
made a deep impression on me, but I only met each of them once
and in rather formal circumstances, so that I cannot trust my
memory to describe them."[4] Trotsky, of course, he never met.
Rubashov has, like Trotsky, a goatee and wears a pince-nez, as
Trotsky did in his youth, and, like Radek, he is short, but how
much of his personality is theirs?

Warren Lerner, in his scholarly biography of Radek, speaks of
him as "brilliant" but also makes use of such words as "sarcas-
tic," "witty," "ingenious," "colorful," "volatile," "notoriously
loose-mouthed," and even "frivolous."[5] According to the GPU
defector Orlov, when Radek was being interrogated on one
occasion, he said that he would confess but would list among his
accomplices his inquisitor, telling the terrified GPU man, "In
order to have at the trial one Radek, Yezhov [the head of the
GPU] will gladly throw into the bargain a dozen like Mol-
chanov!"[6] Whether or not this story is true, it is illustrative of the
irrepressible wit for which Radek was noted. There is also his
statement at the trial, supposedly describing his response to a
message from Trotsky to the effect that capitalism must be
restored in the Soviet Union but making, it would seem, either a
purposeful veiled comment or a carelessly indiscreet one on the
trial itself: "And therefore the conclusion: restoration of capitalism in the circumstances of 1935. For nothing at all, just for the
sake of Trotsky's beautiful eyes—the country was to return to
capitalism. When I read this I felt as if [I were in] a madhouse."[7]
There is nothing at all like this in Rubashov. As for Trotsky, it is
doubtful that anyone, whether a friend or a foe of his, would
recognize in the doubt-ridden, guilt-haunted figure of Rubashov
any similarity to him.

As a matter of fact, although it has not been pointed out,
anyone reading *The Invisible Writing*—the significance of his
self-revelation for *Darkness at Noon* seems indeed to have been
invisible to Koestler—must come to one conclusion: Rubashov is
not a synthesis of Trotsky and Radek; he is Arthur Koestler with
a goatee and pince-nez. Koestler tells of how he was imprisoned
by Franco during the Spanish civil war when he was discovered
to be a Communist agent while acting as a war correspondent of

a liberal British newspaper. Like Rubashov, he was in solitary confinement, expected to be executed, paced his cell constantly, was permitted to walk in the courtyard in the company of other prisoners, wasn't beaten himself but knew that others were being beaten, and saw through the spy-hole in his door men being led to their execution, reliving in his imagination what he saw. He was not asked to make a confession, but he was asked to write a statement of praise for Franco in return for the commutation of his sentence from death to life imprisonment. He did write that Franco was a humanitarian in whom he trusted, but then he took it back, in the kind of bargaining in which Rubashov engaged, to state that he assumed that any commutation of his sentence would be granted because of political considerations.

Koestler speaks of himself as a "guilt-ridden ego," who in Franco's prison experienced a "satisfied craving for punishment,"[8] just as Rubashov walks restlessly about his cell, muttering "I shall pay."[9] He felt that there was a "neat, symmetrical design" in his fate being dependent on a general of whom he had drawn a portrait "with a poisoned pen" in a "fraudulently obtained interview,"[10] just as Rubashov "saw himself through Ivanov's eyes, in the position of the accused, as once he had seen Richard and Little Loewy" (p. 89). When, meaning to say "I have never been a Red," through a slip of the tongue Koestler said to his jailer "I am no longer a Red" (although he did not officially break with the Communist Party until some time after he left Spain, he dates his internal break with it from his prison experience), he felt that this was "the revelation of an unconscious craving to curry favour with the enemy,"[11] just as Rubashov, despite himself, feels a warm glow when Gletkin addresses him as "comrade" (p. 193) immediately before he capitulates completely.

When the British consul asked Koestler if he could prove all of the allegations in his book about the fascists, "it was as if the dentist had touched an exposed nerve with his drill," and Koestler, who had included fictitious atrocity stories, "answered meekly that the authenticity of some of the material concerning atrocities was somewhat doubtful."[12] So Rubashov's toothache returns every time—the symbol is rather too insistent—his conscience smites him.

The meeting between the consul and him, Koestler says, "reflected the clash of two worlds: the world of straight, intellectually limited, unimaginative decency, based on traditional values, and the twisted world of ruse and deceit in the service of an inhuman Utopia."[13] So likewise the tsarist officer in the cell next to Rubashov, who doesn't have the head to study and knows only the subjects of conversation at the officers' mess—women and horses—possesses a simple creed of loyalty and honor. "Honour is to live and die for one's belief," he tells Rubashov in the prisoners' tapping code when he learns that Rubashov has capitulated. "Honour is to be useful without vanity," Rubashov replies. To this the officer responds, "Honour is decency—not usefulness," to be answered by Rubashov's "We have replaced decency by reason" (p. 140). Clearly, we are to take this as the clash of a "world of straight, intellectually limited, unimaginative decency" and a "twisted world of ruse and deceit."

Most significant is Koestler's account of his betrayal in the Soviet Union of a young woman, Nadeshda, with whom he had been having an affair. This parallels Rubashov's betrayal of his mistress, Arlova, whom he denounced when she was apprehended and brought to trial because he thought that it was necessary to preserve himself in order to work for his political ideas. Nadeshda was of the former artistocracy, and Koestler was told by a GPU agent that she and her old aunt were suspected of being spies. Koestler thought that the charge was nonsense and brought Nadeshda and the agent together to prove it to him. Later Koestler suspected that Nadeshda stole a cablegram from his pocket and told this to the agent. Since he came to know what such a statement entailed in the terror that started three years later, he bore a heavy burden of guilt thereafter. "It is no exaggeration," says Koestler, "when I say that I would have died for her readily and with a glow of joy. The Party to which I betrayed her I did not love; I had qualms and doubts about it, and moments of exasperation. But I was part of it, as my hands and guts were part of myself."[14] Rubashov, although he has no such great love for the devoted Arlova (Koestler makes him something like a disembodied intelligence), bears such a guilt imprisoned within him.

Koestler not only has Rubashov's sense of guilt; he has what Rubashov calls his "familiar and fatal constraint to put himself in the position of his opponent" (p. 17). Looking through Gletkin's eyes, Rubashov sees himself as an arrogant, querulous intellectual and, looking through Ivanov's eyes, as a shadow of his former self, to be regarded with a mixture of tenderness and contempt. So Koestler, who speaks freely of his elephantine inferiority complex, says of the British consul's reaction to his admission: "The impression I made at that moment must have been lamentable; I saw it mirrored in the Consul's eyes."[15] Dining with Nadeshda and the humpbacked proletarian GPU agent who he states is the model for Little Loewy, Koestler perceives the suspicion and fear of Nadeshda masked by her reserve; he perceives that the agent, mistaking her frightened stillness for upper-class arrogance, is overcome by a social inferiority complex; he himself feels an intellectual's guilt towards the worker and, unable to reach Nadeshda, emphasizes the intimacy between himself and the agent in solidarity with him. The incident is a display of a hypersensitive ability to put oneself in the position of others.

Like Rubashov, Koestler in what he calls "the solitary dialogue of cell No. 40"[16] emerged with a new way of thinking. Like Rubashov, he experienced the "oceanic sense," the feeling of being at one with the universe and at peace with oneself. Like him, finally, he dreamt of a new society to be constructed in the dim future by a new breed of spiritually regenerated men. In *The Invisible Writing* this dream is voiced by Koestler as follows:

> To change from Lenin's way to Gandhi's was again tempting, yet it was another short-cut, a toppling over from one extreme to the other. Perhaps the solution lay in a new form of synthesis between saint and revolutionary . . . or perhaps we lived in an era of transition comparable to the last centuries of the Roman Empire, which admitted of no solution at all.[17]

In *Darkness at Noon* it is voiced by Rubashov thus:

> Perhaps now would come the time of great darkness. Perhaps later, much later, the new movement would arise—with new flags, a new spirit knowing of both: of economic fatality *and* the "oceanic sense." Perhaps the members of the new party would wear monks' cowls, and preach that only purity of means can justify the ends. [P. 211]

We come, then, to Koestler's thesis that the Bolshevik precept that the end justifies the means brought about Stalinism. Just as Rubashov is not a composite Old Bolshevik but Arthur Koestler, an ex-Stalinist bowed with guilt by his Stalinist past, so the ideas which Koestler attacks are not Bolshevik ideas but Stalinist ideas.

It is interesting that the same epigraph, a quotation from Ferdinand Lassalle's *Franz von Sickingen,* is used in *Darkness at Noon* and in Trotsky's *Their Morals and Ours* to make quite different points. The lines, as given in the translation in *Darkness at Noon* (there is not an appreciable difference in meaning from that in *Their Morals and Ours*), are:

> Show us not the aim without the way.
> For ends and means on earth are so entangled
> That changing one, you change the other too;
> Each different path brings other ends in view.

[P. 196]

Koestler's implication is that the Bolsheviks, mistakenly choosing immoral ways, wandered far from their goals. Trotsky, in denying the existence of a supraclass morality, found that "the dialectical interdependence between means and end is expressed entirely correctly in the above-quoted sentences. Seeds of wheat must be sown in order to yield an ear of wheat."[18] It seems very strange that Koestler, who stated that the Bolsheviks thought every idea out to its logical conclusion—he thought that such logic was self-destructive in ignoring intuitive morality—did not realize that they had perceived that there is a connection between ends and means. They perceived more than that. They perceived that the connection is a dialectical one, that there is no duality between means and ends, that one flows into the other, that an end attained becomes the means to attaining another end. The final end in the Marxist view is the increase of the power of humanity over nature and the doing away of the power of individuals over each other. Only means that really lead to this end, which can be attained only through proletarian revolution, are permissible.

Thus Trotsky says:

> When we say that the end justifies the means, then for us the conclusion follows that the great revolutionary end spurns those base means and ways which set one part of the working class against other parts, or attempt to make the masses happy without their participation; or lower the faith of the masses in themselves and their organization, replacing it by worship for the "leaders." . . . The liberation of the workers can come only through the workers themselves. There is, therefore, no greater crime than deceiving the masses, palming off defeats as victories, fabricating legends, staging false trials, in a word, doing what the Stalinists do. These means can serve only one end: lengthening the domination of a clique already condemned by history. But they cannot serve to liberate the masses.[19]

The end not only justifies the means; it determines the means.

Koestler shows Rubashov as believing that the masses must be fooled for their own good, thereby laying himself open to persuasion to participate in a staged trial. Early in the novel Rubashov writes in his diary: "History has taught us that often lies serve her better than the truth; for man . . . has to be driven through the desert with threats and promises, by imaginary terrors and imaginary consolations, so that he should not sit down prematurely to rest and divert himself by worshipping golden calves" (pp. 79-80). But Trotsky's statement about the crime of deceiving the masses is not merely an attack upon Stalinism; it is an expression of the ideas that lay behind the Bolsheviks' actions.

Here we are fortunate to have preserved the last message of Bukharin, whose "manner of thinking," we may remember, was stated by Koestler to have served as the model for that of Rubashov. Medvedev gives the text of a letter "To a Future Generation of Party Leaders" that Bukharin had his wife memorize a few days before his arrest and that she sent in March 1961 to the Committee of Party Control, which dared not, however, rehabilitate him. In part of it he says:

I have been in the Party since I was eighteen, and the purpose of my life has always been to fight for the interests of the working class, for the victory of socialism. These days the paper with the sacred name *Pravda* prints the filthiest lie, that I, Nikolai Bukharin, have wished to destroy the triumphs of October, to restore capitalism. That is unexampled insolence, that is a lie that could be equaled in insolence, in irresponsibility to the people, only by such a lie as this: it has been discovered that Nikolai Romanov devoted his whole life to the struggle against capitalism and monarchy, to the struggle for the achievement of a proletarian revolution. . . . I ask a young and honest generation of Party leaders to read my letter to a Party Plenum, to exonerate me, and to reinstate me in the Party.[20]

Pravda has a "sacred name" not only because it was the organ of Lenin's Communist Party from prerevolutionary days but because *pravda* appropriately means *truth*. It is improper that lies, which show "irresponsibility to the people," who should be educated, not deceived, should appear in it. A party leadership which has been cleansed of corruption, which can expose the crimes of past years, will be a party leadership which is "honest."

The Bolsheviks, it will be recalled, published the secret treaties with the Allies that they found in the tsarist governmental files.

They "betrayed" the Allied governments by telling the people of Russia and of the world the truth about the imperialist designs of the Allied powers. This action symbolizes the difference between Bolshevik revolutionary morality and bourgeois-democratic morality.

But is any form of action justified against the class enemy? Yes, says Trotsky, but only if it *really* leads to the end. Koestler felt guilty about coming to the Franco government with false credentials, but the Bolsheviks used false passports in their underground work in tsarist Russia without compunction: one is not bound by one's enemy's decision to prevent opposition by declaring it illegal. One wonders if Koestler, who enlisted in the English army during the war with Germany, raised objections to British military ruses and strategems to deceive the enemy. However, use of false atrocity stories about the fascists such as Koestler engaged in does not serve the end of revolution: it endangers the supposed revolutionist's precious credibility among the masses and fosters in him, as he hoodwinks them, contempt for them. It is precisely because it is abundantly clear to revolutionists that fascism crushes the working class and stifles creative thought that they can convince the masses of this in many ways, including the citation of genuine atrocities, of which there is no lack.

But are there not moral precepts holding good at all times, which the Bolsheviks, who talked of morality as a class product, violated, bringing havoc upon themselves and the country they ruled? This is the question which Rubashov asks himself at the end, as he muses about the meaning of his life:

> He had burnt the remains of the old, illogical morality from his consciousness with the acid of reason. . . . Perhaps it was not suitable for a man to think every thought to its logical conclusion. . . . Looking back over his past, it seemed to him now that for forty years he had been running amuck—the running-amuck of pure reason. Perhaps it did not suit man to be completely freed from old bonds, from the steadying brakes of "Thou shalt not" and "Thou mayst not", and to be allowed to tear along straight towards the goal. [P. 209]

Certainly, moral precepts have been worked out in the development of humanity. They are necessary for the normal existence of society. Because of social tensions and contradictions, however, the precepts cannot be absolute. The sharper the class struggle, the less the moral ties between hostile classes hold, and so likewise with imperialist contradictions and the bond between the ruling classes of nations in "civilized society."

The most pervasive and the strongest of the "Thou shalt nots" is "Thou shalt not kill." However, as Trotsky phrases it, "the most 'humane' governments, which in peaceful times 'detest' war, proclaim during war that the highest duty of their armies is the extermination of the greatest number of people."[21] During World War II millions of persons were killed, culminating with Truman's dropping of the atom bomb on Hiroshima and Nagasaki as if their inhabitants were members of a different species—and this, as we now know, primarily "to make," in the words of Secretary of State James Byrnes, "Russia more manageable in Europe."[22] This did not prevent the mass media during Truman's administration from repeating ad nauseam that the root of the evil of communist thought was the dictum that the end justifies the means. Assuredly, thinking things through to a logical conclusion has its advantages. At least, it prevents flagrant self-contradiction. For what other defense can there be for this ghastly slaughter but the defense—however false its application in this instance—that "the end justifies the means"?

Koestler himself not only supported the Anglo-American side in World War II but praised and defended Zionist terrorism immediately after the war. Yet he has Rubashov recoil in moral horror at perceiving that young Kieffer had drawn the supposedly logical inference of planning to assassinate Stalin—for once, it seems, Rubashov has failed to follow an idea to its conclusion— from Rubashov's statement that the overthrow of Stalin, who will be supported by the bureaucracy, will require violent mass action: "Was it possible that this unfortunate youth had in fact drawn the conclusions from his, Rubashov's, line of thought—that he stood there before him in the glare of the reflector as the consequence incarnate of his own logic?" (p. 165).

Only now does Rubashov think things through and acknowledge to himself his own moral guilt:

If the opposition could attain victory against the party bureaucracy and its immense apparatus only by means of a civil war—why was this alternative better than to smuggle poison into the cold snack of No. 1 [Stalin], whose disappearance would perhaps cause the régime to collapse quicker and less bloodily? In what way was political murder less honourable than political mass killing? That unfortunate boy had evidently mistaken his meaning—but was there not more consistency in the boy's mistake than in his own behaviour during the last few years? [P. 169]

Here Koestler's confusion is carried to absurdity. He has Rubashov send Richard, a party comrade and heroic fighter in the antifascist underground, to his death by betraying him to Hitler's Gestapo because Richard dared to disagree with the party; however, Rubashov, who has said, "Honour is to be useful," does not contemplate assassinating No. 1 because of an unthought-out feeling that assassination is not "honourable."

But the Bolsheviks, polemicizing for years against the many Russian terrorists who, at the great risk of their lives, sought to assassinate tyrannical tsars and their detested agents and often succeeded in doing so, had thought things through with regard to terrorism as with other matters. They did not consider it to be dishonorable but, on the contrary, paid honor to the heroism of the terrorists (just as, we may add, comfortable Swiss bourgeois today pay honor to the national hero, the terrorist William Tell); however, they taught that terrorism was mistaken because of a number of reasons: it got rid only of an individual, not of the system, which produces new tyrants; it fostered the idea that liberation can come from the actions of a few heroes, not through mass organization and action; it muddied the question of the responsibility for violence and gave an excuse for further repression. They therefore called upon terrorists to use their idealism and heroism in leading the masses in struggle through the party. Lenin was fond of pointing out how many leaflets could be produced for the cost of a revolver and bullets. If the Bolsheviks did not practice assassination, it was not because they had not thought out the matter.

As for Rubashov's betrayal of Richard, the GPU apparently did denounce deviationists of the German Communist Party to the Gestapo, and during the Hitler-Stalin pact a number of German Communists, including some friends of Koestler's, were transferred from Stalinist concentration camps to Nazi concentration camps, but such perfidious behavior was utterly alien to Bolshevik thought and tradition. No political opponent ever charged the Bolsheviks with having acted as stoolpigeons in the prison camps or in the underground of tsarist Russia.

Rubashov implicitly defends his betrayal of Richard by telling him, in reply to Richard's assertion that the Communist Party must unite with other underground opponents of the Nazi regime,

> You wrote: "When the house is on fire, all must help to quench it; if we
> go on quarrelling about doctrines, we will all be burnt to ashes." That is
> wrong. We fight against the fire with water; the others do with oil.
> Therefore we must first decide which is the right method, water or oil,
> before uniting the fire-brigades. [P. 35]

It is true that Lenin and the Bolsheviks were adamant on the
need for theoretical clarity, insisting that without a worked-out
revolutionary theory there can be no effective revolutionary
practice; but they supported united fronts on specific issues on
which there was agreement between rival parties while each
party was free to criticize the other on points of disagreement. In
the tsarist camps, for instance, the Bolsheviks joined with other
prisoners to fight for the rights of all political prisoners.

For Rubashov, however, the manner in which to determine the
best way to fight fires is not to analyze the methods proposed and
to observe in practice which method works best but to kill the
holders of the rival theory. This is a principal reason for his
acquiescence in the trial: Stalin is only acting in accordance with
Rubashov's own theory, supposedly the Bolshevik theory. Thus
early in the novel Rubashov, commenting on the fact that Stalin
had thirty-one agriculturalists shot because they advocated the
use of nitrates rather than potash, states in his diary:

> In a nationally centralized agriculture, the alternative of nitrate or
> potash is of enormous importance: it can decide the issue of the next war.
> If No. 1 was in the right, history will absolve him, and the execution of
> the thirty-one men will be a mere bagatelle. If he was wrong . . . He who
> is in the wrong must pay; he who is in the right will be absolved. That is
> the law of historical credit; it was our law. [P. 79]

Later in the novel, sure enough, Ivanov repeats this idea,
telling Rubashov that the execution of Rubashov's devoted
follower, Bogrov, to which Rubashov has horrifiedly witnessed
Bogrov being led, was justified because his advocacy of a
relatively few large submarines as against many small ones
would have brought disaster. He adds that the principle of this
justification is a matter of "elementary knowledge" for
Rubashov—whereat Rubashov is persuaded and able, finally, to
go to sleep peacefully.

The absurdity that a party claiming to be governed by reason should settle policy matters in this manner, which must paralyze thought and the free expression of thought by which reason may prevail, is suggested by Rubashov at one point of the discussion, but he forgets about this when Ivanov calls him back to supposed first principles. The truth is, of course, that this absurdity is not the Bolsheviks', for these supposed Bolshevik first principles are entirely fictitious.

The Bolshevik Party, as a matter of fact, took the greatest care in Lenin's day to ensure the freest discussion. Zinoviev, a leader of the Bolshevik Party from its very beginning, who occupied a principal position in one of the show trials, wrote to all the leading party institutions in a letter in 1927 protesting Stalin's violations of the Leninist norms:

> Under Lenin, prior to the congress all members of the party were given the possibility to print in the party press their suggestions, theses, platforms, pamphlets, and books . . . precisely those comrades, or groups of comrades, who had disagreements with the majority of the CC [Central Committee] were accorded the fullest guarantee of remaining in the large centers so that they might come forward with their criticism of the line of the Central Committee in the precongress days as well as to the congress itself.[23]

The Bolshevik Party, encouraging the fullest debate and made up of the boldest, most independent thinkers, inevitably had sharp disagreements within itself. Bukharin, who, we may recall again, was supposed to be the model for Rubashov in his "manner of thinking," had, despite his filial regard for Lenin, many significant differences with him, notably the one over the question whether or not exhausted Russia should sign the outrageous peace treaty the German government presented at the peace negotiations in Brest-Litovsk, with Bukharin arguing for a revolutionary war of self-defense and Lenin, who finally carried the day, for signing the treaty. It is instructive to compare a passage in Bukharin's letter "To a Future Generation of Party Leaders" with the entry in Rubashov's diary, quoted earlier, about the rightness of the method of deciding differences by killing, with history absolving the killer if his judgment proves correct and condemning him if it proves incorrect.

> If, more than once, [said Bukharin], I was mistaken about the methods of building socialism, let posterity judge me no more harshly than Vladimir Il'ich [Lenin] did. We were moving toward a single goal for the

first time, on a still unblazed trail. Other times, other customs. *Pravda* carried a discussion page, everyone argued, searched for ways and means, quarreled and made up and moved on together.[24]

Bukharin had faith that the party would cast off Stalinism, but his attitude toward the party and its role in history differed from that of Rubashov. For Rubashov the party is infallible, the instrument of a history which proceeds along its fated way. "The Party," he tells Richard, "can never be mistaken. . . . The Party is the embodiment of the revolutionary idea in history. . . . History knows her way. She makes no mistakes. He who has not absolute faith in History does not belong in the Party's ranks" (p. 34). Again, Rubashov, supposedly a man who thinks every thought to its logical conclusion, fails to see the implications of what he says. If history makes no mistakes, then whatever is, is right. Whatever faction in the party has won must be right just because it has won. One can be sure of doing the work of history if one simply obeys the commands of the leadership without question. If Rubashov had perceived the logic of his own statements, he never would have resisted No. 1.

Such historical fatalism is, of course, a perversion of the historical materialism of the Marx who wrote, "Men make their own history, but . . . they do not make it under circumstances chosen by themselves, but under circumstances directly encountered, given, and transmitted from the past."[25] Men make their own history—the words are echoed in Bukharin's last signed editorial in *Izvestia*, July 6, 1936, which the Oxford historian George Katkov believes, it seems with good reason, was written as a warning in Aesopian language against Stalinism: "Real history is not that symbolized as Fate, the master of gods and men; real history is made by live men, by millions of these live men."[26]

Bukharin had been trapped by Stalin into collaborating with him. He and others, blocked by Stalin from political activity if they did not publicly recant their views, did so, depleting their powers of resistance and strengthening Stalin. Undoubtedly, their dictated capitulations prepared the way for their forced confessions at the show trials, but these capitulations were accommodations to Stalinism, not acts in the tradition of Leninism.

In extenuation of these former oppositionists, it may be pointed out that Stalin's purge had not yet transformed the composition of the party by putting to death all those of the October Political

Bureau (with the exception of Stalin) who had not already died or been exiled and almost all survivors of the October Central Committee, as well as 70 percent of the Central Committee and the majority of the delegates of the last party congress before the purge, 80 percent of whom had joined the party before 1921.[27] As Robert C. Tucker, no friend of the Bolsheviks, says in *The Great Purge Trial*, "The prime internal political purpose of the Great Purge from Stalin's point of view was . . . to eliminate the Bolshevik habits of criticism and opposition as well as the men who personified these habits."[28]

The false confessions of the Old Bolsheviks did not dishonor Bolshevism; they dishonored only Stalinism, its dialectical opposite. They showed only that even Old Bolsheviks, worn out it must be remembered by the tremendous events which had absorbed their energies, and weakened by their recent capitulations to Stalin, were after all made of flesh and blood, not that they recognized, as *Darkness at Noon* has it, their own moral guilt. Koestler has Rubashov in his final speech echo the phrases of Bukharin's speech about his guilt and contrition to suggest that the Old Bolsheviks had come to feel, as Rubashov said to himself, that they were "caught in the web they had spun themselves, according to the laws of their own twisted ethics and twisted logic; they were all guilty, although not of those deeds of which they accused themselves" (p. 205). But Bukharin's ritualistic phrases were extracted from him by the GPU; such phrases were used also by the Menshevik leaders who falsely confessed to having committed sabotage and having entered into agreements with bourgeois governments to give them portions of the Soviet Union in a 1931 trial that prefigured the trials of the Old Bolsheviks. As Léon Blum said in a 1931 pamphlet analyzing the trial (he himself, we may note parenthetically, was stated in the confessions at the trial to be one of the conspirators abroad, a charge which did not prevent the French Communists, at the behest of Stalin, from entering into the Popular Front with him five years later), "They have confessed volubly, ostentatiously, with a kind of relish for public confession and contrition."[29]

Moreover, it should be said in justice to Bukharin, Koestler omits everything of Bukharin's speech except these ritualistic phrases. In reality, Bukharin, although confessing many of the charges, tried to repudiate some of them, such as murdering Gorki and attempting to murder Lenin in 1918. What he seems to have been seeking to do was, while fulsomely confessing to the charges in general, to pick them apart in detail. Medvedev comments:

> In his final words, Bukharin gave a juridical appraisal of the trial. "Confessions of the accused," he said, "are not essential [for the court to render a verdict of guilty—if, that is, there is sufficient other evidence!—PNS]. Confessions of the accused are a medieval juridical principle." And this was said at a trial entirely based upon confessions of the accused. . . . Today some researchers (e.g., I.A.R.—) believe that Bukharin deliberately sought to show the illegality and falsehood of the trial, without coming into open conflict with the procurator. Brigadier Fitzroy Maclean, a British attaché who was a spectator at the trial, expressed the same point of view in his book.[30]

It is also the view of Stephen F. Cohen in his 1973 scholarly biography of Bukharin, of Katkov, and of Tucker, who, incidentally, was told by the Menshevik leader Boris Nicolaevsky that Bukharin, whom he knew personally, was extremely devoted to his family, a statement in keeping with the story circulated in the Soviet Union, recorded by Medvedev, that "Bukharin began to 'testify' only after the investigators threatened to kill his wife and newborn son" and with Orlov's account of how Bukharin was made to confess.[31] Indeed, it is very difficult to read Bukharin's words today without coming to the conclusion that he was speaking in Aesopian language in his last speech.

At any rate, it is clear that Bukharin's expressions of repentance do not indicate what Koestler makes them indicate for Rubashov: a sense of the moral bankruptcy of Bolshevism, from which, he now recognizes, Stalinism was the inevitable outcome. In *The Invisible Writing*, Koestler goes even beyond the statement that Stalinism is the logical development of Bolshevism and traces its origin to Marx's polemical style:

> Few among the intellectuals in the Party realized at the time [when Koestler was a member] that their mentality was a caricature of the revolutionary spirit; that within the short span of three generations the Communist movement had travelled from the era of the Apostles to that of the Borgias. But the process of degeneration had been gradual and continuous, and the seeds of corruption had been present in the work of Marx: in the vitriolic tone of his polemics, the abuse heaped on his opponents, the denunciation of rivals and dissenters as traitors to the working class and agents of the bourgeoisie.[32]

And to what, we may ask, does Koestler attribute the degeneration of Christianity from the time of the apostles? To Christ's harsh language about rich men, whom he even denied entrance into heaven, to his fanatic insistence that his adherents give up wealth and family to follow him, to his sharp denunciation of pharisaical self-righteousness in words which those today with a holier-than-thou attitude might well remember?

Bolshevism, like Christianity, evolved not in a vacuum but in historical circumstances. It took power in a backward country surrounded by world capitalism and in doing so concentrated upon itself the pressures of Russia's barbaric past and of imperialism's barbaric present, degenerating internally as a result. In the words of Trotsky,

Stalinism . . . is not an abstraction of "dictatorship," but an immense bureaucratic reaction against the proletarian dictatorship in a backward and isolated country. . . . Every reaction regenerates, nourishes and strengthens those elements of the historic past which the revolution struck but which it could not vanquish. The methods of Stalinism bring to the highest tension, to a culmination and at the same time to an absurdity all those methods of untruth, brutality and baseness which constitute the mechanics of control in every class society including also that of democracy. . . . When the representatives of old society puritanically counterpose a sterilized democratic abstraction to the gangrene of Stalinism, we can with full justice recommend to them, as to all of old society, that they take a good look at themselves in the warped mirror of Soviet Thermidor. True, the G.P.U. far surpasses all other regimes in the nakedness of its crimes. But this flows from the immense amplitude of events shaking Russia under the influence of world imperialist demoralization.[33]

Koestler, in contrasting the old world represented by the tsarist officer in the cell next to Rubashov with the new world represented by Rubashov, sterilizes Russia's past. To suggest that the tsarist officer corps, which was permeated by anti-Semitism, chauvinism, and brutality, was a "world of straight, intellectually limited, unimaginative decency, based on traditional values," is ludicrous. The White Guards were not noted for their gentleness and humanity. Nor is it only in primitive Russia that the code of honor of the aristocratic military caste hid brutality and baseness. The Dreyfus frame-up exhibited the rottenness of this caste in France, which not so long ago engaged in the systematic torture of Algerian revolutionists to extract information from them.

The tsarist officer, as we have seen, is derived from the gentlemanly British consul whose repugnance for lies about Franco so shattered Koestler. No doubt Koestler, in having Rubashov write in his diary "A revolution conducted according to the rules of cricket is an absurdity. . . . we have thrown overboard all conventions and rules of cricket-morality" (pp. 78-79), was thinking of this consul. But the British ruling class is not always so reluctant to tell lies. For instance, the Conservative Party used a notorious forgery, a supposed letter written by Zinoviev as the head of the Communist International to the British Trade Union Congress, to whip up an anti-Red hysteria and sweep to victory over the Labour Party. This was not exactly cricket.

It is, moreover, well known that members of the British ruling class have traditionally used "cricket-morality" in playing cricket games among themselves and imperialist morality in dealing with colonial countries. One instance has special piquancy for the readers of *Darkness at Noon*. A *New York Times* news story of November 17, 1971, states:

An official British commission found evidence today of mistreatment of political prisoners in Northern Ireland. . . . The commission said that prisoners were placed in "hooded isolation," subjected to "continuous noise," placed on a bread-and-water diet and deprived of sleep. . . . The committee found that prisoners were forced to stand, legs apart, leaning with hands raised up against a wall for four-hour to six-hour periods.

Here we have the use of methods described in *Darkness at Noon* and other accounts of the GPU prisons, with the addition of the "improvement" of placing black hoods over the heads of prisoners—a most literal "darkness at noon"!—to contribute to their disorientation and of the substitution of the more technologically advanced device, an electronically produced nerve-shattering noise, for the reflector lamp. The commission, it may be added, was established only after a campaign of protest by Amnesty International and other organizations, and it presented its findings with characteristic British upper-class hypocrisy, insisting that these practices constituted "mistreatment" but not "brutality," as it did not find evidence of bodily harm. The "representatives of old society" may well be instructed, as Trotsky said, to "take a good look at themselves in the warped mirror of Soviet Thermidor."

And this is true of the representatives of old society in all countries. The "third degree" is, after all, not a Russian phrase. In his essay "How 'Bigger' Was Born" Richard Wright described how young Blacks had long been routinely made to confess crimes they had not committed.

> He is held for perhaps a week without charge or bail, without the privilege of communicating with anyone, including his own relatives. After a few days this boy "confesses" anything that he is asked to confess, any crime that handily happens to be unsolved and on the calendar. Why does he confess? After the boy has been grilled night and day, hanged up by his thumbs, dangled by his feet out of twenty-story windows, and beaten (in places that leave no scars—cops have found a way to do that), he signs the papers before him, papers which are usually accompanied by a verbal promise to the boy that he will not go to the electric chair.[34]

Such forms of torture, and worse, are now used, according to Amnesty International, by more countries than ever before, most of them under the patronage and tutelage of the United States.

Darkness at Noon, therefore, far from being "a grimly fascinating interpretation of the logic of the Russian Revolution . . . and at the same time a tensely and subtly intellectualized drama," is a faked wrestling match in which Stalinism is misrepresented as Bolshevism and "a sterilized democratic abstraction" as capitalist and imperialist actuality. There is, to be sure, realistic detail which lends the air of authenticity that, in addition to its topicality, contributed to making the novel such a success. The characterization is sharp, if not complex. The figure of Gletkin, with his crackling cuffs, sitting stiffly behind the pile of documents on his desk, stays particularly in the mind. Koestler's knowledge of GPU methods and his expert use of the language of Marxism, which is only employed, however, to caricature it, also helps to give his novel verisimilitude.

But above all, the novel's realistic effect is advanced by its autobiographical elements. Rubashov's daydreams while pacing the floor, for instance, are well handled, Koestler himself having known solitary confinement. Frozen and longing for a cigarette, Rubashov lives over his past life. He dreams of meeting Little Loewy smoking his pipe in the Belgian harbor town, with its cold sea air; he dreams of being beaten into unconsciousness in a Nazi prison and, on being awakened by cold water dashed over him, groping for a cigarette while continuing to lie on the floor; he dreams of No. 1 looking at him with a strangely knowing irony behind the clouds of smoke of No. 1's pipe when, sick of the Soviet political reality, he asks for a new mission abroad; he dreams of himself, once more in the Belgian port, lighting a cigarette at the conclusion of a speech before Little Loewy and the other party longshoremen in which he tells them they must break the worldwide embargo of oil to Italy during the Ethiopian War in order to unload the oil the Soviet Union was sending to that country. It is all skillfully done, as are the other driftings off into daydream and the returnings to the reality of the prison.

Koestler also achieves concentration through keeping the point of view almost entirely Rubashov's. The shift in point of view in the scene with the religious old porter near the end, which exists for the sake of the obscurantist moral "It's not good for a man to work things out too much" (p. 201) uttered by the old man, represented as a figure of simple folk wisdom, is, however, rather obtrusive.[35] The description is held to a bare minimum. Almost everything happens inside the head of a highly intellectualized man.

However, in Rubashov's musing just before he is led away to his execution the mask slips and we realize that the moralizing voice is that of Koestler, not of Rubashov. A "blessed quietness" had sunk over Rubashov just before he began his speech at the trial, a quietness which envelops him from that time until his final moment. Thinking back upon the men of his generation, he perceives their "twisted ethics and twisted logic." At the same time, however, he tells himself, "The best of them kept silent in order to do a last service to the Party—and, besides, even the best had each an Arlova on his conscience" (pp. 204, 205). Does it make sense that, having lied for a last time to uphold what he now perceives as a corrupt system of ideas that denies the best part of humanity, our inner conscience, he should be so at peace? Does it make sense that he should classify himself and the others who lied for the sake of this monstrous system as "the best of them" as against those who lied "to save their wives or sons from the clutches of the Gletkins," their Arlovas and the sons of their Arlovas? It seems that Rubashov, when led by his "silent partner," his subconscious mind, is as little logical as when he is led by his reason. Such are the demands of a false psychological thesis.

7. Norman Mailer's 'The Naked and the Dead': The American Army and Counterrevolution

Norman Mailer's *The Naked and the Dead*, published in 1948 when he was twenty-five, was accorded a sensational reception as the great war novel for which everyone had been waiting. Indeed Mailer's extraordinary talent, his war experience, in which that talent came to a boil, and the literary tradition of Dos Passos, Farrell, and Steinbeck, which he had absorbed, worked together to produce a novel that was unmatched in conveying the terror, the exhaustion, the boredom, the bitterness of the combat troops in the war in the Pacific.

But *The Naked and the Dead* is, as Mailer complained the reviewers failed to realize, more than a war novel. In an essay unnoticed by Mailer critics in the first issue of the *National Guardian*, October 18, 1948, a "progressive" weekly published by allies of the Communist Party from the Popular Front days that subsequently evolved into the present *Guardian*, Mailer spoke of it as "a novel about America's destiny and the historical paths America was to follow after the war" and said of himself, "I suppose that politically I am an ignorant Marxist. I mean by that confession that I cannot in all honesty call myself a Marxist when I have read so few of the basic works of Marxist theory." He was to go beyond this stage to a more profound study of Marxism, manifested in *Barbary Shore*, only, unable, in his need for popular and critical acclaim, to bear the isolation that this involved during the cold war, to turn to "Hip," to the attempt to "divorce oneself from society, to exist without roots, to set out on that uncharted journey into the rebellious imperatives of the self,"[1] while remaining a tolerated radical critic of capitalist culture.

The fading of the prewar dream of social revolution, as we shall see, permeated *The Naked and the Dead* with a sense of hopelessness foreign to Marxism. At the same time the watered-down Marxism which he had absorbed and his artist's insight made it possible for him to reveal the army as the concentrated expression of American society. Alfred Vagts in his authoritative *A History of Militarism* comments that Marx and Engels pointed out that "the division of labor and machinery on a large scale were first used in the army" and adds,

> The labor of later non-Marxist researchers has gone to substantiate, in large part, the [Marxist] contention that . . . war immensely stimulated certain phases of capitalist development, and yet was in turn dependent upon economic conditions. . . . Each stage of social progress or regress has produced military institutions in conformity with [society's] needs and ideas, its culture as well as its economics. . . . That is to say, army conditions reflect the state of society generally.[2]

Shuttling between a reconnaissance platoon and the headquarters of the commanding general, Mailer shows how the army structure reflects the class structure of American capitalism and in its grim starkness prefigures, just as the new national armies prefigured early industrial capitalism, what can be expected in a later phase of capitalism.

The Naked and the Dead presents the war as seen through the eyes of General Cummings in ironic juxtaposition to the war as experienced by the platoon. The platoon, or at least its veterans, has a collective physiognomy. As Lieutenant Hearn, who joins the platoon as its commanding officer late in the book, muses while watching them, "As a group they had a forbidding and rigid quality as though they no longer held an excess bit of weight nor a surplus emotion. . . . Collectively, they lent something to each other, seemed harder and meaner than they would if isolated."[3]

But we also see the men reacting on each other as individuals. For each one, when the focus of interest is on him, Mailer makes use of the Dos Passos device of "The Time Machine," a biographical flashback which shows all of his past life as making him the kind of person that the rigors of combat reveal him to be. Thus the flashback of the life of the nerve-shattered Martinez, the Chicano who imbibed the American fables of success but was relegated to menial jobs by the tall, haughty Texans, comes after he chooses to be with the squad of veterans, where he will get the punishing assignments, rather than to be with the squad of new men, who he fears will, not knowing his superiority as a scout, disobey his commands despite the stripes of which he is so proud; that of the life of the angry, embittered, fascistic Gallagher, a party-machine worker frustrated by the disappointments and the drabness of his life, comes immediately after his tough exterior has been pierced by the news of his wife's death; that of the irresponsible, self-indulgent small-town southerner, Wilson, comes after the army doctor has told him that he will eventually need an operation for the consequences of his venereal disease. Through another device, the "Chorus," we get the distilled essence of soldiers' conversations on the main subjects of interest to them—chow, women, what they will do when they get out of the army—that add up to a collective portrait that is the counterpart of these individual portraits.

Martinez, Gallagher, Wilson, and Red Valsen, who had sought to escape being crushed in the Montana coal mines by becoming a hobo and a drifter—all of them were formed and stamped, moved along the course of their lives, and finally ejected into the army by the various assembly lines that constitute the vast, complex system of industrial capitalism. But it is not only the "under-privileged" who have been so shaped and so molded. Sergeant Brown is of the great middle class. With his snub nose and freckles, he looks like the all-American boy. He was popular at school and became a salesman of farm machinery to business-men, taking them out to golf, where he missed putts to keep them in good humor, to night clubs, and to high-class brothels. "Honestly, Bev," he complained to his wife in a moment of rare intimacy and troubled self-understanding—a moment that came when he heard about the promiscuity of the sister, "slim and crisp and virginal, the older sister—half mother," who had taught him dancing when he was a kid—"Honestly, Bev, keeping up with everything makes me so goddam fast" (p. 432). He produced because that's what they paid off on, but without knowing it he was poisoned by the sickness and corruption of his society. And so Sergeant Brown, who looks like the all-American boy, is bitter and cynical about women, feels guilty about not doing his job properly as sergeant, as he feels a buried guilt about his life, and looks older on second glance than at first, with wrinkles about his eyes and jungle ulcers on his chin.

Perceiving the army as the concentrated expression of American capitalism, Mailer saw the war it was conducting as the imperialist war that it was. Hearn gets a letter from a friend, "a sound Marxian optimist," in the wartime government, in which he says, "Here in Washington you can see all the patterns. The reactionaries are frightened. Despite what they want to believe they know this has become a people's war, and the currents of world revolution are in the air" (pp. 308, 307). Mailer in his article in the *National Guardian* spoke of himself as being "to the left of [Henry Wallace's] Progressive Party and to the right of the Communist Party," that is, as having the political position which most of the readers of the *National Guardian* regarded themselves as having, and he went on to join with the Communist Party and the *National Guardian* in working for the election of Henry Wallace, who had been the vice-president of the United States during the war; but the whole of *The Naked and the Dead* is a testament to the fatuousness of Hearn's Stalinoid friend, the "sound Marxian optimist," whose real-life counterparts were shortly to support Wallace. To have told the veterans of the reconnaissance platoon that they were fighting "a people's war" would only have provoked a bitter guffaw. Even the uncertain, groping Hearn, having seen General Cummings and the military machine at work, knows better. Cummings himself, a reactionary confident of the future and not at all frightened, tells Hearn, "You're misreading history if you see this war as a grand revolution. It's power concentration" (p. 140).

Cummings's observations about the future are often prophetic. He sees the men of power in America as becoming conscious of their real aims for the first time in the history of the United States. "After the war our foreign policy is going to be far more naked, far less hypocritical than it has ever been" (p. 254). Indeed there was after the war, for the first time in American history, talk about the twentieth century being "the American century," and in Vietnam the United States was to put on, contemptuous of world opinion, a remarkably brutal display of power against a small peasant country. However, Cummings, a coldly calculating machine, underestimates the propensity of men to hypocrisy. Just because the power was displayed so nakedly and because the hypocrisy was so transparent, heavier layers of hypocrisy were needed to attempt to cover up the shameless spectacle. Nixon's statement that the war in Vietnam was one of the most altruistic acts of a great nation in the history of mankind reached a height of crazy rationalization.

Cummings dreams of making American society into the same kind of ruthlessly functioning machine the army is. "You can consider the Army, Robert, as a preview of the future," he tells Hearn (p. 255). However, at one point he is afraid that, held up by the Army's system of promoting mediocrities, he will miss his opportunity.

It would be the hacks who would occupy history's seat after the war, the same blunderers, uncoordinated, at cross-impulses. . . . There would be few Americans who would understand the contradictions of the period to come. The route to control could best masquerade under a conservative liberalism. The reactionaries and isolationists would miss the bell, cause almost as much annoyance as they were worth. [P. 556]

After the wild hysteria of McCarthyism served its purpose of arousing an unreasoning fear of communism but then proved counterproductive in its unrestrained witch-hunting that finally proceeded to the military hierarchy, the ruling class did indeed turn to "conservative liberalism" or, as it came to be called, "cold-war liberalism." The United States became the world gendarme of counterrevolution, intervening, both secretly and openly, on the side of the reactionary status quo all over the world while presenting an aspect of liberalism, made possible by an armaments-sustained prosperity, at home. There was fine talk of a "new frontier" while an army organized, financed, and trained by the CIA was sent against Cuba and while counterinsurgency soldiers were being trained for action elsewhere; and popguns were lined up in a "war against poverty" while murderously powerful armaments were being devoted to the real war.

Where Cummings góes wrong—and here he is at one with the ordinary military mediocrity whom he despises—is in his belief that motivation counts for next to nothing in war. Wars, he believes, are won by superior armaments and soldiers who are sufficiently broken to do what is demanded of them. "The Army functions best when you're frightened of the man above you, and contemptuous of your subordinates" (p. 139). Like the American general staff, which kept believing that just some more military force would defeat the "gooks," Cummings has no idea of the energies released by a revolution, and so his theory does not explain why the National Liberation Front and the Democratic Republic of Vietnam troops fought with such remarkable heroism and effectiveness that, despite the enormous difference in materiel and numbers, they could not be beaten, while the South Vietnamese soldiers of the same country but fighting for a reactionary regime, could not stand up to them despite South Vietnam's great advantages.

Mailer has Cummings at the end succeed in a way that ironically demonstrates his inability to attain the omnipotence, based on a rational understanding of all the factors involved in a situation, to which he aspires. Major Dalleson, Cummings's unimaginative and intellectually limited operations officer, as a result of a series of responses that he is forced to make while Cummings has gone to Army Headquarters to seek to get the destroyers for the combined frontal assault and invasion from the rear he thinks necessary to win the campaign, finds himself blundering into an offensive that unexpectedly causes the collapse of the Japanese: their food, ammunition, and medical supplies had been, without the knowledge of the Americans, utterly exhausted.

Norman Podhoretz in a 1959 *Partisan Review* article found this turn of events to be artifically contrived:

> He [Mailer] had no alternative but to violate the emotional logic of his novel by destroying them [Cummings and Sergeant Croft, the platoon leader, Cummings's enlisted-man counterpart, who finds in combat and killing the satisfaction of his powers] as best he cóuld. The destruction of Croft is spread thin throughout the novel, but the disposal of Cummings is only effected at the end, when Mailer contrives by a shocking twist of plot to rob him of credit for winning the campaign.[4]

But Cummings's defeat is as well prepared for as is Croft's. War, Cummings tells Hearn early in the novel, is like chess, but Hearn, although conscious of Cummings's intellectual superiority in his attempts to answer Cummings's exposition of his theories, stubbornly replies that it is really like "a bloody football game. You start off with a play and it never quite works out as you figured it would" (p. 143). Cummings cavalierly rejects this, asserting that war, although more complicated than chess, comes to the same thing, but at other times he is not so sure that things must work out as you plan them. In his journal he speculates that the asymmetrical parabola, the path of any projectile, a comparatively swift descent after a gradual ascent, is the basic curve of the rise and fall of cultures, of tragedy, of sexual arousal and detumescence, of life itself. It is his overpowering ambition to control this curve: "It was all there if only he could grasp it. To mold . . . mold the curve." The path of the projectile would be symmetrical if only the unvarying force of gravity were operating on it, but wind resistance, a varying force incapable of being measured precisely at a given moment, is also at work. "In the larger meanings of the curve, . . . wind resistance would be the resistance of the medium . . . the mass inertia or the inertia of the masses through which the vision, the upward leap of a culture is blunted, slowed, brought to its early doom." This is why there are different kinds of asymmetrical parabolas but only one symmetrical parabola. The thought depresses him. "It had all been too pat, too simple. There was order but he could not reduce it to the form of a single curve. Things eluded him" (p. 444).

It is "mass inertia or the inertia of the masses" which, he comes to realize, is his enemy, exerting a force that takes him by surprise. After he halts the advance of his troops in order to finish a road, he finds that they take the opportunity to make themselves comfortable, improving their bivouacs and building drainage pits and overhead covers on the foxholes, and are reluctant to be moved, engaging in only desultory combat patrols, advancing slowly and relinquishing ground readily, retreating to their bivouacs. "The shock cut deeply into the General's confidence. . . . No matter how he molded them now the men always collapsed into a sodden resultant mass like dishrags, too soft, too wet to hold any shape which might be given them" (p. 237). Molding the curve is inhibited by "the resistance of the medium."

This disturbs his elation for a moment over his victory over Hearn, in which he makes Hearn pick up his cigarette under threat of court martial. Will he make 6,000 men do what he wants, Hearn asks, by bringing them all over to his tent and making them pick up his cigarette butts? He hasn't imposed his will on the troops, he admits to himself. "Hearn he had been able to crush, any single man he could manage, but the sum of them was different still, resisted him still" (p. 257). Just so it is the "resisting weight of the platoon" (p. 258) that helps to bring Croft down from his ascent up the challenging steepness of Mount Anaka, like the projectile brought down by the combined forces of gravity and the resisting medium of the air: "He had the mountain to fight and the men dragging upon him" (p. 539).

The defeat of Cummings and Croft, however, is balanced by the defeat of Hearn and Red Valsen, Hearn's enlisted-man counterpart, who, like him, regards the preservation of his integrity, his commitment not to back down in an ultimate confrontation, as his chief value. Red, with Croft's rifle pointing at him, knowing that Croft would be happy to kill him, obeys his command that he go with the squad up the mountain, just as Hearn picks up Cummings's cigarette, knowing that he will go through with his threat to have Hearn court-martialed and sent to the stockade for years. The defeat of each is prefigured early in the book when

Cummings, in response to a liberty Hearn has taken in one of their discussions, has Hearn salute him and, replying to Hearn's statement about the unfairness of his behavior, says,

> You've seen too many movies. If you're holding a gun and you shoot a defenseless man, then you're a poor creature, a *dastardly person*. That's a perfectly ridiculous idea, you realize. The fact that you're holding a gun and the other man is not is no accident. It's a product of everything you've achieved, it assumes that if you're . . . you're aware enough, you have the gun when you need it. [P. 67]

In his 1959 *Partisan Review* article Podhoretz saw the defeat of Hearn and Valsen as evidence that "American liberalism is bankrupt":

> The trouble with Hearn and Valsen is their inability to transcend the terms of the given; they know perfectly well that these terms are intolerable, yet they cannot envisage any conditions other than the ones before their eyes, and therefore they are reduced to apathy, cynicism, and despair. . . . Hearn and Valsen shrug helplessly at the sight of the peaks: like liberalism itself, they lack the vision and the drive to push toward the top of the mountain.[5]

Valsen, of course, is not a liberal, being contemptuously aware of how illusory is the idea of significant change within the system at the same time that he cynically rejects the possibility of changing the system itself, but it is true that Hearn is a type of the "left" liberal who prates of the need for a new society but is fundamentally doubtful about it and can think only of a few timid, uncertain steps to be made toward it. It is piquant, however, that this should have been said by the Norman Podhoretz who, after "making it" as editor of *Commentary,* reached the point where, speaking at a meeting of the American Jewish Committee, he "decried the tendency of Americans to downgrade themselves" and said: "If people will not produce for profit, experience has shown they will not produce at all" (*New York Times,* May 5, 1975).

Mailer himself was, of course, aware of the inadequacies of Hearn and Valsen. Hearn, the son of a midwestern industrialist, against whom he is in rebellion, is not sure about anything and is made aware by Cummings that he does not even feel strongly about social justice; but he seeks to hold on to his insecure beliefs, knowing that the only alternative is to make peace with the principles of his father. He finds in himself as commander of the reconnaissance platoon the urge for power of Cummings and Croft, which Cummings had said was in him, and he decides to give up his commission. But even this decision is marked by wavering. His real reasons for it, he tells himself, are probably lousy, and when he becomes an enlisted man he will probably fit into Cummings's fear ladder as well as anyone else. And when, the next morning, he feels good in the cheerfulness of the sunshine and in the exercise of his command, it is by no means sure that he will persist in his decision—but ironically, a half hour later, through Croft's treachery, he walks into the fatal machine-gun fire of the Japanese and is not given the opportun ity to act one way or the other.

Red Valsen is a far more appealing character. A confirmed loner who has always told himself that he will not take any crap from anyone, beneath his hard-boiled cynicism he is easily the most compassionate person in the novel, but he restrains his feelings for others in order not to tie himself down and to avoid the hurt when the inevitable disaster comes to the one toward whom he feels sympathetic. He knows from the first that it will come to a showdown between Croft and himself, and nerves himself for it, but he has been worn down by the wear and tear he has suffered during a lifetime of rolling along on his own. "You kept fighting everything," he comes to realize, "and everything broke you down, until in the end you were just a little goddam bolt holding on and squealing when the machine went too fast" (p. 548).

Although Mailer is aware of the inadequacies of Hearn and Red, he himself has no revolutionary vision to offer. He was quite mistaken concerning the inner meaning of his novel when he said of it in his *National Guardian* article, significantly entitled "A Credo for the Living,"

> It has been called a novel without hope. I think actually it is a novel with a great deal of hope. It finds man corrupted, confused to the point of helplessness, but it also finds that there are limits beyond which man may not be pushed, and it finds that even in man's corruption and sickness there are yearnings and inarticulate strivings for a better world, a life with more dignity.

The inability of Cummings to mold his soldiers and the inability of Croft to gain the peak of Mount Anaka indeed indicate that there are limits beyond which man may not be pushed, but the resisting inertia of the men yields no hope for a replacement of a system of oppression by any other system. The bolts of the machine squeal if it goes too fast, but they remain bolts turning without their own volition. As for the yearnings and inarticulate strivings of men for a better world of which Mailer speaks, they are shown with a sense of hopelessness about achieving it. This is conveyed in a key passage of startling beauty that stands out amid the ugliness, anguish, and horror of the novel. As the platoon approaches the island of Anopopei in its landing craft, the men look upon it in the sunset with a strange rapture.

> The sunset was magnificent with the intensity and brilliance that can be found only in the tropics. . . . The men stared and stared. The island hovered before them like an Oriental monarch's conception of heaven, and they responded to it with an acute and terrible longing. It was a vision of all the beauty for which they had ever yearned, all the ecstasy they had ever sought. [P. 353]

But this vision cannot last, and, as the sunset fades, they are left with the reality of the terror and blackness of life: "After a little while, there was only the gray-black ocean, the darkened sky, and the evil churning of the gray-white wake. Bits of phosphorescence swirled in the foam. The black dead ocean looked like a mirror of the night; it was cold, implicit with dread and death" (pp. 353-54).

The island of Anopopei, which presented itself as a bright vision, proves to be a nightmare. It is the mysterious world in which men live, a world working in unfathomable ways to confuse, terrify, and destroy them. Tony Tanner has written eloquently of it in his *The City of Words*:

> The military concept of a "connected line" vanishes in the impenetrable jungle—"no army could live or move in it." The mountain which dominates the island dominates the men with its motionless hostility. The sea around them wears all things down and is full of death. The land itself becomes terrifying in its "somnolent brooding resistance." It seems as if there is a cosmic conspiracy against men, as if something working through the various forces of nature is seeking to bring them to a standstill, erase their identities, annihilate them altogether.[6]

The only ones to whom Anopopei is not terrifying are Cummings and Croft, for each of them believes that life contains a pattern, which he seeks to control or identify with, not a fearsome mystery. Cummings, as we have seen, seeks to grasp this pattern through reason; Croft, on the other hand, seeks to grasp it through intuition. When Red Valsen and Croft observe young Hennessey, going into combat for the first time, following the rule-book in each particular, taking no chances, each is seized with the certainty that Hennessey is going to be killed. When Hennessey is indeed killed, each reacts in a significantly different way. "It gave Red a moment of awe and panic as if someone, *something*, had been watching over their shoulder that night and laughing. There was a pattern where there shouldn't be one" (p. 35). For Red, who at eighteen, remembering his father's body crushed almost flat underneath the blanket after he had been brought home from the mine-slide, found that he didn't believe in a God, for whom life was a series of random events, of which one could be sure only that he would end up getting "the shitty end of the .stick" (p. 160), and for whom Hennessey had been a kid whose naïveté excited compassion—for Red, the sense for a moment of Hennessey's death as fitting a pattern could only mean the glimpse of some malign supernatural force, something above people that watches and laughs. For Croft, the confirmation of his intuition means an exultant sense of power. "Hennessey's death had opened to Croft vistas of such omnipotence that he was afraid to consider it directly. All day the fact hovered about his head, tantalizing him with odd dreams and portents of power" (p. 35).

But in failing to reach the peak of the mountain Croft has failed to attain a grasp of the pattern. It eludes him, as it does Cummings. "Croft kept looking at the mountain. He had lost it, had missed some tantalizing revelation of himself. Of himself and much more. Of life. Everything" (p. 552). Is there, however, really a pattern—or, if there is one, can people find it and work with it? In the very first pages of the book Croft is in a poker game, where he plays shrewdly, with a knowledge of the odds and of the psychology of the men he is facing, but with an appreciation of the role of luck and "a deep unspoken belief that whatever made things happen was on his side" (p. 11). When, after a night of mediocre hands, he gets a potentially powerful set of cards, he gains the intense conviction that he is going to win the pot—"a certainty as vivid as this one had to mean something" (p. 11)—but to his utter disgust and bewilderment he doesn't get the card he needs. Just so, in the last pages of the book, Cummings bitterly broods over Dalleson's victory:

For a moment he almost admitted that he had had very little or perhaps nothing at all to do with this victory, or indeed any victory—it had been accomplished by a random play of vulgar good luck larded into a casual net of factors too large, too vague, for him to comprehend. He allowed himself this thought, brought it almost to the point of words and then forced it back. But it caused him a deep depression. [P. 555]

Even for Cummings and Croft, therefore, there are fears that there is no pattern in life. The action and dialogue as well as the setting and atmosphere suggest, however, the presence of the malign supernatural power which the intimation of a pattern meant for Red. The suggestion of such a power, which Mailer need not have literally believed in, is his means for conveying a sense of human powerlessness. An exchange between Hearn and Cummings is significant:

"Well, what do you want me to admit, that you're a God?"
"You know, if there is a God, Robert, he's just like me."
"Uses the common denominator techniques."
"Exactly." [P. 145]

The "common denominator techniques" refers to Cummings's assertion a moment earlier that in the army the idea of individual personality is just a hindrance, that in commanding military operations one is concerned only with the effectiveness of military units, not the differences between the men who make them up. "I work with grosser techniques, common denominator techniques" (p. 143). The phrase "common denominator" is used again in the climactic portion of the book, when we are told of Ridges and Goldstein, bearing the wounded Wilson on the improvised litter: "Their fatigue had cut through so many levels, had blunted finally so many of their senses that they were reduced to the lowest common denominator of their existence. Carrying him was the only reality they knew" (p. 501). And of the squad simultaneously climbing the mountain with Croft, we are told: "Like the litter-bearers, they had forgotten everything; they did not think of themselves as individual men any longer" (p. 512). God, it seems, is indeed like General Cummings, unconcerned with the personalities and fates of individual men and reducing them to the point where they cease to be individuals. As the cynical petty racketeer Polack responds to the question, "Listen, Polack, you think there's a God?" which young, immature Wyman blurts out to him as they are about to resume their climb of the mountain, "If there is, he sure is a sonofabitch" (p. 472).

All of these suggestions of a malign supernatural power receive their sharpest expression in a passage of intensely ironic juxtaposition. As Red regards the battlefield debris of gutted tanks looking like lizard skeletons and rotting corpses without heads and limbs, he thinks to himself, "The way a bunch of ants would kill each other" (p. 172). At the same time in the battalion area Wyman is absorbed in the thrashing about of a caterpillar, which he has stabbed with a twig and then subjected to the heat of a burning cigarette. The simpleminded religious southern poorwhite farmer, the illiterate Ridges, tells him that is no way to treat a "bug," and they get involved in a controversy about killing "bugs" and killing Japanese. Ridges points out that the Japanese, as heathen, can be killed by Christians, but he is troubled by the questions that are raised until he grabs hold of an idea that, although irrelevant, is reassuring, and the following exchange takes place:

> "You believe man got a soul?" he asked Wyman.
> "I don't know. What the hell is a soul?". . .
> "The soul's what leaves a man after he dies—that's what goes up t' heaven. . . ."
> "Who the hell knows," Wyman said. He felt philosophical.
> The insect was dying under the last handful of earth he had poured over it. [P. 173]

Red's comparison between armies of ants and armies of men, the philosophical discussion about the killing of insects and the killing of men, like the philosophical discussions on a higher level between Cummings and Hearn as Cummings sent men to their deaths (or like those which might occur on a still higher level between a supernatural General Cummings and his aide), the writhings of the caterpillar tortured by young Wyman and the dead bodies on the battlefield "frozen in the midst of an intense contortion" (p. 166)—one is forcibly reminded of the words in *King Lear* of the blinded Gloucester in his pain, "As flies to wanton boys are we to the gods; / They kill us for their sport."

The climb up the mountain and the long haul of carrying Wilson bring to the men an epiphany in which they attain a fleeting vision of a cruelly indifferent God. It is this experience which gives the title to the novel. Mailer has used the word "naked" several times earlier to mean open, vulnerable. Thus Brown in the grove with Wilson has his brain "washed clean of . . . the protecting calluses . . . of memory."

He was at once more vulnerable and less bitter. Something in the limitless darkness of the night, the tenuous protection of the grove, and the self-absorbed suffering of the wounded man beside him had combined to leave him naked, alone, a raw nerve responding to every wind and murmur that filtered into the wood from the bare gloomy hills in the blackness about them. [P. 418]

So too when Goldstein leaves the "haven" of conventional Brooklyn Jewish middle-class married social life, we are told that "in the bare alien worlds of the barracks and the bivouacs" he "fumbles for a new answer, a new security. And in his misery the old habits wither away like bark in winter, and he is left without a garment" (pp. 383-84). Searching in the very depths of his consciousness, he finds "the concretion, the heritage" (p. 384), the defensive shell of his grandfather's belief that the Jews are born to suffer for humanity.

Each of the men, in fact, has some kind of shell. Throughout the novel we have the irony of men fumbling to make contact with each other but, misunderstanding each other, drawing back after having for a moment opened up. Even Cummings, a human being with human weaknesses, after all, despite his almost successful attempt to make of himself a machine, is unable, would-be controller of the island though he be, to control himself and briefly reveals his homosexual impulses: "'Are you, Robert, are you really? Does anything ever touch you?' For that single instant the General's voice was naked" (p. 144).

At the climax of the novel the men are stripped finally of all defenses and exposed to the scorching truth of their experience. When Roth, utterly worn out during the climb up Mount Anaka, is clouted across the back of his head and called a "Jew bastard" by Gallagher, we are told: "All the protective devices, the sustaining façades of his life had been eroding slowly in the caustic air of the platoon; his exhaustion had pulled out the props, and Gallagher's blow had toppled the rest of the edifice. He was naked another way now" (p. 515). "Naked another way now" refers to Roth's sensitivity to the platoon's taunts, against which he has been unable to grow a "protective shell." Now he has to bear "all the faults of a religion he didn't believe in, a race which did not exist." He has been stripped of his last protective illusion: the belief that anti-Semitism is a myth nurtured by Jews with Old World memories. It is with this despair that Roth plunges to his death.

Ridges and Goldstein too have their protective illusions

stripped from them when, after the excruciating agony of carrying Wilson on his stretcher for what seems an eternity, he dies and is swept away in a rapid stream they are fording. Ridges, whose whole life had been governed by his religious faith, has an intense revulsion against the providence which he had accepted. The loss of their burden after so much effort seems to him to epitomize his whole life of harsh labor scratching away unavailingly at the barren soil. "God's way. He hated it suddenly. What kind of God could there be who always tricked you in the end? The practical joker. He wept out of bitterness and longing and despair; he wept from exhaustion and failure and the shattering naked conviction that nothing mattered" (p. 531). The protective garment of his religious belief torn away, all that remains to him is this "naked conviction."

So too Goldstein had found shelter in the belief that the Jews had been assigned to act as the conscience of humanity, that this is God's reason for their suffering. In the extremity of his pain and fatigue, his mind was "both blunted and exposed, naked and stupified" (p. 524). The loss of Wilson destroys forever the shelter to which Goldstein's naked, vulnerable mind can retreat.

All the suffering of the Jews came to nothing. No sacrifices were paid, no lessons were learned. . . . All the ghettos, all the soul cripplings, all the massacres and pogroms, the gas chambers, lime kilns—all of it touched no one, all of it was lost. It was carried and carried and carried, and when it finally grew too heavy it was dropped. That was all there was to it. [P. 531]

For Ridges, the experience is "the beginning of a deep and unending bitterness" (p. 530); for Goldstein, it is "the origins of a vast hopelessness" (p. 531). Ridges and Goldstein are left exposed to the numbness of despair; Roth and Wilson find the cessation of their agony in death. These men who attain the ultimate in suffering and pain are the naked and the dead.

Although it is buried deep in their being, the men are unable to hold onto their epiphany. They sleep for a day before the landing craft picks them up, and drowse for hours on the return trip. "The events of the patrol had receded already, become a diffused wry compound of indistinct memories" (pp. 546-47). The journey with the litter seems remote to Goldstein as he lies on his bunk. The feeling he experienced is "encysted" (p. 548) in his brain: a new membranous sac has been formed for his bitterness and despair to protect his consciousness from it. And yet the experience which, while it lasted, seemed to the men to constitute their entire existence, colors their whole view of the future as they emerge from the stupor of their fatigue.

> The patrol was over and yet they had so little to anticipate. They were still on the treadmill; the misery, the ennui, the dislocated horror. . . . Things would happen and time would pass, but there was no hope, no anticipation. There would be nothing but the deep cloudy dejection that overcast everything.[P. 547]

The bawdy song they sing together to cheer themselves up is ironically significant:

> Roll me over
> In the clover.
> Roll me over,
> Lay me down
> And do it again.
>   [P. 550]

We are reminded of Red's bitter musing just before the mountain ascent: "Even if we do get back we'll get a fuggin. What did it matter if they ever got out of the Army? It would be the same thing on the outside" (p. 449). The one thing the men can be sure of is that they will keep on getting screwed.

That Mailer could have said of *The Naked and the Dead* that "it is a novel with a great deal of hope" shows how far wrong an artist can be about his own creation. At the same time that he profited from Marxist insights into the nature of the army, Mailer, while proclaiming himself a Marxist, evinced deep distrust of the attempt, the very essence of Marxism, to deduce laws from the workings of human society, a part of the universe and subject like it to the governance of law. The savage, in the face of the mysterious forces of nature, peoples the world with fearsome spirits, which, since he cannot control, he must appease; the intellectual, in the face of the immense radiating and subterranean power of American capitalism, sees it, unless he has a revolutionary theory, as incomprehensible and therefore unconquerable, and even enlarges his view to include a numinous universe.

Hearn, whose inadequacies Mailer displays, is nevertheless very close to Mailer in his skepticism concerning any kind of theorizing and in his hopelessness. "No one ever really comprehends it, the vast table of America, and the pin points, the accretions, the big city [of Chicago, center of America] and the iron trails leading to it. The nexus," says Mailer at the beginning of the Hearn "Time Machine" sequence (p. 258); and Hearn muses at its conclusion, "Always there was the power that leaped at you, invited you. . . . And all the bright young people of his youth had butted their heads, smashed against things until they got weaker and the things still stood" (p. 278). The incomprehensible power, the threats, the blandishments, the seeming invincibility of American capitalism—these left Hearn impotent and apathetic. Why knock one's head against a wall that will not come down?

Revolutionary dedication needs the support of Marxist understanding. Marxist theory does not consist—as Mailer implies in his description of Hearn's brief political honeymoon with the Stalinist doctrinaires of the Harvard John Reed Society—of dogmatic phrasemongering and of the repetition of simple formulas that take the place of thought. This is a caricature of Marxism. Marxists do not claim to be the keepers of a mystic truth who have been ordained by an infallible pope.

A prognosis [as Trotsky said] is not a promissory note which can be cashed on a given date. Prognosis outlines only the definite trends of the development. But along with these trends a different order of forces and tendencies operate, which at a certain moment begin to predominate. All those who seek exact predictions of concrete events should consult the astrologists. Marxist prognosis aids only in orientation.[7]

Reality is richer and more complex than theory, which has to be constantly revised to keep pace with changing reality; but without the working models constructed by a theory derived from the scientific method of Marxism, one cannot begin to comprehend reality.

The best that Hearn can reply to the dogmatic assertions of the Harvard Stalinists is "That's a little too farsighted for me. . . . It seems to me you just do the thing that seems best at the moment and worry about the rest of it later" (p. 270), just as he later says to Cummings (p. 252), "I don't go in for the long views." From such disorientation the next step is the despairing apathy in which he says to himself: "There were no answers you could find, but perhaps there were epochs in history which had no answers. Rely on the blunder factor. Sit back and wait for the Fascists to louse it up" (p. 456). This is said in the midst of the slaughter of millions upon millions of persons brought about by the victory of fascism in Germany!

With this one can compare Trotsky's brilliant prognosis before Hitler came to power. In "Germany, the Key to the International Situation" (November 26, 1931), he wrote: "On the direction in which the solution of the German crisis develops will depend not only the fate of Germany herself (and that is already a great deal) but also the fate of Europe, the destiny of the entire world, for many years to come."[8] He called upon the German Social Democratic Party and the German Communist Party, which commanded the great German working class, to form a united front against the Nazis. Instead, the Social Democratic leaders continued their policy of supporting "the lesser evil," finally supporting Hindenberg, who gave the reins of power to Hitler; and the Communist leaders continued to denounce the Social Democratic Party as "social fascism," "the moderate wing of fascism,"[9] making it impossible to attract the Social Democratic workers to a united-front policy. Both paid for their mistakes with their lives when the German working-class movement was crushed in the concentration camps of Hitler, who had come to power without a struggle.

Hearn's light-minded "Sit back and wait for the Fascists to louse it up"—inexcusable when it was uttered with fatuous confidence in the German Communist Party in the form of the well-known saying "After Hitler, our turn,"[10] and even more inexcusable when it was uttered by Hearn with a self-indulgent despair after the consequences of Hitler's assumption of power were seen—was actually a "long view" based on a theory of history. Those who are skeptical of theory nevertheless find themselves formulating theories, ill conceived and confused as they are. Such contradictions abound where there is a lack of theoretical clarity. Mailer, despite the hopelessness of *The Naked and the Dead* and its raillery of "sound Marxian optimists," joined with the Communist Party and its periphery in supporting Wallace, adopting the old Social Democratic policy of "the lesser evil." It was, after all, in keeping with the novel's picture of society as a machine in which the parts may squeak, causing the drivers of the machine to let up on their speed, but in which the parts can only continue to make the machine go.

We need not, however, accept Mailer's politics to appreciate *The Naked and the Dead* as a novel which expresses most powerfully not only the horror of war but the oppressiveness of the society of which the army is an epitome. That is a great achievement.

8. George Orwell's '1984': A Worldwide 'Managerial Revolution'?

George Orwell, who was as staunch in both his radicalism and his anti-Stalinism as was his friend Silone, believed that the construction of a society based on the principles of socialist humanism was the one hope for humanity. The experience that left an indelible impress on him was his fighting in the POUM* militia in Spain. Here he saw how the Stalinists hunted down and killed their revolutionary and left-centrist working-class opponents, how they let loose a flood of lies about them, and how Stalinoid radicals in England acquiesced in the overwhelming of the truth.

At the same time in revolutionary Barcelona and in the POUM militia he was imbued with a feeling of what socialism means:

Socialism means a classless society, or it means nothing at all. And it was here that those few months in the militia were valuable to me. For the Spanish militias, while they lasted, were a sort of microcosm of a classless society. In that community where no one was on the make, where there was a shortage of everything but no privilege and no boot-licking, one got, perhaps, a crude forecast of what the opening stages of Socialism might be like. And, after all, instead of disillusioning me it deeply attracted me. The effect was to make my desire to see Socialism established much more actual than it had been before.[1]

On leaving Spain, he wrote to a friend: "I have seen wonderful things and at last really believe in Socialism which I never did before."[2] Through the years, while Orwell's vision of socialism receded, it was never obliterated. It was not joined, however, to a

---

*The POUM (Workers Party of Marxist Unification) was a left-wing socialist party led by Andres Nin, a founder of the Spanish Communist Party and an ex-Trotskyist. Its militia was made up of working-class militants fired by a revolutionary spirit. The POUM was attacked by the Stalinists as a Francoist fifth column. Nin was kidnapped and murdered at the command of the Soviet secret police.

Marxist analysis of capitalism, fascism, and Stalinism.

Orwell's *1984*, published in 1949, when the cold war was getting under way, was immediately seized upon as a major weapon in that war. Its nightmare vision of a worldwide, all-powerful totalitarian society of the future was used in a campaign of terror directed at frightening the people of the western capitalist countries into forgetting the Soviet Union as an only recently lauded ally and seeing it as a monstrous threat to civilization. The mass media broadcast its "message," simplified and distorted, with volume turned up high so that it assumed the proportions of a deafening and horrifying shriek. Thus, ironically, *1984* became what is called in it "prolefeed," adulterated artistic sustenance for mass consumption; and, like the savage music composed for Hate Week, it helped to turn off mass hatred for one country and turn it on, unreasoningly, for another, as with the turning of a dial.

Orwell was perturbed to find his novel being used as a defense of capitalism against the idea of socialism. On his deathbed, he wrote,

> My recent novel [*1984*] is NOT intended as an attack on Socialism or on the British Labour Party (of which I am a supporter) but as a show-up of the perversions to which a centralized economy is liable and which have already been partly realised in Communism and Fascism. . . . [T]otalitarian ideas have taken root in the minds of intellectuals everywhere, and I have tried to draw these ideas out to their logical consequences.[3]

A few critics pointed out that the society of *1984* has features that resemble those of English and American capitalism, that Orwell was not simply ranging himself on the Anglo-American side of the cold war, but their voices were drowned out in the roar of the mass media. We are now, however, in a position to understand it better.

The society of *1984*, as a number of commentators have pointed out,[4] is based on the analysis of the contemporary world in James Burnham's *The Managerial Revolution*. Orwell in an essay on this book and on Burnham's *The Machiavellians* summarized Burnham's argument in what reads like a description of *1984*'s Oceania. In brief, Burnham, a renegade from Trotskyism who is now an editor of the arch-conservative *National Review*, stated that capitalism is giving way not to socialism, but to a new form of society, the managerial society. The managerial society is dominated by a new class, the managers, the technical experts, the governmental and industrial bureaucrats. In the United States, this class, growing within capitalist society, has achieved dominance as a result of the divorce between stock ownership and management and control. In Nazi Germany, it has achieved dominance by a totalitarian dictatorship which has reduced the nominal owners of property to subservience to the wielders of governmental power. In the Soviet Union, where the means of production are nominally under collective ownership, it has achieved dominance by its absolute control of the state, which owns the means of production. Each is going in the same direction, although the United States has not proceeded so far as the other two. The probability is that this process will culminate in perhaps three super-states fighting for possession of the world but unable to conquer one another.

Orwell said of the concept of the managerial society, "as an interpretation of what is *happening,* Burnham's theory is extremely plausible to put it at the lowest."[5] But, he went on to say, as a prognostication of the future there are many objections to be made to it. The interesting thing is that each of these objections applies to *1984* if we regard it as literal prophecy. Burnham's prognostications, Orwell noted, are based not on a study of possibilities but on a projection of what is occurring at the moment. In *The Managerial Revolution,* written when the German army was triumphant on the Continent, he predicted a Nazi victory over England, to be followed by an attack on the Soviet Union, which would crack and split apart; in an article, "Lenin's Heir," written when the Russian army was advancing rapidly in Eastern Europe, he predicted that it would conquer all of Eurasia and go on to threaten England and the United States. Moreover, Burnham telescopes and compresses history, looking for sweeping changes to occur in an impossibly short time. Finally, Burnham exaggerates "managerial" efficiency and makes it invincible. But only a totalitarian regime like Nazi Germany, closed to discussion, could have made such a colossal error as attacking the Soviet Union while the war with England was still going on and when it was clear that the United States was preparing to enter it. "The Russian régime," Orwell concluded, "will either democratise itself, or it will perish. The huge, invincible, everlasting slave empire of which Burnham appears to dream will not be established, or, if established, will not endure, because slavery is no longer a stable basis for human society."[6]

In a review of Burnham's *The Struggle for the World* published

at the end of March 1947, seven or eight months after he had
begun work on *1984,* he continued to speak coolly of Burnham's
prognostications, which had now taken on a feverish quality.
Burnham, he pointed out, was now speaking of America, the land
of the free, as an old-line conservative instead of as the proponent
of the theory of the managerial revolution that was doing away
with the decadent old order. Warning that the Soviet Union must
soon develop an atomic bomb, Burnham urged the formation of
an American empire, union with Great Britain, the rigorous
repression of Communists and their sympathizers in the American domain, and, implicitly, said Orwell, a preventive war
against the Soviet Union. To this Orwell replied that it was not at
all clear that the danger was as acute as Burnham made it out to
be: "We do not know how strong the Russians are, how badly
they have been crippled by the war." What Burnham calls the
Communist infiltrators are not as rigidly fanatic as he makes out:
the turn-over of the Communist Party membership in England is
very great, and there are large numbers of disillusioned fellow-
travelers as well as of former party members. Suppression of the
Communists would only strengthen domestic authoritarianism.
An alternative to Burnham's program is to seek "to make
democratic Socialism work" in Western Europe and Africa.[7]

How, then, did Orwell, who stated that Russia must liberalize
itself or perish, that Communists are not necessarily inhuman
zombies, that even totalitarian regimes do not change human
beings and the fabric of life overnight, come to write *1984,* in
which the omnipotent state of Oceania—the unification of the
United States and Great Britain which Burnham called for has
been effected—apparently crushes "the last man," "the guardian
of the human spirit,"[8] only thirty-five years after the appearance
of the novel? One answer is that he was a dying man when he
was in the latter stages of its composition. Undoubtedly, the
awful description of Winston Smith's ravaged, debilitated body at
the conclusion of the novel came from Orwell's awareness of his
own body, ravaged and debilitated by tuberculosis.

But a dying man does not desperately race against death to
produce a book unless he feels that it contains a vision which he
must communicate to the world. The truth is that Orwell had long
accepted the general view of *The Managerial Revolution,* which
was not at all original with Burnham, and, while he bravely
continued to call for a genuine socialism, always had his fears
that it would not be realized, becoming more pessimistic than
ever after the war. Thus, reviewing in May 1940 Franz Borke-

nau's *The Totalitarian Enemy*—one of a number of books published before the war and during the period of the Hitler-Stalin pact that purported to show that the totalitarian dictatorships of Germany and the Soviet Union were not symmetrical phenomena, but identical—he said: "The two régimes [Germany and the Soviet Union], having started from opposite ends, are rapidly evolving towards the same system—a form of oligarchical collectivism."[9] "Oligarchical collectivism," it will be recalled, is the term used by the supposed Emmanuel Goldstein to describe the society of Oceania. In June 1941, Orwell wrote that "a collectivized economy is bound to come" but that he believed that the "non-militarized countries," Western Europe and the Americas, India and China, "will know how to evolve a form of Socialism which is not totalitarian," adding, however, that this belief "may be no more than a pious hope."[10] By July 1947 he was able to say that a Socialist of that time was like a doctor treating an all but hopeless case. It is his duty to continue to fight to keep the patient alive on the chance that he will survive, but, facing the facts as a scientist, he knows that the patient will probably die: the "odds" are "against the survival of civilization within the next few years."[11]

Orwell had supported the war against Germany, believing that Nazi totalitarianism was the main enemy and that England, to defend herself more efficiently, would effect a socialist revolution. At the end of the war he found England continuing as before in a kind of "semi-anaesthesia," a horrible devastation on the Continent, a new super-weapon, the atomic bomb, which might wipe out humanity, and a menacing hostility making itself manifest between the Soviet Union and the United States. He, like many leftist intellectuals of the time, accepted the dictum that all totalitarian states are by nature expansionist and saw the Soviet Union as "preparing for war against the western democracies," this despite the fact that his good sense made him wonder about its strength after the havoc of war.[12] Although, unlike many of these intellectuals, he did not, as we have seen, permit himself to be stampeded into joining the holy crusade against Communism, he did regard the Soviet Union as the epitome of all the authoritarian trends that he found in the "western democracies." These developments, the death of his wife, and his own illness made him see the world in darker colors than ever before.

1984, then, is an urgent warning of the kind of society that may come about. To the very end, Orwell insisted that it was just that, a warning, not a prophecy of what must be. As a warning, Orwell put the time of his novel not in some reassuringly distant future but in the lifetime of many of his readers, certainly in the lifetime of their children. Whatever its immediate fate, the intention of the book was neither to paralyze action nor to galvanize hysterical action, but to arouse thoughtful action. And so, although the artist may have been partially overcome by his own sombre vision, he sounds, as we shall see later, a thin but clear note of hope that, lost though it may be in the crashing conclusion, is of the utmost importance. It is a note that has been generally missed by the critics.

With the exception of its out-of-balance conclusion, *1984* is masterfully planned. It is divided into three parts. In the first part we see the situation of Winston Smith, isolated, sick, weak, and miserable in a society which he abhors but from which he cannot escape. He does not know if anyone else shares his feelings. He does not know if this society will endure forever. But, hate this society as he does, he himself is poisoned by it. Blocked by not being accustomed to communicate truly with himself or anyone else, he is for a while unable to write in the diary he has acquired, itself an act of rebellion, but then the words gush from his pen in a stream of automatic writing, omitting capitals and punctuation, telling of a war film he saw—a "very good one of a ship full of refugees being bombed," with "a wonderful shot of a childs arm" (p. 11) reaching up out of the water—without a hint of horror or compassion.

In the second part we see Winston grow in spiritual strength and understanding. He has an affair with a young woman. At first he is simply prompted by sexual desire and a desire to commit a political act against the Party, but then he grows to love her. The room which he has discovered as a refuge becomes a world apart. The experience is symbolized by the beautiful hemispherical glass paperweight with a piece of coral embedded in the center, an object of the past, that he has acquired. "The paperweight was the room he was in, and the coral was Julia's life and his own, fixed in a sort of eternity at the heart of the crystal" (p. 122). The Thought Police who come tramping into the room at the end of this section smash the paperweight to pieces on the hearthstone.

In the third part we see Winston internally broken and reduced to an empty husk. The third part is a countermovement to the second. Whereas in the second part Winston, the process of life no longer being intolerable to him, ceases to drink gin at all hours and to have coughing fits in the morning, puts weight on his scrawny body, and finds that his varicose ulcer, the physical symbol of his psychic wound, has subsided to become only a brown stain, in the third part he is starved into a living skeleton, with this varicose ulcer "an inflamed mass with flakes of skin peeling off it" (p. 223). But he is more than beaten into verbal submission. The "few cubic centimeters inside your skull" (p. 26), which at the beginning of the book he believed would at any rate always be his, mask his thoughts at all times as he must, are infused with the thoughts and feelings the Party wants him to have. Terrified at the idea of being devoured alive by rats, he calls out that Julia should be substituted for him, giving up his love, his humanity, his inner self. Having given up that inner self, he can cast himself upon the "loving breast" (p. 245) of Big Brother. At the beginning of the novel he had written his private thoughts in his diary in a "small but childish handwriting" (p. 11), the sign of his emotional stuntedness; at the end he writes "the thoughts that came to his head," the various slogans of the Party, in "large clumsy capitals" (p. 228), the sign that he has been deprived of a personality and of thoughts of his own.

The conclusion is the more harrowing in that it comes after the period of Winston's developing psychological health. His progress was to no avail. For seven years, ever since the first glimmering of an idea of opposition to Big Brother, the Thought Police had watched him "like a beetle under a magnifying glass" (p. 228). They knew each action of his, each move, each thought. Even his most intimate moments with Julia were observed. His growth as a human being, his opposition to Big Brother only occurred because they were part of a game which the omnipotent Inner Party had been playing with him.

The defeat of Winston is, of course, presented as inevitable from the beginning. Orwell, however, sustains the reader's interest by a series of ironic surprises: Julia, whom Winston had regarded as unalterably orthodox and probably an agent of the Thought Police or a patriotic spy, turns out to be a rebel against the Party and interested in having an affair with him; Mr. Charrington, the antique dealer, who had seemed to be a relic of the past, turns out to be a member of the Thought Police; Parsons, the fatuous Party zealot, whom Winston thought was one of those you could be sure would never be "vaporized," is apprehended for having uttered rebellious words in his sleep, having been denounced by his little daughter, of whose work in the children's organization, the Spies, Parsons was so proud; O'Brien, the Inner Party member with whom Winston felt such a rapport and whom he thought to be a

leader in the Brotherhood, the secret opposition party, turns out
to be the inquisitor, teacher, and priest who inducts him into the
worship of Big Brother. These surprises are no mere spy-thriller
devices. They contribute to the sense of the groping uncertainty
of the individual isolated in this world of lies, the phantasma-
goric quality of life in it, and the lunatic lengths to which it will
go in enforcing absolute conformity.

Another means Orwell uses to sustain the reader's interest
while traveling with Winston along the road which he knows has
but one end is suspense. Various teasing questions are raised in
the course of the book, whose answers we await. What is the
meaning of O'Brien's words, "We shall meet in the place where
there is no darkness" (p. 24), in Winston's dream? What is the
meaning of the dream in which his mother and baby sister look
up at him, out in the light and air, from some dark, subterranean
place? What is the suppressed memory that comes to the edge of
Winston's consciousness at the sight of the Inner Party chocolate? What lies behind the wall of darkness in his recurring
nightmare? What is there in room 101? Again, this suspense is
not merely a plot device. The answers to these questions are part
of a series of revelations to Winston concerning himself and his
world, of his human weakness, exemplified in his selfish,
childish snatching away of the last morsel of food from his
mother and sister, an adumbration of his later giving up of Julia,
and of his society's ability to use that weakness to crush him.

One of these revelations is the reading of the book supposedly
written by Emmanuel Goldstein, whose Jewish name, physical
description, and position as the hated arch-heretic suggest Leon
Trotsky. Some critics have felt that the material contained in this
book is imperfectly integrated into the text and should have been
relegated to an appendix such as the appendix "The Principles of
Newspeak" that Orwell added to his novel. But *the book* comes
at just the right moment. Winston has been progressively freeing
himself from Big Brother. In the first part, during the Two
Minutes Hate period, he felt a rage that veered from Goldstein to
Big Brother and back to Goldstein. Now he has joined the
Brotherhood. He has, moreover, the contentment and the security
of the room he shares with Julia, where he thinks he is unob-
served. Here he can sit back luxuriously and give himself up to
the book that articulates for him the ideas he had already
imperfectly shaped for himself. It performs a similar function for
the reader of *1984*, bringing together the bits and pieces of the life
of Oceania he has seen through the eyes of Winston and shaping

them into a pattern whose elements are shown to have been derived from his own day ("by the fourth decade of the twentieth century all the main currents of political thought were authoritarian") (p. 168).

Because the book is purportedly Goldstein's, it has generally been taken to be a paraphrase of Trotsky's *The Revolution Betrayed*, and Irving Howe, who edited a selection of Trotsky's writings, has found it to be a brilliant imitation of Trotsky's style.[13] However, the doctrine it propounds is Burnham's, not Trotsky's. Trotsky saw the governing stratum of the Soviet Union as a parasitic growth upon the workers' state established by the revolution, a bureaucracy that came to power as a result of the isolation of the revolution in a backward country. He compared the Soviet Union to a trade union undemocratically administered by a conservative bureaucracy more intent on preserving its position than fighting for the membership: the trade union remains a workers' organization even though its leadership must be combated if the workers' power is to manifest itself truly. Burnham, however, regarded the Russian revolution, as we have seen, as a revolution not of the proletariat, but of a managerial class, and this is the way the Ingsoc revolution is presented in "Goldstein's" *The Theory and Practice of Oligarchical Collectivism*.

The style of *The Theory and Practice of Oligarchical Collectivism* too is modeled on that of Burnham, not of Trotsky. Howe quotes one analogy between a law of natural science and a law of human society and also one "compressed paradox" from "Goldstein" and asserts that these are characteristic of Trotsky. It is indeed true that Trotsky, seeing human society as a particle of the material universe, subject, like it, to general laws, drew frequent analogies between natural laws and social laws, and that, seeing "the law of combined development" working in the evolution of society, he frequently showed in one compressed, vivid phrase the old and the new existing incongruously together. However, Howe's examples are not typical of "Goldstein's" style, and Burnham, influenced no doubt by his former mentor, himself makes occasional ornamental use of such analogies and paradoxes.

The general tone is that of *The Managerial Revolution*, dispassionate and with something of the flatness of a textbook, not that of *The Revolution Betrayed*, which—its very title stands in contrast with the other two titles—is charged with feeling as well as with thought. The difference in tone between Burnham and

Trotsky is indicated in the statement of intention of the two. Burnham states that his purpose is not to make "any *moral* judgment" but to "elaborate a *descriptive* theory" able to explain the present and predict the future (Burnham's italics).[14] Trotsky too says that his purpose is "to estimate correctly what is, in order the better to understand what is coming to be," but he does not pretend that he is a neutral observer and that man's consciousness and actions do not play a part in history: "This book will be critical. Whoever worships the accomplished fact is incapable of preparing the future."[15]

The point is important because if "Goldstein's" book had been written in Trotsky's style it would have had a revolutionary élan that would have struck a jarring note. Winston believes that the book was written by the old revolutionist, and he anticipates that later on it will reveal how the revolution will be made, presuming that it will state that it will be through the proles, led by the Brotherhood. But Orwell did not want to write persuasively on behalf of the Brotherhood or to arouse sympathy for it. He was against Lenin's concept of a vanguard party, accepting Burnham's thesis that Stalin was truly Lenin's heir and the thesis of *Darkness at Noon*, which undoubtedly influenced *1984* although Orwell condemned Koestler's "pessimistic Conservatism,"[16] that the Bolsheviks' destructive amoralism in believing that the end justifies the means brought about Stalinism. This is the significance of Winston's unquestioning acceptance of any means necessary for the purpose of the revolution, including throwing sulphuric acid in a child's face, when questioned by O'Brien, posing as a leader of the Brotherhood. The suggestion is that the Brotherhood can produce only another Big Brother.

"Emmanuel Goldstein's" book is therefore written in an impersonally expository manner and contains nothing of revolutionary optimism or of revolutionary indignation. On the contrary, at one point it says that "the Party has been able—and may, for all we know, continue to be able for thousands of years—to arrest the course of history" (p. 177). The irony is that we discover in part 3 that the book was actually written by O'Brien in collaboration with other Inner Party members. O'Brien tells Winston that the description of Oceanic society he has read is entirely true but that the idea of revolution is nonsense.

Orwell in his essay on *The Managerial Revolution* had said that Burnham in his projection into the future of the strength first of the Hitler dictatorship and then of the Stalin dictatorship, was prostrating himself before power, as was indicated by the tone of "fascinated admiration" in which he wrote of Stalin's crimes. In this he was only revealing "the power worship now so prevalent among intellectuals."[17] O'Brien is the high priest in this power worship, in which one gains power through prostrating oneself before it. If one, he says, "can make complete, utter submission, if he can escape from his identity, if he can merge himself in the Party so that he *is* the Party, then he is all-powerful and immortal" (p. 218).

Orwell had written that Burnham's underlying assumption is that the desire for power has always been present in people and always will be.

It is curious that in all his talk about the struggle for power, Burnham never stops to ask *why* people want power. He seems to assume that power hunger, although only dominant in comparatively few people, is a natural instinct that does not have to be explained, like the desire for food. . . . The question that he ought to ask, and never does ask, is: Why does the lust for naked power become a major human motive exactly *now*, when the dominion of man over man is ceasing to be necessary?[18]

This is the question that Winston had asked himself: what was the ultimate motive of the Party in its huge imposture of building and continuously altering a world of lies? "I understand HOW: I do not understand WHY." It was the question which "Goldstein's" book had failed to answer for him. It is the question which O'Brien finally answers, but the answer is tautological, is really not an answer but the baffling reply, "It's so because it's so": "The Party seeks power entirely for its own sake. . . . The object of persecution is persecution. The object of torture is torture. The object of power is power."

In his review of Burnham's *The Struggle for the World*, Orwell stated that if the American empire Burnham called for were to come into being, "the strongest intellectual influence in it would probably be that of the Catholic Church."[19] It was at about this time, it may be recalled, that Bishop Fulton J. Sheen was acting as the father confessor for a number of leading ex-Communists and had a weekly television program in which he called for a crusade against the absolute evil of Communism, citing the forced confessions of the Moscow trials as evidence of how Communism destroys men's minds and souls—conveniently forgetting as he did so the Spanish Inquisition. O'Brien, whose Irish name suggests Roman Catholicism, says of himself and his fellow Inner Party members, "We are the priests of power" (p. 217).

He uses the language of religion throughout. When, as a supposed leader of the Brotherhood, he asks a series of questions about what enormities Winston and Julia will commit for the sake of the revolution, he presents them as "a sort of catechism" (p. 142). When he appears as Winston's inquisitor, he has "the air of a doctor, a teacher, even a priest, anxious to explain and persuade rather than to punish" (p. 203). "You have failed in humility, in self-discipline" (p. 205), he tells Winston. But Winston will not gain any martyrdom. The Inquisition of the Middle Ages failed because it conferred martyrdom on heretics by killing them when they were unrepentant. "We do not destroy the heretic because he resists us. . . . We convert him, we capture his inner mind, we reshape him" (p. 210). Abject submission will not suffice; surrender must be of one's own "free will" (p. 210). And in his final mad vision, in which the more powerful the Party becomes, the less tolerant it is (just as Stalin said that the closer to communism the Soviet Union gets, the more frenzied and dangerous the counterrevolutionary forces get, and the more pitiless should be the state's repression), he sees the drama that he has played out with Winston repeated generation after generation, using the same religious terms: "Always we shall have the heretic here at our mercy, screaming with pain, broken up, contemptible—and in the end utterly penitent, saved from himself, crawling to our feet of his own accord" (p. 221).

In his adoration of power, in his unquestioning acceptance of power as the ultimate goal in life, in his association with the Catholic Church, O'Brien, then, is Burnham, who, incidentally, was called a "secularized Catholic" in Trotsky's polemic against him.[20] The author of *The Struggle for the World*, the opponent of communism, is himself the Inner Party man of the party modeled on the Russian Stalinist party! For to Orwell the oppressor is always the same, whatever the oppressive society calls itself. "The real question," he said in his essay on *The Managerial Revolution*, "is not whether the people who wipe their boots on us during the next fifty years are to be called managers, bureaucrats, or politicians: the question is whether capitalism, now obviously doomed, is to give way to oligarchy or to true democracy."[21] This is why in addition to the familiar features of Stalinism—the purges, the confessions at the public trials, the falsification of history, including the role of Big Brother in the revolution—there are also features of life in English capitalist society: the debased mass culture ("rubbishy newspapers, containing almost nothing except sport, crime, and astrology, sensational five-cent novelettes, films oozing with sex, and sentimental songs which were composed entirely by mechanical means") (p. 39), the pubs, from whose "grimy swing doors, endlessly opening and shutting, there came forth a smell of urine, sawdust, and sour beer," and the gambling, which for millions of proles "was the principal if not the only reason for remaining alive" (pp. 72-73).

The society that contains these features of Stalinist Russia and capitalist England, but carried to the nth degree, is mad, as is indicated by the many references to the "lunatic enthusiasm" (p. 211) of O'Brien and the statement in *The Theory and Practice of Oligarchical Collectivism* that the exercise of "doublethink," necessary to maintain the society, means that the "prevailing mental condition must be controlled insanity" (p. 178). There is no such thing as external reality, says O'Brien, no material universe governed by natural laws; reality is "only in the mind of the Party, which is collective and immortal. Whatever the Party holds to be truth *is* truth" (p. 205).

"Always, at every moment, there will be the thrill of victory," says O'Brien, "the sensation of trampling on an enemy who is helpless. If you want a picture of the future, imagine a boot stamping on a human face—forever" (p. 220). Jack London used this image in *The Iron Heel* to characterize the centuries-long period of despotism during which the American capitalists were able to stave off socialism. Orwell spoke of this novel as a prophecy of fascism, and there can be little doubt that he got his image from it (there are a number of references to the "iron-shod boots" (pp. 183, 189) on the feet of the black-uniformed guards, who are reminiscent of the SS troops and who use their boots freely to kick their victims into agonizing pain). Jack London, however, made his ruling class convinced that it was guarding civilization against the barbarian masses, for he knew that in order to preserve its élan it needed such a rationale. This is a point that Orwell himself made in writing of *The Iron Heel*.[22] In *1984*, however, where Orwell, immersed in the irrationalities of totalitarianism, partly lost his sense of social reality, the Party does not rationalize its material interests.

O'Brien has the last word in *1984*. His "forever" has been generally accepted, and *1984* has been regarded, in the words of Stephen Spender, as "a confined, absolute, dead-end world of despair, like Sartre's *Huis Clos* in which there is no way out."[23] Certainly, the atmosphere of *1984* is heavily oppressive, and its conclusion is overwhelming. There can be no doubt that we are to feel at the end that history may very well be frozen for eternity. Yet, if we retain the novel as a whole in our minds, I believe that we have hope that O'Brien's lunatic exultation about the world that will be built by the Inner Party is like the ravings of a certain dictator about a thousand-year Reich—a dictator whose regime was destroyed only three years before the completion of *1984*.

For one thing, there is the matter of corruption within the Party. "Perhaps," Winston thinks when he is with Julia, "the Party was rotten under the surface, its cult of strenuousness and self-denial simply a sham concealing iniquity" (p. 104). She has had sexual relations with Party members scores of times, she tells him, and, as for the Inner Party members, she wouldn't have any with "those swine," "but there's plenty that *would* if they got half a chance. They're not so holy as they make out" (p. 104). It seems as if the thoughts of the priests in the worship of power are not always confined to that worship—and without the single-minded devotion of these priests the society which they have built for the glory of the God who is Power must crumble.

Then there is the question of the youth. Julia hates the Party. She likes to have good times, and "they" seek to rob her of her pleasures. Winston wonders vaguely "how many others like her there might be in the younger generation—people who had grown up in the world of the Revolution, knowing nothing else, accepting the Party as something unalterable, like the sky, not rebelling against its authority but simply evading it, as a rabbit dodges a dog" (p. 109). Julia herself suggests that there may well be many others. The indoctrination about chastity, she says, no doubt works in a lot of cases, but "of course you never can tell; people are such hypocrites" (p. 110). It is she who enables Winston to grasp "the inner meaning of the Party's sexual puritanism": "How could the fear, the hatred, and the lunatic credulity which the Party needed in its members be kept at the right pitch except by bottling down some powerful instinct and using it as a driving force? The sex impulse was dangerous to the Party, and the Party had turned it to account" (p. 111). But if Julia is indeed representative of what we call today an alternative youth culture, the Party is losing its driving force.

Moreover, there is Parsons. Even this indefatigable Party zealot had, unknown to himself, "bad stuff" within him, as he puts it, and called out "Down with Big Brother!" in his sleep (pp.

192-93). If such as Parsons cannot rid themselves of unconscious revolt against the Party, who can be free of it, and can the Thought Police, with all its powers of surveillance, continue to nip revolt in the bud?

But most of all, there are the proles. Orwell has been condemned not only by Stalinist critics but by such a discerning non-Stalinist radical critic as Raymond Williams for his presentation of the proles, which they have characterized as insulting to British workers.[24] What they failed to see was that the proles are presented through the eyes of Winston and that Winston's attitude toward them undergoes a progressive development, which, it may be added, duplicates Orwell's own experience. In *The Road to Wigan Pier* he tells of how at the age of six he was forbidden by his parents, struggling to retain their middle-class gentility, to play with the plumber's children because they were "common." [25] Before this, he says, his chief heroes were working-class people—fishermen, blacksmiths, bricklayers—because they did such interesting things. Perhaps the sudden setting up of the class barrier had the traumatic effect that, we are told, southern white children often suffer when they reach the age at which they are ordered to give up their Black playmates; at all events, Orwell in later years continued to seek to enter the working-class world and to feel at home in it. He tells of one such experience, in which he lived in coal miners' homes for months, ate with them and their families, drank in their pubs, talked for hours at end with them, and shared their bedrooms. Nevertheless,

I was not one of them, and they knew it even better than I did. . . . Whichever way you turn this curse of class difference confronts you like a wall of stone. Or rather it is not so much like a stone wall as the plate-glass pane of an aquarium; it is so easy to pretend that it isn't there, and so impossible to get through it.[26]

To Orwell as a child and a prep-school boy, however, the working class seemed not only alien but almost outside of humanity, bestial.

To me in my early boyhood, to nearly all children of families like mine, "common" people seemed almost sub-human. They had coarse faces, hideous accents and gross manners, they hated everyone who was not like themselves, and if they got half a chance they would insult you in brutal ways. That was our view of them, and though it was false it was understandable.[27]

He came, however, through reading and experience to see the working class entirely differently:

> In a working-class home—I am not thinking at the moment of the unemployed, but of comparatively prosperous homes—you breathe a warm, decent, deeply human atmosphere which it is not easy to find elsewhere. . . . [The worker's] home life seems to fall more naturally [than the home life of an "educated" man] into a sane and comely shape.[28]

In *1984* the Party view is that the proles "are not human beings"; they are "natural inferiors who must be kept in subjection, like animals" (p. 61). Regarding the proles as beneath suspicion, the Party does not seek to impose its doctrine and way of life on them. "Left to themselves, like cattle turned loose upon the plains of Argentina," the proles "had reverted to a style of life that appeared to be natural to them, a sort of ancestral pattern." The Party slogan is "Proles and animals are free" (pp. 61-62).

Winston at the beginning too sees the proles as animals, even after he has written in his diary, "If there is hope, it lies in the proles" (p. 60). The little houses in which they live remind him of "rat holes." When a rocket-bomb attack occurs, they scoot into doorways "like rabbits." The proles, for their part, stiffen when he walks past them in his Party uniform in their working-class neighborhood, "as at the passing of some unfamiliar animal" (pp. 70-71). Each is on a different side of the aquarium glass pane and sees the other as a member of an alien species.

However, after Winston has progressed in psychological health, he comes to see the proles differently. When he finally recalls in his dream his mother clasping his starving baby sister to her breast after he had snatched away the chocolate, he remembers how the refugee woman in the war film had instinctively made the same protective gesture with her arm even though it could be of no help to protect her child against the bullets. In describing the war film in his diary, he had told of how there was applause from the Party section during the bombing but how a prole woman was thrown out of the cinema for loudly exclaiming that the film should not have been shown before children. Now, although he does not refer to this incident, when he reflects that only two generations ago individual relationships and private loyalties existed as they do not today, his mind turns to the proles.

The proles, it suddenly occurred to him, had remained in this condition. They were not loyal to a party or a country or an idea, they were loyal to one another. For the first time in his life he did not despise the proles or think of them merely as an inert force which would one day spring to life and regenerate the world. The proles had stayed human. They had not become hardened inside. They had held onto the primitive emotions which he himself had to relearn by conscious effort. . . . "The proles are human beings," he said aloud. "We are not human." [P. 136]

Ironically, then, the proles, whom he, like the other members of the Party, had regarded as not human, he now regards as the only genuine human beings, just as Orwell, as a boy, had regarded workers as "almost subhuman," but then had come to see them as living in a "deeply human atmosphere." In fact, they are human just because they are animal, that is, they are not automatized beings but possess natural, spontaneous feelings. So Winston regards himself and Julia, humanized by their love, as animals: their "room was a world, a pocket of the past where extinct animals could walk" (p. 124).

When Winston, just before he and Julia are caught in their room, observes the sturdy, middle-aged prole woman in the yard hanging up her washing and singing a sentimental love song with a happy spontaneity, he comes to a profound conviction:

The proles were immortal; you could not doubt it when you looked at that valiant figure in the yard. In the end their awakening would come. And until that happened, though it might be a thousand years, they would stay alive against all the odds, like birds, passing on from body to body the vitality which the Party did not share and could not kill. . . . You were the dead; theirs was the future. [Pp. 181-82]

The prole woman is like Wordsworth's Highland Lass, whom he observes singing and reaping, seeming a part of immortal nature, her song like that of the cuckoo bird or the nightingale. So the prole woman's song is compared to that of the thrush which Winston had watched with a "sort of vague reverence" (p. 103) singing at the edge of the lonely wood, the Golden Country of his dreams.

In the hands of O'Brien, his mind as broken as his body, Winston forgets his conviction about the proles, but are we to do so? In their final dialogue, in which, with his last spark of resistance, Winston feebly seeks to speak up against the view of the future offered by the intellectually superior O'Brien, only to be crushed in argumentation, O'Brien brusquely dismisses the proles as a revolutionary hope: "They are helpless, like the animals. Humanity is the Party. The others are outside—irrelevant" (p. 222). A moment later, however, he implicitly concedes that the Party is not humanity. When Winston says that the spirit of man will finally defeat him, O'Brien asks if Winston considers himself a man and, on receiving an affirmative, replies, "If you are a man, Winston, you are the last man. Your kind is extinct; we are the inheritors. Do you not understand that you are *alone*? You are outside history, you are non-existent" (p. 222). Repeating "You are the last man. You are the guardian of the human spirit," O'Brien confronts Winston with his own physical, intellectual, and moral puniness. This, it is implied, is what humanity comes to! But, if we recall Winston's words, "The proles are human beings. We are not human," as we should, we remember that he regarded himself as only working towards being what the proles are. It is not Winston who is representative of humanity; it is not the Party which is humanity; it is the proles. And they, unlike Winston, have not been defeated. It is true, however, that our final impression is of an utterly crushed Winston. The final sentences, "He had won the victory over himself. He loved Big Brother," are devastating. The conclusion is rather out of balance with the pattern of the novel.

Do the events of the twenty-five years since Orwell wrote *1984* give warrant to the note of hope in it, or do they give warrant to Burnham's prophecy of the completion of the "managerial revolution," which for Orwell meant "1984"? First of all, it must be said that Soviet society has evolved away from the world of *1984* rather than toward it. Here Orwell was more nearly correct in his critique of Burnham's *The Struggle for the World* than he was in *1984*. One possibility that Burnham has not considered, he wrote, is that "the Russian regime may become more liberal and less dangerous a generation hence, if war has not broken out in the meantime. Of course, this would not happen with the consent of the ruling clique, but it is thinkable that the mechanics of the situation may bring it about."[29]

The Yugoslav and Chinese revolutions and the "revolution from above" in the Eastern European states broke the isolation of the Soviet Union. At the same time industrialization and the extension of education produced a new proletariat and a new intelligentsia. The primitive religious worship of Stalin, the pervasive terror, and the draconian labor laws were no longer appropriate in a society which felt the need to modernize itself.

Millions were released from the slave labor camps. Many who had become "unpersons" were restored to history and even to life in the society from which they had been excluded. The "memory holes" had not obliterated them, after all.

On the other hand, *1984*, in which Oceania, while in continuous warfare with one or the other of the two other superstates, does not really seek to vanquish them, seems to be closer to the reality of the Soviet Union's foreign policy than the review of Burnham's *The Struggle for the World,* in which Orwell accepts Burnham's premise that the Soviet Union is an expansionist power. Such historians as Isaac Deutscher, David Horowitz, Gabriel Kolko, and D. F. Fleming have found that the cold war was initiated not by the Russians but by the Americans. Indeed, as Deutscher says, the idea that the Soviet Union, bled far more white than any other country by the war, was thinking of starting a new one against an America more powerful than ever before, was an utter fantasy.[30] Since then, while the United States has been backing regimes of reaction throughout the world with massive aid and direct military intervention, the Soviet bureaucracy, heading a different social system but intent only on defending its own narrow, nationalistic interests, has given limited aid to opponents of these regimes, seeking at the same time to make deals with the United States by using this aid to manipulate and restrain them. The conservatism of the Soviet bureaucracy, the American playing off against each other of the Soviet Union and China, and the weakened international position of the United States are the basis for the so-called détente.

While the Soviet Union has done away with the unrestrained terror and the large-scale purges of Stalin, it has retained its totalitarian framework. Here *1984* has proven unduly pessimistic about the staying power of intellectuals, for a courageous band of dissidents has been fighting for civil rights and freedom of artistic expression, circulating manuscripts, statements, and news chronicles from hand to hand, as was done with "Goldstein's" book. These intellectuals are preparing the way, but only the "proles" are capable of restoring a socialist democracy.

In the United States, the theory of the managerial revolution has not been proven with time. On the contrary, G. William Domhoff says concerning this theory in *Who Rules America?,*

The circumstantial evidence developed by TNEC [The United States Senate Temporary National Economic Committee], Sweezy, Perlo, Lundberg, Kolko, and Villarejo points to only one conclusion—the biggest shareholders in large corporations are actively involved in determining the general policies and selecting the managers of these companies.[31]

As for the Nazi "New Order," it has disappeared from the face of the earth, but the pre-World War I Krupps, Thyssens and other big business families and even the Hohenzollerns and other members of the Junker nobility remain in their positions of authority.

Instead of the vaunted efficiency of the managerial society that was to have developed out of capitalism, after a prolonged period of postwar prosperity, maintained, as in Oceania, by an enormous military budget, the classic problems of capitalism have reemerged: unemployment, inflation, labor unrest, and intensified competition between the capitalist states, to say nothing of the depletion of energy-producing and other natural resources, ravaged by the anarchic pursuit of profit. For the "continuous war" waged by the United States against the Soviet Union and China—in the form of the cold war and of the hot war against North Korea and the Democratic Republic of Vietnam—did not solve its problems, as it did in the world of *1984*; they were submerged, only to surface at a later point. In the meantime, just as in *1984*, armaments research and armaments production goes on, even though each side has in the hydrogen bomb a weapon capable of annihilating the other side.

But what is of more interest than the comparison between our world and the world of *1984*, which was not intended as literal prophecy in any case, are Orwell's enduring psychological insights into contemporary society. He presents O'Brien, for instance, as an insane leader of an insane society, and we now know from Khrushchev's revelations that Stalin was quite paranoid at the end. He has O'Brien tell Winston, strapped down in bed, with a white-coated attendant present to obey O'Brien's orders, that he is mentally deranged, but that he will be cured. Just so, Soviet dissidents are declared to be mental cases and are forcibly administered drugs. The "symptoms" of the dissident's mental illness are his actions in challenging the authority of the bureaucracy. "Sanity is statistical" is a saying that holds true in the Soviet Union as well as in Oceania. Again, Winston's feeling for O'Brien—"he was the tormentor, he was the protector, he was the inquisitor, he was the friend" (p. 201)—recalls Bruno Bettelheim's shocking revelation that some of the broken prisoners in the Nazi concentration camps fell in love with their guards.

But the insights of *1984* are applicable to the United States as

well. Erich Fromm in his *The Insane Society* has stated that the
United States is an insane country. He cites such madness as the
state spending billions on armaments but not spending to
"produce houses and other useful and needed things," as its
restricting agricultural productivity to "stabilize the market"
while millions go hungry, and as the churning out by the mass
media, despite our 90 percent literacy level, of "the cheapest
trash, lacking in any sense of reality" and full of "sadistic
phantasies."[32] Paul A. Baran and Paul M. Sweezy cite other
manifestations of what they call "the irrational system": "idle
men and idle machines coexist with deprivation at home and
starvation abroad"; "poverty grows in step with affluence";
"enormous amounts of resources are wasted in frivolous and
often harmful ways."[33] It might also be pointed out that the
insane O'Brien's method of "curing" Winston's supposed madness anticipates the "clockwork orange" behavioral modification
techniques experimented with in some American prisons and the
CIA experiments with drugs on unsuspecting persons.

Instances of American "doublethink" analogous to those of
Oceania abound. An economic system dominated by a few giant
corporations is spoken of as a "free enterprise" system. A society
in which a national minority comprising millions of people found
it necessary to raise the cry "Freedom Now!" is called a "free
society." The expression "the free world" is used for America's
allies and dependents, most of which are dictatorships, just as
"Freedom is Slavery" is the slogan in Oceania. War alliances are
changed almost as quickly and propaganda reversed almost as
abruptly as in *1984*: "Ich bin ein Berliner," proclaimed Kennedy
in Berlin. A shameful war was waged in the name of national
honor, and the most destructive bombing in the history of
humanity was conducted on the pretext of preventing a blood-
bath later. The department which supplied the armaments in this
war against a small peasant country is called the Defense
Department, just as it is called the Ministry of Peace in Oceania.
Deceptive war news and statements sighting "the light at the end
of the tunnel" were constantly issued, as in Oceania. War films
were shown on television during the family dinner hour with the
same callousness as they were shown in Oceania.

But most important of all is the sense of the isolation and
alienation of the individual conveyed through Winston. In his
diary Winston speaks of living in "the age of uniformity" and
"the age of solitude" (p. 27). David Reisman was to give a name
to the people of our age—"the lonely crowd"—indicating that

Winston's plight is only a projection of the plight of many today. Not only is Winston unable to communicate with others. The conditions of his work are alienating. He does his work alone, but the Records Department, only a branch of the Ministry of Truth, is, with its many subsections, in which "swarms of workers [are] engaged in an unimaginable multitude of jobs," a "huge complexity" (p. 38) that is coordinated and directed by anonymous men from on top. "There is no doubt," says George Woodcock, who was a friend of Orwell's, "that [Orwell's] experience at the BBC provided him with the basic raw material that went into the portrayal of the Ministry of Truth and the devising of the propaganda of Newspeak in *Nineteen Eighty-Four*."[34]

About us is the story written. *1984* has greater significance for us than ever.

IV

RUSSIAN REEXAMINATION OF REVOLUTION IN THE "THAW"

Introduction to Section IV

The modernization of society and the extension of education in the postwar Soviet Union produced a new intelligentsia which had, for the more efficient operation of that society, to be given more leeway than hitherto, as had been predicted by Deutscher at a time when the Stalinist dictatorship seemed to other observers to be incapable of abandoning its rigidity.[1] During the brief "thaw" that followed Khrushchev's speech attacking Stalin, intellectuals hoped for genuine freedom of expression. This, however, the bureaucracy could not allow, and it continued a modified, attenuated Stalinism. But the boldest of the Soviet intellectuals questioned the continuing restraints of the bureaucracy, explored the roots of Stalinism, and reexamined the idea of revolution itself. This reexamination, published in *samizdat* and abroad, ranged from a revival of Leninism (Grigorenko, Plyushch, Roy Medvedev) to a rejection of Marxism (Solzhenitsyn, Sakharov, Amalrik). The present economic difficulties of the West, predicted in 1960 by Ernest Mandel,[2] may be expected to affect that reexamination and to cause the West itself to conduct one of its own.

9. Boris Pasternak's 'Doctor Zhivago': The Russian Revolution and The 'Hereditary' Intelligentsia

When Boris Pasternak's *Doctor Zhivago* was published in 1958, it had received one of the greatest publishing buildups in history. The circumstances—the cold war, the internationally known poet who had long been silent, his secret work on the novel over the years, its theme of the free personality opposed to a dictatorial regime, the accidental manner in which an Italian radical publisher acquired the manuscript while it was being considered by a Soviet publishing house, the bungling efforts of the Soviet bureaucracy to suppress it—all of these raised interest in the novel when it appeared to a fever pitch. In this atmosphere critics such as Edmund Wilson, Frank Kermode, and V. S. Pritchett hailed it as, in Wilson's words, "one of the great events in man's literary and moral history."[1]

Despite the extraordinary praise it received, *Doctor Zhivago* is a failure as a novel. A political novel written by an antipolitical poet, it is, moreover, not any better as political commentary than it is as a novel. But before discussing its deficiencies, let us first look at its plot and its themes, preliminary to seeing how Pasternak handled them.

Yura Zhivago is a ten-year-old when we first see him. The son of a wealthy industrialist who has become bankrupt, he lives as a boy after the death of his mother and father at the home of Alexander Gromeko, a university professor. He becomes a physician and a poet and marries Gromeko's daughter, Tania. Shortly after a son is born, Zhivago is drafted to go to war.

At the front he meets Lara, who has gone there to search for her husband, Pasha Antipov, missing in action. With the coming of the revolution, Zhivago returns home to Moscow. He and his wife decide that it would be safer to leave Moscow, and they go to the former estate of Tania's grandfather, who was a wealthy landowner and ironmaster. In town he again meets Lara, whose husband has become a revolutionary army leader under the name of Strelnikov, and has an affair with her.

173

As he is seeking to make up his mind to tell his wife and give up Lara, he is kidnapped by a partisan band to act as its doctor. After a year and a half goes by, he escapes it to find that his family has gone to Moscow. Subsequently he learns that they have been exiled abroad. He lives with Lara and her daughter in the deserted estate where he and Tania had lived before. One day Komarovsky, a business lawyer who seduced Lara when she was a school girl, comes to warn them that they will be apprehended by the government and to offer to spirit them out of the country. By a ruse Zhivago, unwilling to accept this favor himself, gets Lara to go, renouncing her for her sake.

Zhivago returns to Moscow, where he deteriorates greatly. Finally, he dies in 1929 from a heart attack. However, Lara and his half-brother Evgraf gather together his poems and publish them. This is his legacy to his friends and his country.

The idea underlying the novel is that although Zhivago seems to have been so much at the mercy of events and of other men, he and Lara alone truly lived, and his poems and his example tell other men how to live. Pasternak propounds the philosophical doctrine by which he justifies this idea not only through his authorial comments but through many characters, each time clearly signaling to the reader to recognize the character as a voice for the doctrine. In addition to Zhivago, who Pasternak stated in an interview spoke for him,[2] there is Zhivago's Uncle Kolia, whose books greatly influence Zhivago; Lara, who shares Zhivago's thoughts; Sima Tuntseva, who has been influenced by Uncle Kolia and who, says Lara, thinks a good deal like Zhivago; Zhivago's friends Gordon and Dudorov, who at the end become Zhivago's intellectual heirs. Indeed, one of the novel's weaknesses is the presence of such shadowy characters as Uncle Kolia and Sima Tuntseva, who exist solely for the statement of the philosophical doctrine.

The entire universe, Zhivago says, is alive, continually changing and continually renewing itself. "All the time, life, one, immense, identical throughout its innumerable combinations and transformations, fills the universe and is continually reborn."[3] Those people who really live are able to commune with this living universe of which they are a part. They can do so through sensitivity to nature. The countryside, we are told,

was dearer to [Lara] than her kin, better than a lover, wiser than a book. For a moment she rediscovered the purpose of her life. She was here on earth to grasp the meaning of its wild enchantment and to call each thing by its right name, or, if this were not within her power, to give birth out of love for life to successors who would do it in her place. [P. 66]

"To call each thing by its right name"—to sense the rich differentness of things and their interrelations in a marvelously complex and changing universe—is echoed in Pasternak's statement about Zhivago's study of literature, history, and science: "Everything in the world, all the things in it were words in his vocabulary. He felt he was on an equal footing with the universe" (p. 76).

People can also commune with the universe through sexual love.

Never, never, even in their moments of richest and wildest happiness, were [Zhivago and Lara] unaware of a sublime joy in the total design of the universe, a feeling that they themselves were a part of that whole, an element in the beauty of the cosmos. This unity with the whole was the breath of life to them. [P. 417]

Those like Zhivago who are able to enter into such communion with the universe have a gift for life. "Talent," says Zhivago, "in the highest and broadest sense means talent for life" (p. 60). The "pockmarked Caligulas [an anachronistic reference to the pockmarked Stalin?]," says Uncle Kolia (p. 13), "do not suspect how untalented every enslaver is." A "talent for life" is only possible for the "free personality," a conception born in the Christian era (p. 13). "It is possible to be an atheist," says Uncle Kolia (p. 13), ". . . and yet believe . . . that history as we know it began with Christ, and that Christ's Gospel is its foundation." Christ's mother, says Sima, brought forth

the miracle of life, the "universal life," as He was afterwards called. . . . Something in the world had changed. . . . The duty, imposed by armed force, to live unanimously as a people, as a whole nation, was abolished. Leaders and nations were relegated to the past. They were replaced by the doctrine of individuality and freedom. Individual human life became the life story of God, and its contents filled the past expanses of the universe. [P. 343]

It is on the basis of this philosophical doctrine that the revolution is first hailed by Zhivago and then condemned. Zhivago during the wonderful summer of 1917, when "Mother Russia" was "on the move," thought that everyone and everything was being "revived, reborn, changed, transformed" (p. 124), but he became bitterly disappointed. Marxism, he came to feel, detaches man from the "universal life," giving him a false eminence. "The elevation of man above the rest of nature, the modern coddling and worshipping of man, never appealed to [Zhivago and Lara]. A social system based on such a false premise, as well as its political application, struck them as pathetically amateurish . . ." (p. 417).

Zhivago keeps saying that he does not know much about either politics or Marxism, but this does not prevent him from rejecting both. Revolutionists, he says, have never truly been in touch with life. They talk of building the future, but "man is born to live, not to prepare for life" (p. 248).

> Reshaping life! People who can say that have never understood a thing about life—they have never felt its breath, its heartbeat . . . They look on it as a lump of raw material . . . But life is never a material, a substance to be molded. If you want to know, life is the principle of self-renewal, it is constantly renewing and remaking and changing and transfiguring itself. [P. 282]

Marxists seek to impose an abstract doctrine on living reality. They are themselves robots, lacking the vital force which would enable them to enter into the life of the universe and failing to perceive the life of the society whose evolution they would disturb. "Revolutionaries," says Zhivago, ". . . are like machines that have got out of control, like runaway trains." History, he reflects, is, like nature, organic. "The forest does not change its place, we cannot lie in wait for it and catch it in the act of change. . . . And such also is the immobility to our eyes of the eternally growing, ceaselessly changing history, the life of society moving invisibly in its incessant transformations" (p. 378). But such is not the change forced upon society by revolutionists, "fanatical men of action with one-track minds," locomotives capable of moving only in a single direction, smashing through the forest of history. "All customs and traditions," says Lara, "all our way of life, everything to do with home and order, has crumbled into dust in the general upheaval and reorganization of society. The whole human way of life has been destroyed and ruined" (p. 335).

Yet Pasternak's attitude toward the revolution is more complicated and indeed self-contradictory than has been generally understood. Sima says that in gains for the workers and women against "the power of money," "our revolutionary era is a wonderful, unforgettable era of new, permanent achievements," but she condemns its "interpretation of life" and "philosophy of happiness" (pp. 343-44). Moreover, the revolution was, after all, a part of history. It is equated with the snowstorm that sweeps about Zhivago as he buys the extra announcing the establishment of the dictatorship of the proletariat: "There was something in common between the disturbances in the moral and in the physical world" (p. 162). Storms are natural phenomena which one must endure in the expectation of fair weather. In his musing on the organic character of history, just before he tells himself that revolutionists are men with one-track minds, Zhivago thinks, "Wars and revolutions, kings and Robespierres, are history's organic agents, its yeasts" (p. 378). For this moment revolution is regarded not as mechanical, after all, but organic!

And in the epilogue, when Dudorov and Gordon are talking together during the Second World War, Dudorov says:

The war came as a breath of fresh air, a purifying storm, a breath of deliverance. . . . Its real horrors, its real dangers, its menace of real death were a blessing compared with the inhuman reign of the lie. . . . The war has its special character as a link in the chain of revolutionary decades. The forces directly unleashed by the revolution no longer operated. The indirect effects of the revolution, the fruit of its fruit, the consequences of the consequences, began to manifest themselves. Misfortune and ordeals had tempered characters, prepared them for great, desperate, heroic exploits. [P. 422]

Again, the revolution is conceived of as organic—the heroic resistance of the Russian people is "the fruit of its fruit." And at the conclusion, when Dudorov and Gordon meet again some time after the war, this organic development is seen as promising freedom: "Although victory had not brought the relief and freedom that were expected at the end of the war, nevertheless the portents of freedom filled the air throughout the postwar period" (pp. 431-32). At the price of some self-contradiction Pasternak voices his philosophy of cosmic optimism and of wise passivity: spring comes after winter, not as a result of human exertion but because it is in the nature of things for it to do so.

Pasternak's philosophic doctrine is the doctrine of romantic idealism of the poets and philosophers of the early nineteenth century, particularly the Germans, with whom he probably became acquainted during his study of philosophy in Germany at the University of Marburg in 1912. His ideas of the "free personality," the wisdom to be derived from the communion with nature, the superiority of the organic over the mechanic, the superiority of the individual and the particular over the abstract and the general, the rich differentness and the interrelatedness of things in a wonderfully complex and continuously growing universe, wise passivity in a world of change, the organic character of history, and the need to observe custom and tradition closely follow the ideas of this school.

John Herman Randall, Jr., points out that the "emphasis on the continuity of tradition" became "a potent instrument of reaction," especially in Germany, in the hands of "conservatives shocked by the spirit of the Enlightenment enforced by revolutionary assemblies."[4] So too Ernst Fischer comments:

> The [German] Romantic idealization of everything "organic," everything that had grown or taken form "naturally," became a reactionary protest against the outcome of the [French] revolution: the old social classes and relationships were regarded as "organic," the movements and conditions created by the new classes as wickedly "mechanical."[5]

An English radical romanticist such as William Hazlitt could, however, use the natural-mechanical opposition to describe the salutary effect of the French revolution upon English poetry, as Pasternak on occasion presents the Russian revolution as an organic development, not a mechanical imposition. The "sentiments and opinions which produced [the French] revolution," he says in *Lectures on the English Poets,* gave an "impulse" to English poetry, which had become "mechanical . . . in the hands of the followers of Pope," acting to "stir it up" and make poets look for what was "natural and new."[6]

Pasternak himself attacked romanticism in *Safe Conduct,* but he was referring to the romantic rebelliousness of the life-style and the poetic style of Mayakovsky and Essenin, as the later Wordsworth objected to the rebel romanticist Byron. In fact, Wordsworth offers many striking parallels to Pasternak. Intoxicated initially by the French revolution, he sharply reacted against it afterwards, denouncing "systems built on abstract rights" and "upstart Theory" and exalting "the vital power of social ties / Endeared by Custom."[7] Like Zhivago, he regarded it as the function of the poet, "who rejoices more than other men in the spirit of life that is in him,"[8] to communicate the wonder and joy of life. Like Lara, he found "more of wisdom" in nature than in "books."⁹ Like Lara, who was for Zhivago "the inarticulate principle of existence" become "sensitive and capable of speech" (p. 325), even when she was performing the most mundane household chores, the young woman whom he describes in "She Was a Phantom of Delight" was for him "a spirit, yet a woman too," with "household motions light and free." Like Pasternak, he deplored "what man has made of man"¹⁰ but, feeling "a sense sublime" of a "motion and a spirit, that impells/All thinking things, all objects of all thought," retained his optimistic faith that "Nature never did betray/The heart that loved her," that "'tis her privilege/Through all the years of this our life, to lead/From joy to joy."¹¹ And, like Pasternak, he published a work—*The Excursion*—which he regarded as his crowning achievement but which, written in a form alien to his talent, was an inferior production.

The virtues of *Doctor Zhivago* are the characteristic romantic virtues—beautiful descriptions of nature, lyrical intensity, concrete detail of ordinary everyday life, which makes one experience the turmoil of the years of the revolution and the civil war; its defects are the characteristic romantic defects—weakness of structure, deficiency of characterization, feebleness of dramatization. The lyrical intensity, which reaches its peak in the chapter where Zhivago and Lara are alone on the great estate, happy in each other but aware of the dangers outside, and the nature description are illustrated in this paragraph in that chapter:

> The stillness that surrounded Yurii Andreievich breathed with happiness and life. . . . Outside, the frosty winter night was pale blue. To see it better, Yurii Andreievich stepped in the next room, cold and dark, and looked out of the window. The light of the full moon on the snow-covered clearing was as viscid as white of egg or thick white paint. His heart was at peace. He went back into the warm well-lit room and began to write. [P. 363]

The use of concrete detail of everyday experience is illustrated by the household tasks which Zhivago and Lara have to perform on the estate, the description of which gives a realistic underpinning to the lyricism.

However, scattered lyrical passages do not make a novel. The Russian émigré critic William Weidle in a 1928 essay reprinted in Donald Davie's and Angela Livingstone's anthology of Pasternak criticism wrote:

In poetry as in prose the only thing he can do is to point to things. Thus it is not surprising that the elements of plan, structure and unity in his work are so weak, and so forced, which is really the same thing. . . . Pasternak's still unfinished novel in verse, *Spektorsky,* is unlikely to be held together by anything more than a plot that artificially couples unequal fragments.[12]

This is entirely true of *Doctor Zhivago,* which is "held together" by the "forced" coincidences of its plot. Each chapter is made up of numbered sections, like the stanzas of a poem, which constitute vignettes, bald summaries (often substituting for necessary dramatization of character development or conflict), and extended conversations or monologues. Sometimes there is an interval of years between two sections, sometimes no time interval at all. The narrative proceeds by bumps and jolts over the "unequal fragments" of the sections. Pasternak himself told an interviewer that "the novel had been built around its lyrical passages and that it had been difficult for him to join them in narrative sequence."[13] It shows.

The plot which yokes these sections together is full of extraordinary coincidences, too numerous and pervasive to recount, over which the author and his characters constantly exclaim. The rationale for such coincidences was given by Pasternak in a letter to Stephen Spender:

The nineteenth century applied the incontestable doctrine of causality, the belief that the objectivity was determined and ruled by an iron chain of causes and effects. . . . There is an effort in the novel to represent the whole sequence of facts and beings and happenings like some moving entireness, like a developing, passing by, rolling and rushing inspiration, as if reality itself had freedom and choice and was comprising itself out of numberless variants and versions. . . . Hence the frank arbitrariness of the "coincidences" (through this means I wanted to show the liberty of being, its verisimilitude touching, adjoining improbability).[14]

The point of the coincidences, then, is that in this wonderful world of ours there is no "iron chain of causes and effects" and just about anything can happen. Whereas for Malraux the unpredictability of the universe is reason for anguish and for Mailer it is reason for hopelessness, for Pasternak it is reason for a joyous acceptance of life.

Pasternak is not consistent, however, in his comments on the coincidences. In the novel Lara and others often remark of a coincidence that it must be a result of predestination. Thus she exclaims when she discovers that the same Komarovsky who seduced her swindled Zhivago's father and instigated him to commit suicide: "It isn't possible! It's extraordinary! Can it really be true? So he was your evil genius, too! It brings us even closer! It must be predestination!" (p. 333). This and other coincidences are, it seems therefore, not to be attributed to "the liberty of being," the chance results of the freedom of choice of "reality itself," but to an unseen vast design.

At the beginning of the novel we are told that the passengers on the train from which Zhivago's father jumped are part of the "general stream of life which united them all" and are governed by a "higher sense" that teaches them that "all human lives were interrelated, a certainty that they flowed into each other" (p. 15). This "higher sense" is justified by the fact that on the train, besides Komarovsky, are the boy Misha Gordon, who will later meet Zhivago and become his friend, and Tiverzina, whose son will also play a role in the lives of Zhivago and Lara. Moreover, watching the train from a distance and not knowing that the reason it has stopped is that the old Zhivago has just jumped off it, is his brother-in-law Uncle Kolia, visiting on the estate of Kologrivov, who is later to be a benefactor to Lara. At the very same moment the ten-year-old Yura, praying for the soul of his dead mother, forgets to pray for his father, as his mother had instructed him to do, and decides to let it go for another time, not knowing that his father has just committed suicide. These relationships, in which lives flow into each other, would seem intended to give the impression of design, not chance, as rivers join each other by following their set courses, not by "rolling and rushing" along every which way.

At the conclusion of the novel, however, the coincidence attendant upon the death of Zhivago would seem to suggest chance, not design. Zhivago is on a trolley that keeps breaking down. He notices an old lady whose course is parallel to that of the trolley. Each time the trolley stops, she overtakes it, and then the trolley, temporarily set right, in turn passes her. Zhivago

> tried to imagine several people whose lives run parallel and close together but move at different speeds, and he wondered in what circumstances some of them would overtake and survive others. Something like a theory of relativity governing the hippodrome of life occurred to him. [P. 408]

Here individual lives are conceived of not as rivers joining each other but as racehorses and their riders proceeding in parallel lines on a broad track, intermittently coming close to each other but never joining. It is a race in which one never knows who will overtake the other. Zhivago has a heart attack, breaks through the crowd on the trolley, and collapses in death on the sidewalk. The old lady, Mademoiselle Fleury, the former keeper of a boardinghouse in which Zhivago had stayed, whom Zhivago had not recognized and who does not recognize him, stops only briefly to look at the corpse surrounded by a crowd. "So she walked on, overtaking the trolley for the tenth time and quite unaware that she had overtaken Zhivago and survived him" (p. 409). We do not know the people against whose lives our own lives brush in random encounter.

But whether we are to think of the coincidences as exhibiting the wonderfully strange possibilities of life or as a wonderfully complicated design of which we catch glimpses, they do not work. When we get repeated coincidences over which the characters exclaim or which the novelist presents with a flourish, none of them hits us with a jolt and, in fact, we get to anticipate them. Thus when we are told that Zhivago, on his return to Moscow, was accompanied everywhere by a good-looking young peasant boy, with the author asking rhetorically "Who was his young companion?" (p. 388), we immediately start to review mentally the people whom Zhivago met in the course of his travels, knowing full well that it must be one of them. When in the epilogue Dudorov says of Tania, the laundry girl, "Have you noticed the way Tania smiles, all over her face, like Yurii? You forget the snub nose and the high cheekbones, and you think she's quite pretty and attractive. It's the same type, you see it all over Russia" (p. 423), we immediately infer that Tania has Zhivago's snub nose and smile because she is his daughter by Lara, born unknown to him. The living universe of which Zhivago speaks, ever-changing and full of surprises, becomes, ironically, predictable, mechanical.

We may compare Pasternak's failure with the "prosy" Bennett's conveyance of the sense of the inexhaustibility of life. The last book of *The Old Wives' Tale* is entitled "What Life Is." Arnold Kettle has condemned this title as a dogmatic assertion that Sophia's thoughts concerning her wasted life and the futility of all life as she contemplates Gerald's dead body is the final word on human existence.[15] But later in the book we are told of Constance, "When she surveyed her life, and life in general, she would think, with a sort of tart but not sour cheerfulness: *'Well, that is what life is!'*" (p. 609). The two sisters' different views of life just before their respective deaths are the outcomes of their different experiences. Neither is represented as having the ultimate answer to "the riddle of life" (p. 573). It is one of the ironies of the novel that both Constance and Sophia from the time they are sixteen and fifteen—"when, if one is frank, one must admit one has nothing to learn: one has learnt everything in the previous six months" (p. 8)—keep thinking that now they have learned all there is to know. Constance, sleeping with Samuel in the same bed in which her father and mother had slept, in which her father had died, and which her mother had left to live apart, broken by grief, "esteemed that she knew what life was" (p. 51), but when she becomes a widow twenty years later she thinks back upon the "naive ignorance of life" (p. 255) of Samuel and herself when they were married. Sophia in the glittering Parisian restaurant to which Gerald takes her after they are married is conscious "that she was no longer a virgin, but the equal in knowledge of any woman alive" (p. 310); but when she is being nursed back to life by Madame Foucault, the now decayed courtesan who had overawed her in the restaurant (Bennett has his own unobtrusive coincidences), she regards herself as having been "ingenuous and ignorant" at the time (p. 378). Such ironies are far more suggestive concerning the constant unfolding of new knowledge and experience in life than Pasternak's rhapsodic utterances and philosophical disquisitions about life's wonderful unpredictability and strange coincidences.

So too does Pasternak fail in characterization. The characters of this author who believes in a living universe do not for the most part come alive. Andrei Sinyavsky, the Soviet critic later imprisoned and then exiled for his dissidence, says in his sensitive introduction to Pasternak's poetry that Pasternak is not concerned with characterization in his long narrative poems of the 1920s, so much so that in *Spektorsky* "even the person whose name is the title of the poem is really of little interest to us."[16] In a historical novel such as *Doctor Zhivago* this is disastrous.

Pasternak himself said that the lack of individualization of his characters was purposeful. "I purposely did not fully characterize the people in the book," he told Ralph E. Matlow. "For I wanted to get away from the idea of causality."[17] In this ever-changing universe people's characters do not remain the same. Here too, however, Pasternak is not consistent. In an authorial comment in *Doctor Zhivago* he speaks of the "archetype that is formed in every child for life and seems for ever after to be his inward face, his personality" (pp. 286-87). People, then, are now said to have an essential personality despite the changes they undergo.

But the characters in Pasternak's novel do not change while retaining a central core of personality. Instead, they undergo complete transformations, the reasons for which are unexplained. "Human nature, and particularly woman's," Zhivago tells Lara (p. 333), "is so mysterious and so full of contradictions." But Pasternak does not show these contradictions resolved into any kind of unity, and, unlike Bennett, he does not show them in conflict within his characters so that we can follow their evolution. Moreover, their traits are all too often stated, not dramatized. In none of their metamorphoses do they come across clearly and distinctly. What we have instead are blurred shadows constantly changing in shape. But we cannot become interested in a blur.

An example is Nika Dudorov. We are introduced to him when he is fourteen years old, and the author comments (p. 19), "He was a strange boy. When he was excited he talked aloud to himself, imitating his mother's predilection for lofty subjects and paradox." He has a secret inner life, hiding to be alone to pursue it. The next we see him he is in the yard neighboring Lara's, participating in the workers' 1905 uprising. He is now described as "proud, straightforward, taciturn" (p. 45). The adjectives are tossed out without any attempt to reconcile this boy with the strange, secretive, excitable boy we had previously seen.

When Zhivago returns from the front, Dudorov is a guest at a party given by the Zhivagos. He is now presented as rather comical, a subject of humorous story-telling among his friends. He had been drafted into the army by mistake, was constantly punished for absentmindedly forgetting to salute officers, and then after being discharged would raise his arm automatically whenever he saw an officer. During this period he proposed to a young woman at first sight and was divorced within a year. But he shows up at the party with a new personality. "Like Gordon, he had become the opposite of what he had been. He had always been flippant and featherbrained; now he was a serious scholar" (pp. 148-49). He talks to people as if he is delivering a lecture and addresses his childhood friend Zhivago in a formal manner. Not only is the change in him unexplained but we have never seen him as the "flippant and featherbrained" person he is said to have "always" been!

Dudorov's next appearance occurs when Zhivago returns to Moscow, having lost Lara. He and Gordon are now represented as being unable to "carry on a conversation naturally and intelligently." "At a loss for words, they . . . gesticulated and repeated themselves" (p. 400). This is the man who talked excitedly in paradox as an adolescent and spoke fluently, albeit with pedantic solemnity, at a later period. Zhivago now finds that his lifelong friend, whose adolescent musings resembled his own near-pantheistic belief ("How wonderful to be alive . . . God exists, of course. But if He exists, then it's me" [p. 19]), exhibits "intellectual poverty" (p. 400). It is not explained why the harmless pedant we saw last should have been imprisoned for political reasons, but so he was, and he speaks sincerely of having been politically reeducated, sickening Zhivago with his love for his own bondage.

When we next see Dudorov in 1943, we learn that the former clown, the former pedant, the former intellectual robot has been in the worst of the penal camps of the Soviet Union, evidently for political dissidence. How did he come to throw off his bonds? We are not told. Having lost his tonguetiedness, he speaks eloquently of "the inhuman reign of the lie" (p. 422).

Finally, he and Gordon are presented as the disciples who are faithful to the gospel of Zhivago's book of poetry which they "almost knew by heart" and about which they "read and talked and thought" as they look out upon Moscow at the close of the novel (p. 431). These two men, of whom Zhivago once thought (p. 400), "how desperately commonplace you are," now are the only ones who perceive the historical significance of the portents of freedom of the postwar period.

An analysis of Gordon would show similar contradictions. But these contradictions are not confined to the minor characters. Pasha Antipov, when we first see him as a boy, is described as "gay and sociable," with "a great sense of humor" (p. 33). Later, he is described as having been a "shy, mischievous, and girlish child" (p. 98). The "shy" does not jibe with the "gay and sociable" of the previous description, in which, furthermore, there had been no hint of effeminacy.

When the war is over, Pasha does not return to Lara and his daughter, whom he loves dearly, but becomes a Red Army leader in the civil war. He, who had a "malleable, easygoing character" (p. 46) as an adolescent, now has a more commanding personality than anyone Zhivago has ever encountered and is "entirely a manifestation of the will" (p. 208). Although he is a man of honor and integrity, in his absolute dedication to his principles he is ruthless.

How did this transformation occur? We are told only that "his fanaticism was . . . a natural consequence of all his previous life" (p. 209). So there is causality in character development, after all—but it is unexplained. Pasha was the son of a revolutionary worker, but in his first appearance in the novel he mimics the droning voice of a radical orator for the amusement of Tiverzin's old mother, who is scornful of the radicals. He and Dudorov participate in the street fighting in 1905, but we are told that for them it was really a boyish game. As a student, Pasha, a poor boy trying to make good, pays attention only to his studies and does not participate in any radical activities. We are not shown him repressing any sense of social injustice. As a teacher, he is concerned only with his academic career. Just before he commits suicide, he tells Zhivago that Lara, wronged by Komarovsky, representative of all that was bad in the old society, was for him "a living indictment of the age" (p. 384), but we are never shown him burning with indignation. On the contrary, on the one occasion we are admitted into his thoughts, when he decides to enlist in the army during the war, he does so because he believes that Lara does not love him and is not even sure if he loves her. He does not for a moment in his brooding think of her wrongs or of avenging them against society.

Although Lara and Zhivago are much more logically drawn characters (causality operates for them at any rate), they only fitfully come to life, and there are puzzling questions of characterization with them too. Zhivago at one point tells Lara, "Perhaps there is something in your loathing that keeps you in subjection to [Komarovsky] more than to any man whom you love of your own free will, without compulsion. . . . Someday he will take you away, just as certainly as death will someday separate us" (p. 333). Sure enough, after Lara leaves with Komarovsky, thanks to Zhivago's deceiving her into believing he will follow, she becomes once more Komarovsky's mistress. The fascination Komarovsky holds for her, however, never becomes real, and we do not see the process by which she is subjected to him. And we wonder how Zhivago, possessed of this insight, ever concurred in the deception of Lara.

In his portrayal of the revolution Pasternak is as muddled and confused as in his portrayal of character. Like the changes in individuals, the revolution is a transformation of society without explanation. "It's petty to explore causes of titanic events. They haven't any," says Zhivago of the revolution in his first amazement at its sweep and grandeur. "What is truly great is without beginning, like the universe" (p. 153).

After Zhivago's first flush of enthusiasm, the revolution is presented not as a "marvel of history," a "revelation" (p. 164), but as a cataclysm bringing everything down before it. Pasternak graphically depicts how ordinary life was turned upside down, but we don't see the forces at work that have caused this. As Isaac Deutscher says, "We are hardly able to guess that Moscow [during the months of Zhivago's stay in it] is already being cut off by the Whites from food and fuel bases in the south: and so famine and chaos appear as the results of an apocalyptic breakdown of moral standards."[18] We may add that there is no indication at all that the civil war with all its horrors might have been averted, given the overwhelming defeat of the old ruling classes; only the military intervention and aid of fourteen nations, headed by Britain and the United States, enabled the Whites to keep on fighting. So does a lack of exploration of the causes of titanic events distort history!

Deutscher also points out that

in the years 1918-1921 Zhivago and Lara are already revolted by the tyranny of the monolithic regime which in fact was not formed until a decade later. . . . The "forced enthusiasms," the deadly uniformity in art and science, the "singing of the same tune in chorus," and the degradation of Marxism to an infallible Church—all this fits the fully-fledged Stalin era but not the years in which these words are spoken. Those were years of *Sturm und Drang,* of bold intellectual and artistic experimentation in Russia, and of almost permanent public controversy within the Bolshevik camp.[19]

We may sympathize with Pasternak in his description of Zhivago's distress in these circumstances (characteristically, his greatest distress is his aesthetic repulsion by the turgid prose to which he is subjected), realizing how it expresses his feelings under Stalinism, but in projecting these feelings back to the years of the revolution he is presenting a false picture.

The fact is that Pasternak himself did not have at the time the sentiments he attributes to Zhivago, his literary alter ego. Robert Payne, who had the advantage of conversations about Pasternak with Pasternak's friend, the poet Anna Akhmatova, says in *The Three Worlds of Boris Pasternak*:

He was elated by the excitement of the revolution, he sympathized with the aim of the revolutionaries, and in the twenties he was prepared to place his poetry at the service of the revolution, characteristically celebrating the triumphs of the Bolsheviks by writing poems to the revolutionaries of another age. By 1926 or 1927 he was already disenchanted.[20]

From the fact that *The Lofty Malady,* one of his epic poems of the 1920s, received its last revisions in 1928 and was published in 1929, we can perhaps infer that the disenchantment came somewhat later. For *The Lofty Malady* concludes with some stanzas about Lenin which, Sinyavsky says, "recreate the irrepressible energy of Lenin's thought and belong among the best depictions of him in Soviet literature."[21] They contain the lines: "He was like the thrust of a rapier, / Hunting for the last spoken word. / But the curve of his body breathed / With the soaring flight of the bare essential/As it tears through a senseless layer of lies."[22] How far different this is from Zhivago's statement during the civil war period: "The men in power . . . are so anxious to establish the myth of their infallibility that they do their utmost to ignore the truth. Politics doesn't appeal to me. I don't like people who don't care about the truth"! (p. 216).

"I too think that Russia is destined to become the first socialist state since the beginning of the world" (pp. 153-54), says Zhivago in his inspired speech to his dinner guests just before the October revolution. "When this comes to pass, the event will stun us for a long time, and after awakening we shall have lost half our memories forever. We'll have forgotten what came first and what followed, and we won't look for causes." No doubt something like this happened to Pasternak's memory of the first years of the revolution—a poet's impressions, not a political thinker's analysis—when he awoke from his enchantment with the revolution to a new view of it. "Life around us is ever changing," he told Olga Carlisle in 1960, "and I believe that one should try to change one's slant accordingly—at least once every ten years. The great heroic devotion to one point of view is very alien to me—it's a lack of humility."[23] But Pasternak's change of vantage-point only confused his view.

Borne along by the mighty force of the revolution, Pasternak had been a "fellow traveler" before he fell silent in the 1930s. The reversals, circlings, and zigzags of the revolution in the Stalin era, however, threw overboard this basically antipolitical poet. The Soviet critic A. Lezhnev in a 1927 essay characterized Pasternak as a "spokesman of the highly cultured summit of the intelligentsia, the 'hereditary' intelligentsia, on which the ruling class has set its indelible stamp" but which "considerably surpasses the bourgeoisie in respect of culture" so that "its representatives often regard the bourgeoisie with disdain," "intelligent, talented, fine-feeling people, certainly not indifferent and certainly not egoists, but limiting their world to love and art."[24] He noted that "Pasternak has been trying to break out from the chamber-music quality of his poetry" to "a social orientation" but that this is very difficult for anyone, especially for someone like Pasternak, "a poet who is honest to the end, who can either write one hundred per cent sincerely, or else not write at all."[25] Pasternak, unable to follow his new path to the end, chose not to write at all and retraced his steps to work in secret on *Doctor Zhivago*, an apologia for the "hereditary," materially secure intelligentsia, which retained the stamp of the bourgeoisie but regarded it with disdain.

"We Gromekos lost our acquisitive passion a generation ago," says Zhivago's father-in-law (p. 203), with whom Zhivago is very close. Gromeko and Zhivago are not at all like the swindling Komarovsky, intent only on his material and sensual gratification. Indeed, although *Doctor Zhivago* is, as Pasternak himself said, not the highly symbolic novel some of its critics made it out to be, something like a parable emerges from it: Lara, Mother Russia ("And what was [Lara] to [Zhivago] . . .? . . . Russia, his incomparable mother . . . martyred, stubborn, extravagant, crazy, irresponsible, adored Russia") (p. 325), violated by Komarovsky (the old order), makes a mistaken marriage to Antipov-Strelnikov (the revolution) but in a liaison with Zhivago (the liberal, humanistic old intelligentsia) has a daughter (the child of "Russia's terrible years") (p. 431), who will be looked after and educated by Zhivago's half-brother Evgraf (the perpetuator of Zhivago's ideas).

Gromeko and Zhivago are sympathetic to progress, decent, kind, and humane. "You must be frozen" (p. 55), says Gromeko solicitously to the coachman who has been waiting for him a long time. Similarly, Zhivago, back from the front, is magnanimous, telling the ingratiating porter, who has come running to "welcome the young master," "How are you, Markel? Let's embrace. Put your cap on, you eccentric" (p. 142). When the nursemaid, Niusha, "greeting him respectfully" (p. 146), offers to help him carry his wicker hamper upstairs, he thanks her, saying that he can manage.

The family accepts the new times cheerfully. When Markel speaks derogatorily of the Bolshevik government, Tania tells Zhivago, "He's talking like that only because he thinks you like it," and, addressing Markel, says, "Time you were sensible. After all, you know what kind of people we are" (p. 142). She informs Zhivago that "only" the housekeeper and the nursemaid—she forgets to mention Markel—remain, the other servants having had to be discharged. When she goes on to say that she has let the Agricultural Academy have some of the rooms of their house, it being too expensive to heat in the winter anyway, Zhivago replies, "There really was something unhealthy in the way rich people used to live. Masses of superfluous things. . . . I'm very glad we're using fewer rooms. We should give up still more" (p. 143). Other doctors leave the hospital after it comes under Bolshevik administration because the pay is not good enough, saying superciliously to Zhivago, "So you're working for *them?*" but he replies, "I am proud of our privations and I respect those who honor us by imposing them on us" (p. 166). And even after Zhivago and Gromeko have internally broken with the revolution, Gromeko says, "Their philosophy is alien to me, their regime is hostile to us, I have not been asked if I consent to all this change. But I have been trusted, and my own actions, even if they were not freely chosen, put me under a certain obligation" (p. 202).

Yet Pasternak unconsciously shows the limits of their progressivism. Observing the war-weary soldiers whom a Kerensky army commissar is trying to persuade to perform their "soldierly duty," Zhivago reflects, "Four months of wooing by the Left and Right had corrupted these unsophisticated men" (p. 129). The political debate by which the Bolsheviks won the soldiers to their side is regarded by him as a process of corruption! "Unsophisticated men," it seems, are not supposed to think. This is the opinion of one who, although not arrogant in his behavior, considers himself in the romantic manner as a unique individual and thinks little of the common person.

Although Pasternak says of Zhivago "the originality of his vision was remarkable" (p. 57) (he is opposed to Strelnikov, who has "brilliance" but not "originality" [p. 208]), he and Gromeko do not have the capacity to transcend the society to which they have been accustomed. Gromeko may have been solicitous toward his coachman, but he never questioned—let alone, did anything about—a social system which permitted the privileged few to have an entourage of servants who waited humbly on them. Zhivago may have been "democratic" in his manner with Markel, but the cheap irony of the statement that Markel told people that the Gromekos and the Zhivagos had "kept him in ignorance all these years and deliberately concealed from him that man is descended from apes" (p. 179) shows how far the author and his hero are from appreciating that a position of subservience fosters resentment as well as obsequiousness.

Zhivago feels guilty at the party he gives on his Moscow homecoming that none of his bourgeois neighbors has the good fortune of being able, as he is, to provide wild duck and vodka.

> Their party was a kind of betrayal. You could not imagine anyone in the houses across the street eating or drinking in the same way at the same time. Beyond the windows lay silent, dark, hungry Moscow. Its shops were empty, and as for game and vodka, people had even forgotten to think about such things. [P. 148]

And how about those who had never dined on wild duck in the past and who had drunk the cheapest vodka in squalor to induce forgetfulness, not on festive occasions to heighten conviviality? Zhivago is not shown to have been stricken with guilt at that thought before the revolution. Certainly, if he had, he had done nothing about it.

The first of Zhivago's poems, "Hamlet," is a justification of his passivity. "Hamlet," said Pasternak in his essay on translating Shakespeare, "gives up his will in order to 'do the will of him that sent him.'"[26] *Hamlet* is not the drama of a man who lacks character but a drama of duty and self-renunciation. In Zhivago's poem the speaker is a person in whom three figures are superimposed on each other: Hamlet, the actor playing Hamlet, nerving himself to step on the stage, knowing that in the darkness a thousand binoculars are trained upon him, and Christ ("If thou be willing, Abba, Father, / Remove this cup from me" [p. 433]). There is heroism in taking what life has to offer, playing to the end the role that has been allotted to him: "I stand alone. All else is swamped by Pharisaism. / To live life to the end is not a childish task" (p. 433).

Yet in the novel Zhivago, despite the laudations of him by the author and the other characters, does not appear so heroic. "Some are trying to get out, they talk of going south, to the Caucasus, or farther still. I wouldn't want to do that, myself. A grown-up man should share his country's fate," he tells his wife (pp. 143-44) when he comes home—but then he later goes with her to her father's former estate in the Urals. During the October insurrection Uncle Kolia comes bursting in to announce there is fighting in the streets, and there is this passage of seemingly unconscious irony: "'Hurry up, Yura! Put your coat on, let's go. You've got to see it. This is history. This happens once in a lifetime.' But he stayed talking for a couple of hours. Then they had dinner" (p. 160). They never do go out.

Most remarkable of all is an incident that takes place when Zhivago is involuntarily acting as a doctor for the partisan band. They are attacked by a White force made up for the most part of young volunteers from the universities. As the Whites advance across an open field, "their expressive, handsome faces seemed to belong to people of his own kind. . . . With all his heart he wished them success. They belonged to families who were probably akin to him in spirit, in education, in moral discipline and values." He thinks of running out and giving himself up to them, but that would be too dangerous: he would be shot by the partisans, incensed by his betrayal, and by the Whites, ignorant of his intention. Not to defend his life, but "submitting to the order of events" (p. 278), he takes a rifle, although the partisans did not demand his participation, and shoots in the general direction of the advancing Whites. "You had to do what everyone was doing" (p. 279). However, he aims at a tree, taking care to fire only when there is no one in front of his target. "But alas!— however carefully he tried to avoid hitting anyone, every now and then a young attacker would move into his firing line at the crucial moment. Two of them he wounded, and one who fell near the tree seemed to have lost his life" (p. 279). Even after he has wounded someone, he keeps on firing! Although this would not seem to be the author's intention, the incident is an epitome of Zhivago's submission "to the order of events," which brings pain and sorrow to both Tania and Lara, and a revelation of the utter impotence of the well-off intelligentsia, vacillating in its sympathies between the Reds and the Whites.

Even when Zhivago hailed the revolution, he never truly understood it. "Only real greatness," he exclaimed, "can be so unconcerned with timing and opportunity," so unconcerned with waiting for "the old centuries to finish before undertaking to build the new ones" (p. 164). The Bolsheviks' study of previous revolutions and of their own society, the debates about the possibility of a proletarian revolution in Russia, Trotsky's theory of the permanent revolution, Lenin's April theses and his winning the party over to them, the Bolshevik strategy for revolution and their preparation of the actual insurrection, their hope of the revolution spreading to other European countries—all of this is for Zhivago as if it had never been.

Similarly, his view of Marxism as regarding life not as something constantly changing but as inert material to be molded by the social planner is entirely mistaken. Marxism is above everything else a doctrine of evolution. It is only by perceiving the laws of social evolution as they are manifested in his own time that the social planner can make his plans and carry them out. Revolutionists do not, as Lara says of Pasha, sulk at the course of events or quarrel with history; they perceive their place in history and work patiently in time of reaction for the revolutionary morrow. They do not seek to destroy the organic development of history; they preside over the birth of the new order which has been growing within the old one. To be sure, the skill of the obstetrician is not inconsequential.

As for Zhivago's statement that for revolutionists "transitional periods, worlds in the making, are an end in themselves. . . . Man is born to live, not to prepare for life" (p. 248)—how can people live if they are poor, brutalized, and ignorant? The privileges which enabled Zhivago to cultivate his sensibility and become steeped in culture so that he "was drawn, as irresistibly as water funneling downward, to dream, to think, to work out new forms, to create beauty" were held by only a few in tsarist Russia. If a "talent for life" was to become more than the characteristic of a rare few, then there had to be preparation for life.

But those who engaged in this preparation for life were not merely building the future; they were also living. Zhivago, telling of his poetic creativity, says that "he felt himself to be only the occasion, the fulcrum" by which "poetry in its present stage" was raised to "the one to come" (p. 364). While building the future, he was also living and creating. The same is true of the revolutionist.

But while building the future of society as Zhivago was building the future of poetry, the revolutionists lived as Zhivago did not have the inner capability of living—as participants in a common struggle. This sense of solidarity in struggle was well described by Larissa Reisner, in whose honor Pasternak wrote a poem at her death of typhus at the age of thirty-one in 1926. An outstanding figure in the revolution at twenty-one, serving as a military spy, as a political commissar, and as a journalist, she was present at the stand at the legendary Svyazhsk, of which she wrote:

Brotherhood! Few words have been so abused and rendered pitiful. But brotherhood does come sometimes, in moments of direst need and peril, so selfless, so sacred, so unrepeatable in a single lifetime. And they have not lived and know nothing of life who have never lain at night on a floor in tattered and lice-ridden clothes, thinking all the while how wonderful is the world, infinitely wonderful! That here the old has been overthrown and that life is fighting with bare hands for her irrefutable truth, for the white swans of her resurrection, for something far bigger and better than this patch of star-lit sky showing through the velvet blackness of a window with shattered panes—for the future of all mankind. . . . Everybody, including the cowardly and the nervous and the simply mediocre workers and Red Army men—everybody, without a single exception, performed unbelievable, heroic deeds; they outdid themselves, like spring streams overflowing their banks they joyfully flooded their own normal levels.[27]

It is interesting that so many of the themes, symbols, and images of *Doctor Zhivago* are present in this quotation: the wonder of life, resurrection, the window as an opening upon freedom and life, the spring streams. But the topic of the quotation—fraternity in struggle—is alien to Zhivago. In this respect, for all of his vaunted "talent for life," he was one of those who "have not lived and know nothing of life."

10. Alexander Solzhenitsyn's 'Cancer Ward': The Betrayal of the Russian Revolution

Thanks to *The Gulag Archipelago*, his various letters, and his Harvard commencement address, Alexander Solzhenitsyn's present political position is well known.[1] He is a strongly anti-Bolshevik Great Russian nationalist of Russian Orthodox faith who believes that Marxism is the chief source of the world's evil. What he advocates for the Soviet Union is a benevolently authoritarian regime that would return Russia to religion and decentralize it on a predominantly agricultural basis.[2]

Many have inferred that he came to his present beliefs during his eight years in Stalinist labor camps.[3] *Cancer Ward* shows him, however, in transition from his previous Leninism to his present position. Solzhenitsyn himself, to be sure, in appearing before the secretariat of the Board of the Union of Soviet Writers in September 1967 to urge its publication, denied that it was in any way a criticism of Soviet society. The title, he alleged, is not "some kind of symbol," as it was charged with being. "The fact is that the subject is specifically and literally cancer."[4]

> Moreover, [he continued,] it is not the task of the writer to defend or criticize one or another mode of distributing the social product, or to defend or criticize one or another form of governmental organization. The task of the writer is to select more universal and eternal questions, the secrets of the human heart and conscience, the confrontation of life with death, the triumph over spiritual sorrow.[5]

It is not minimizing Solzhenitsyn's extraordinary courage in fighting the Soviet bureaucracy to say that on this occasion he engaged in rather disingenuous temporizing. Of course, the novel is not an elaborate allegory and gives a most realistic description of a cancer ward with patients afflicted by different kinds of cancer; but the ward, containing persons of all classes and nationalities, becomes a microcosm of Soviet society sickened by the bureaucratic parasitic growth upon it. The protagonist, Oleg

Kostoglotov, even makes an explicit analogy between the ills of Soviet society and cancer: "A man dies from a tumor, so how can a country survive with growths like labor camps and exiles?"[6] Of course, Solzhenitsyn is concerned in his novel with "universal and eternal questions," but these questions are raised in the context of Soviet society, and the way in which they are dealt with has the deepest implications for that society.

More in keeping with Solzhenitsyn's view of the social duty of the artist was his statement to a Czech journalist, Pavel Licko, in March 1967: "A writer is able to discover far earlier than other people aspects of social life. . . . It is incumbent upon the writer to inform society of all that he is able to perceive and especially all that is unhealthy."[7]

In 1969 at a meeting of writers he quoted Tolstoy as saying "The disease that we are suffering from is the murdering of people. . . . If we could recall the past and look it straight in the face—the violence we are now committing would be revealed"[8] and related this to the need for telling the truth about Stalin's crimes. The disease metaphor with regard to society in these two statements is significant for *Cancer Ward*.

Some anti-Bolshevik students of Russian literature have suggested that the references to Lenin and Leninism in the dialogue of *Cancer Ward* were inserted by Solzhenitsyn to make the novel acceptable to the literary dictators and get it published. The suggestion does not do honor to Solzhenitsyn. It is most unlikely that Solzhenitsyn, who has a high sense of mission (in *The First Circle* one of his characters states that a great writer is a second government), would have violated the artistic integrity of his novel even though he was ready to temporize to get it published. He himself said in challenging Sholokhov's authorship of *The Quiet Don*, "Over the years Sholokhov has given permission for numerous unprincipled corrections to *The Quiet Don*—political and factual. . . . Of the two mothers of the disputed child, the true mother was the one who preferred to hand the child over rather than have it mutilated."[9]

The great question of *Cancer Ward* is asked early in the novel by one of its characters, Yefrem Podduyev. Yefrem is a shrewd operator who has knocked about all of his life, secure in his "grip on life," making good money as a foreman in the construction industry in one section of the Soviet Union after another, spending it readily, and abandoning woman after woman. He is proud of his physical strength and independence and has never been sick in his life. When his cancer appears, he laughs it off as an insignificant growth, boasting to his pals that nothing can scare him; but inwardly he is afraid. "The whole of his life had prepared Podduyev for living, not for dying." When he has to recognize, however, that he has cancer and is going to die, he walks about the ward restlessly, getting grim satisfaction from making dire predictions to all about their fates, but puzzled by his sense of the meaninglessness of his life. One day he seeks to escape his emptiness by reading a book of short stories by Tolstoy that Kostoglotov has forced upon him. To his astonishment—Yefrem has always considered literature as something no intelligent man takes seriously—he finds that the story "What Men Live By" makes him think about what life is and what his own life has been, asking the question he has been seeking to formulate and giving him the answer.

He asks every one in the ward to give what he thinks is the answer to the question "What do men live by?" No one at first understands that the question means what principles of conduct make life meaningful, and they give such answers, depending on their backgrounds, as water and food, pay, professional skill, and, in the case of a long-suffering, gentle young Tatar, homeland. Rusanov, however, whom Yefrem detests as a smugly arrogant milksop, gives a different kind of answer, which takes Yefrem by surprise. Rusanov is busy eating chicken which his wife had brought him, together with other delicacies not to be obtained on the hospital menu, when he undertakes to answer the question. "Pavel Nikolayevich did not put himself out in the least. He barely looked up from the chicken. 'There's no difficulty about that,' he said. 'Remember: people live by their ideological principles and by the interests of their society.' And he bit off the sweetest piece of gristle in the joint" (p. 103). Yefrem, to his annoyance, cannot respond to this, for he knows that "when it came to ideology it was better to keep your trap shut." Moreover, he is disturbed by something else: "He was furious that the bald man had almost guessed the answer. It said in the book that people live not by worrying only about their own problems but by love of others. And the pipsqueak had said by 'the interests of society.' Somehow they both tied up" (p. 104).

The suggestion is that, although the relationship is not worked out, the Marxist humanist philosophy is closely related to the Tolstoyan gospel of love but that for the Rusanovs this philosophy has been drained of all meaning. It has been reduced to a series of formulas which they glibly repeat by rote while they are intent on finding the "sweetest piece" of everything for themselves.

In the political discussions there emerges also the suggestion that Leninism, which has been betrayed by the bureaucracy, has much that is right but that it needs to be modified by Tolstoyism. In one such discussion there is comment about a newspaper item about an official who built himself a villa with government funds. Kostoglotov asks how the existence of such graft can be explained. The orthodox intellectuals in the ward, a nameless professor of philosophy and the young geologist Vadim, respond with the orthodox answer, "Survivals of bourgeois mentality," and Rusanov adds, "If you dig deep into such cases you'll always find a bourgeois social origin" (pp. 404-5). Kostoglotov is roused to a rage by Rusanov's dogmatic statement. He states that he is the son of a small merchant but has worked hard all of his life. Did his father give him a different kind of blood? This is racism, not Marxism. On the other hand, it doesn't matter if Rusanov had ten proletarian grandfathers: as they said in the twenties, where are the calluses on his hands?

As the argument grows more impassioned and Kostoglotov accuses Rusanov of being concerned only with maintaining his large salary and getting a special pension, the professor of philosophy informs Kostoglotov that socialism provides for differentiation in the wage structure.

"To hell with your differentiation!" Kostoglotov raged, as pigheaded as ever. "You think that while we're working toward communism the privileges some have over others ought to be increased, do you? You mean that to become equal we must first become unequal, is that right? You call that dialectics, do you?" [P. 407]

When the professor of philosophy replies that it is necessary to distinguish between those who wash hospital floors and those in charge of the health service, there is an unexpected interruption. Shulubin, the new patient who has made everyone uneasy with his unbroken silence, his intense scrutiny, his gloomy mien and worn face, intervenes to quote a point from Lenin's April theses, the revolutionary program Lenin brought back from exile in April 1917, that the professor did not remember from his textbooks: "No official should receive a salary higher than the average pay of a good worker." "That's what," he tells the surprised professor, "they began the Revolution with" (p. 408).

The "pigheadedness" of Kostoglotov is evidently the stubborn-
ness of the rebel who will not swallow without examination the
rationalizations of those who have abandoned the original ideals
of the revolution. His words, "Who's got the bourgeois mentality?" (p. 410) after he has described the special privileges of the
officer corps in the army, in which he served during the war, are
dramatized in the chapter "Why Not Live Well?" In this chapter
Shulubin enters the ward as a new patient and with him comes
another new patient, Chaly, who is his polar opposite. Chaly is a
hearty, ebullient fellow who has two wives, each unknown to the
other, who bring him delicious provisions, which he shares with
his neighbor, Rusanov. Rusanov, depressed that the second
anniversary of Stalin's death has been treated with such little
ceremony by *Pravda*, is as drawn to Chaly by his optimism, his
cheeriness, his love of the good things of life as he is repelled by
Shulubin. Chaly, it turns out, is one of those entrepreneurs who
live in the interstices of the system, bribing its officials to make
his livelihood, against whom Rusanov has so often inveighed.
Their having been equalized by both being patients in this
gloomy ward and the good-fellowship which has sprung up
between them make him, however, regard Chaly in the flesh
rather differently than in the abstract. In a finely ironic passage
he remonstrates with Chaly, his mildness contrasting with the
fury he felt against Kostoglotov in his arguments with him:

"But is it right, what you're doing?" Pavel Nikolayevich pressed him.
"It's all right, it's fine!" said Maxim reassuringly. "Now have a bit of this
delicious veal. We'll guzzle some of your compote in a minute. You see,
Pasha, we only live once, so why not live well? What we want to do is live
well!" Pavel Nikolayevich could not help agreeing with this. Maxim was
quite right. We only live once, so why not live well? It was just that . . .
"You see, Maxim, people don't approve of . . . " he reminded him gently.
[P. 319]

Within the system Chaly's profiteering is not socially approved,
but the bureaucrat and the businessman are really brothers under
the skin. Each, despite the external differences of Rusanov's
austerely forbidding demeanor and Chaly's cheery one and of
Rusanov's timidity in the face of authority and Chaly's breezily
assured enterprise, is dominated by selfishness and greed.*

---

*Although the bureaucrat has a mentality similar to that of the
businessman, the system in which he operates is quite different. Rusanov's special privileges are largely based on influence, not money. He does

The implicit condemnation of both capitalism and the bureaucratic rule over Soviet society is made explicit by Shulubin. Shulubin, however, although he was a Bolshevik in 1917, is no orthodox Marxist-Leninist. Throughout the twenty-five years of Stalin's era he had joined in the mass denunciations of the current supposed enemy agents even though he knew that the charges against Lenin's old guard and the rest were nonsense— first for the sake of his wife, who died, then for the sake of his children, who grew up to be cold and indifferent to him, and finally for the sake of his own miserable self. During these years he acceded to the dictates concerning his teaching at the university, to being reduced to a librarian in a remote region, to secretly burning the books he was told to burn. But during all of this time of fear and shame he has been thinking. "Why not?" he says wearily. "Haven't I earned the right to a few thoughts through my suffering, through my betrayals?" (p. 444).

The result of his thinking he confides to Kostoglotov when they are alone on the hospital grounds, saying that he never would have dared to speak anywhere else as he had done in the ward and that he would not even here dare tell anyone what he is now telling him if there were a third person present and if he were not

---

not have the "right" which everyone (with money) has in the United States: to engage a private hospital room with superior accommodations and to hire a private nurse. However, he does have contacts whom he thinks to use to get admitted to a hospital in Moscow rather than one in his own region, and he seeks to use his position to intimidate the hospital staff into giving him special treatment. Although his standard of living, which includes a fine apartment, well furnished, and official automobiles at his service, is far greater than an ordinary person's, he does not, despite the bonuses which supplement his salary, have a private fortune that would enable him to retire. He hopes, however, to get one of the special pensions granted to prominent officials. He got his son into law school and found him a good appointment on graduation, but he is afraid that his son by not being sufficiently ruthless in his governmental investigations and by not cultivating the proper people or by making the wrong marriage will deprive him of all of those things for which Rusanov is dependent on those in higher authority, on whom he fawns. All in all, Rusanov aptly illustrates the validity of Trotsky's words (*The Revolution Betrayed*, pp. 249-50), "The bureaucracy enjoys its privileges under the form of an abuse of power. It conceals its income; it pretends that as a special social group it does not even exist. . . . All this makes the position of the commanding Soviet stratum in the highest degree contradictory, equivocal and undignified, notwithstanding the completeness of its power."

to be operated on in two days. What caused the reaction from the revolutionary ideals and the general acceptance of this reaction? he asks. He speaks of people's unthinking acceptance of authority and of conventional phrases and formulas, Francis Bacon's "idols of the tribe," but he is not sure that he has really got the full answer. "I fought in the Civil War. You know, we did nothing to protect our lives, we were happy to give them for world revolution. What happened to us? How could we have given in? What was the chief thing that got us down? Fear? The idols of the market place? The idols of the theater?" (p. 439).

But of one thing he is certain. When Kostoglotov, in response to his question if he has lost faith in socialism, answers that he does not know, Shulubin says:

Don't ever blame socialism for the sufferings and the cruel years you've lived through. However you think about it, history has rejected capitalism once and for all! . . . If private enterprise isn't held in an iron grip it gives birth to people who are no better than beasts, those stock-exchange people with greedy appetites completely beyond restraint. Capitalism was doomed ethically before it was doomed economically, a long time ago. [P. 440]

Socialism must, however, be built on ethical foundations, not on the production of an abundance of material goods; it must be permeated by the spirit of love, not of hatred. It is not enough merely to change the mode of production. Shulubin differentiates his concept of "ethical socialism" from "democratic socialism," which is concerned only with the structure of the state that introduces socialism, not its ethical foundations, and from the "Christian socialism" of the Catholic parties in postfascist Germany and Italy, which, he indicates, were not made up of the proper sort of people. "Ethical socialism," he states, is peculiarly Russian: "I should say that for Russia in particular, with our repentances, confessions and revolts, our Dostoyevski, Tolstoy and Kropotkin, there's only one true socialism, and that's ethical socialism. That is something completely realistic" (p. 441). And yet, despite his statement that "ethical socialism" is completely realistic, he is at another point uncertain that socialism can ever be attained because of man's exceedingly resistant human nature; despite his statement about the need for private enterprise to be held in an iron grip, he later says that ethics should come first and economics afterwards; despite his rejection of the phrase "Christian socialism," he expresses his certainty that man has an immortal soul.

The Marxist-Leninist egalitarian ideal and belief in the need to do away with private property in the means of production; Tolstoy's religiosity and gospel of love; Dostoyevski's Slavophilism; Kropotkin's anarchist creed of social cooperativeness; an underlying skepticism, born of disillusionment, concerning the possibilities of humanity, tempered by the belief in the possibility of the individual attaining goodness ("only human beings can feel affection for each other, and this is the highest achievement they can aspire to" [p. 443])—these constitute the mixed, self-contradictory elements of Shulubin's "ethical socialism." In view of Yefrem's confused perception of a relationship between Marxism and Tolstoyism, of the presentation of the spiritual kinship of Rusanov and Chaly, and of, as we shall see, the presentation of the inadequacy of the lives of the various characters because they have not known what men live by, we can say that Shulubin's ideas are projected by the novel itself. The novel's conclusion, we shall furthermore see, bears out this inference.

The many characters of *Cancer Ward* are seen from within and without. The point of view is that of each character when he becomes the center of the action. Consequently, we see each of them as he sees himself, as the others see him—and, usually indirectly but sometimes through direct statement, as the author sees him. The author's attitude is predominantly one of unrelenting irony, in large part derived from the relationship of each person's cancer to his attitude towards life. This is true of each of the major characters among the patients except for Kostoglotov and the sixteen-year-old Dyomka, who, as we shall see, serve other functions.

Yefrem has cancer of the tongue.

> It was Yefrem's tongue that had been hit—his quick, ever-ready tongue, which he had never really noticed, but which had been so handy in his life. . . . With it he'd talked his way into pay he'd never earned, sworn blind he'd done things when he hadn't, stood bail for things he didn't believe in, howled at the bosses and yelled insults at the workers. . . . He lied to hundreds of women scattered over the place that he wasn't married, that he had no children, that he'd be back in a week and they'd start building a house. "God rot your tongue!" one temporary mother-in-law had cursed him, but Yefrem's tongue had never let him down. [Pp. 93-94]

Rusanov and his wife tell themselves that "they served the People and were ready to give their lives for the People," but they could not stand the crowds on streetcars, busses, and trains, always pushing and often dressed in dirty overalls whose grime was rubbed off on their coats, and so they traveled by limousines and taxis and then, as they advanced in position, by their own automobile.

> They became wary of people who were badly dressed, impudent, or even a bit drunk. . . . So although there was nothing in the world Rusanov feared, he did begin to feel a totally normal, justifiable fear of dissolute, half-drunk men, or, to be more precise, of a fist striking him a direct blow in the face. [Pp. 193-94]

When he hears the rumor that the former fellow-worker whom he had secretly given false testimony against to get the apartment they shared has been rehabilitated, his first thought is that his victim will return to "punch him in the face" (p. 194).

Rusanov's cancer is on his neck, "pressing against him like an iron fist" (p. 195), the fist of retribution he fears. When Shulubin looks at him with his hard, unflinching gaze, Rusanov "could physically feel that eagle owl staring at him from the corner, like a stubborn, reproachful pressure on the side of his head" (p. 308). "His fate lay there, between his chin and his collarbone. There justice was being done. And in answer to this justice he could summon no influential friend, no past services, no defense" (p. 196).

Shulubin has cancer of the rectum. His lower intestine is going to be surgically removed, and he tells Kostoglotov that he kept silent during the Stalinist terror "for the sake of my own sinful body" and now "my body is a bag full of manure—they're going to drill a hole for it on one side" (p. 437). His shame and his self-disgust for the conduct of his life are expressed in his words about his cancer:

> My disease is something specially humiliating, specially offensive. . . . If I live—and it's a very big if—simply standing or sitting near me, like you are now, for instance, will be unpleasant. Everyone will do their best to keep two steps away. Even if anyone comes closer I'll still be thinking to myself, "You see, he can hardly stand it, he's cursing me." [Pp. 431-32]

The professor of philosophy has cancer of the throat. A person of formerly dignified bearing, he has become abject and terrified in the face of death. When Kostoglotov learns that he is a professor, he cannot forebear exclaiming, "A lecturer, and it's your throat!" To himself Kostoglotov thinks, "What did he churn out in his lectures anyway? Perhaps he was just clouding people's brains? And what was the point of all his philosophy if he was so completely helpless in the face of his illness? . . . But what a coincidence—in the throat, of all places!" (p. 149).

Chaly, the lover of good food and drink, has cancer of the stomach. He cheerfully announces that three-quarters of his stomach is going to be hacked out, but he does not realize he has cancer and has no concept of what the operation entails. Despite the doctors' orders, he drinks vodka, which he regards as a cure for all illnesses, and plans to drink a bottle of alcohol just before his operation. "Let the others croak if they want to," he tells Rusanov. "You and I'll have a good time!" (p. 317).

The twenty-six-year-old Vadim is entirely devoted to his geology. He confidently tells Yefrem he knows what men live by: creative work. His highly solicitous mother, a physician, aware that the large birthmark on his leg could degenerate and become malignant, had in her overzealous care continually probed it and engaged a top surgeon to perform a preliminary operation, which was precisely the wrong thing to do. Vadim had neglected the resultant degeneration while he was absorbed in his fieldwork, and the walking and riding in the mountains had aggravated it. Now he knows that he will die before too long, and in the few months that are left to him he intends to give his time to working out a new method for discovering ore deposits. Thus he will atone for his early death and die reconciled.

Vadim is a much more attractive person than Rusanov or Chaly, but Solzhenitsyn points up the inadequacy of his values. When Vadim says that his work is the most interesting thing he knows in the world, Shulubin replies, "Interesting—that's no argument. . . . Business is interesting. . . . If that's your explanation science becomes no different from the ordinary run of selfish, thoroughly unethical occupations" (p. 378). A member of the scientific elite and a Communist Party member, Vadim is unconsciously selfish. Like Rusanov, he is downcast when *Pravda* does not do "justice" by Stalin on the second anniversary of his death. For Stalin had pampered him, as had his mother. In Vadim's view Stalin "had exalted science, exalted scientists and freed them from petty thoughts of salary or accommodations. Science itself required his stability and his permanence to prevent any catastrophe happening that might distract scientists or take them away from their work."

Vadim finds that, after some weeks of intense study, he cannot continue as he had confidently planned. He feels acutely the tragedy of his dying before his talent is fulfilled and has a throbbing sense of loneliness because no one "had any idea how much more important it was for him to survive than for the others." He finds that he is not fully grasping what he is reading. "He would read a whole page and then realize he hadn't understood it. He'd grown heavy, he could no longer scale other people's thoughts as a goat scales a mountain. . . . His leg was in a trap, and with it his life" (p. 377). The cancer on his leg, the consequence of the pampering he had received, will not permit him to climb mountains for geological fieldwork or to scale the mountains of other people's thought.

Finally, there is another representative of Soviet youth, the seventeen-year-old Asya. When the serious-minded Dyomka asks her in his hesitant, embarrassed manner Yefrem's question, "What . . . what *do* people live for?" she looks at him as if not quite sure whether he is playing a joke on her. "What for? What do you mean? For love, of course." But "love" for her is not what it is for Tolstoy; it is erotic gratification. She, like her classmates, was initiated into sex early and is amused that Dyomka is still a virgin. "The earlier you start, the more exciting it is. . . . Why wait? It's the atomic age!" It is to this girl, who has been admitted into the hospital for what she thought was a routine examination, that there comes the news that she will have to have a breast removed. She is heartbroken. "'What have I got to live for?' she sobbed. . . . She could never show herself on the beach again. . . . Living had lost all meaning."

So summarized, Solzhenitsyn's irony towards his characters may seem heavily didactic. It is not, however, insistently obvious, Solzhenitsyn often cleverly delaying information about the nature of the cancer or something else so that when we come to recognize the relationship between the patient's cancer and his or her attitude toward life it hits us with a jolt. And with the irony, there is, except in the case of Rusanov, a deep compassion, especially evident in the scene in which Asya offers the breast that is to be amputated to Dyomka to kiss so that he, at least, will remember its beauty.

In addition to these patients, there are a number of others less important in the narrative, many of them of non-Russian nationalities. In the ward can be seen the falsity of the official propaganda that in the Soviet Union all nationalities are of equal importance. This falsity is summed up when Rusanov, entering the ward and feeling too weak and low to protest Yefrem's pessimistic utterances about their chances of living, looks about for help. "There was no one in the room to rein him in. All the others there seemed either pathetic wrecks or non-Russians" (p. 10). The mental observation is indicative of both the actual status of the non-Russian nationalities and Rusanov's contempt for them.

Many doctors are also portrayed. They form their own little society, a representative bureaucratic planning commission, as they meet in a conference presided over by the "senior doctor." Many of them are highly devoted and capable, but many are not, and the "senior doctor," a man of imposing appearance but vain and incompetent, who has saddled the staff with its other incompetents, is a heavy drag on the enterprise. But then, thinks the surgeon who is the center of strength of the hospital, "administrators were seldom efficient in their actual profession" (p. 355).

Despite the multiplicity of characters and Solzhenitsyn's own statement about the "polyphonic novel" he was seeking to write, in which the author "gives preference to none" of the "dozens of heroes" he creates,[10] *Cancer Ward*, as we have said, has a protagonist, Kostoglotov, and an antagonist, Rusanov. The contrasting curves of the fortunes of these two men supplies a pattern to the novel, a kind of progress chart of the ups and downs in Soviet society in the early de-Stalinization period, which ends with their discharges from the hospital. It is their respective fates which determine the note upon which it concludes.

Kostoglotov had been arrested with a group of students because they dared, in talking politics, to make some critical remarks about Stalin. He had been sentenced to seven years in labor camp and lifelong exile. He had contracted cancer near the end of his sentence in labor camp, had been neglected, and had come to the hospital at the point of death, insisting upon and gaining immediate admission despite the rules, knowing that no hotel in town would allow him, an exile without the proper internal passport, to stay there.

Kostoglotov's life has been blighted by his inquiring mind, but he remains determined to understand everything that comes within his field of vision and he is not cowed by authority. He demands that the doctors, contrary to their usual practice, explain his treatment to him and that he make decisions concerning his own welfare. Toughened by his experience in the camps, he is nevertheless sensitive and compassionate despite his hard exterior. Genuinely strong, questioning everything, not given to self-deception, he is in every way the opposite of Rusanov, who likes to think of himself as a strong "new man" but is nothing of the sort.

When Rusanov is admitted to the hospital, terrified of the tumor which he persists in telling himself is not cancer, Kostoglotov has been there for twelve days and has revived remarkably. He was exceptionally able to sustain large amounts of X rays, and his cancer has consequently diminished considerably. Rusanov's cancer and his fear, however, continue to grow. When Kostoglotov says of Rusanov's remonstrances about Yefrem's self-questionings, "Why try to stop a man's mouth just when he has started to think about the meaning of life, when he himself is on the borderline between life and death?" Rusanov thinks bitterly, "It was all very well for Bone-chewer [the derogatory nickname he uses in thinking of Kostoglotov] to talk about death. *He* was getting better" (pp. 136, 138).

When Rusanov reels back to the ward after his wife tells him during her visit of the rumor that the worker he betrayed long ago has been rehabilitated, he sees the nurse Zoya "flirting with the uncouth Bone-chewer and paying scant attention to the patients" (p. 184). An attraction has indeed sprung up between Zoya and Kostoglotov, who has continued to improve in health. The chapter recounting the development of this attraction is entitled "Passions Return . . ."; the next chapter, which tells of the terrors engendered in Rusanov by his wife's story, is entitled " . . . and So Do the Specters."

The terrors reach their climax in the nightmare Rusanov has after his second injection. This injection comes immediately after Rusanov has read in *Pravda* that the entire membership of the Supreme Court, all those who administered justice for a quarter of a century, has been dismissed, a sign of a momentous political change in the offing. Kostoglotov read the paper just before, and his exclamation as he read had alerted Rusanov to look for the seemingly insignificant item set in small type. The hands of each trembled as they read, but for different reasons. Two days later the same thing happens in reverse. Rusanov feels the earth rumbling underneath him and involuntarily exclaims as he reads that Malenkov has been relieved of his duties, and when the doctor comes just then to give him another injection Kostoglotov seizes the paper. To Kostoglotov it is as if he heard the four Beethoven chords of fate thundering from the sky.

But then the two curves alter their courses, Rusanov's now ascending and Kostoglotov's descending. The last chapter of the first of the novel's two parts is entitled "The Shadows Go Their

Way." In it the specters haunting Rusanov are dispelled by his daughter Aviette, who comes to visit him. Aviette is his pride and joy, unlike her brother, who does not know how to get ahead in the bureaucratic world. She is cheerful, energetic, and knowledgeable. Rusanov has given himself up to the weakness that has overcome him following his third injection, but she revives him with her briskness, her sensible views about the immorality of the wholesale releases of prisoners, and her reassuring inside information that the law against false evidence is not going to be invoked for past cases. He feels "as if even his tumor had eased a little" (p. 278). She tells him about the prevailing political atmosphere: "Though they talk about 'the cult of personality,' in the same breath they speak of 'the great successor.' So one mustn't go too far in either direction. Generally speaking, you have to be flexible, you have to be responsive to the demand of the times" (p. 279). Her last words are "Fight hard, go on with the treatment, get rid of your tumor, and don't worry about *anything*. . . . Everything's going to be all right, *everything*" (p. 287).

In the next chapter, some weeks later, Kostoglotov, after his initial euphoria, is suffering from constant acute nausea as a result of the prolonged X-ray treatment. Rusanov's tumor has been greatly reduced as a result of the injections, and he is no longer afraid of dying. He is, however, made very weak by them. The two of them lie side by side unspeaking, Rusanov listless and Kostoglotov nauseous. Their curves have intersected, as Rusanov's rises and Kostoglotov's falls.

After Chaly comes, Rusanov mends rapidly. Kostoglotov, however, learns from Zoya that the injections he is now being given are hormone therapy, deemed necessary to save his life, but at the price of rendering him impotent in the future. He refuses to take them, and Rusanov thinks, "If Bone-chewer was fool enough to refuse injections, well, let him get worse. . . . As for himself, Rusanov now knew for certain he wasn't going to die" (p. 372). He has just been assured by the doctor that his tumor is going well and that he will get over his weakness in time.

Rusanov is finally discharged from the hospital in a chapter ironically entitled "Happy Ending . . ." He has his son blow the horn of the automobile in which his family is taking him home at Kostoglotov, walking in the middle of the road, so that Kostoglotov has to leap aside to avoid being run over. Rusanov feels triumphant. He has overcome his illness, proving himself "a man of courage, stronger than circumstances" (p. 461). He does not

know, however, that the doctors "still expected an outbreak of
tumors in many of his glands" and that "it depended on the
speed of the process whether or not he would live out the year" (p.
454). The Stalinist bureaucrat is resuming his former position
and way of life, but his doom, whatever his flexibility in adapting
himself to "the demand of the times," awaits him, however long
or short the process will prove to be.

Kostoglotov, who has acceded to taking the hormone therapy,
is also discharged from the hospital. Since he cannot go to a
hotel, his doctor, Vera Gongart, with whom he has fallen in love,
invites him to stay the night at her place. Before doing so, he
spends the day wandering through the town, getting intense
pleasure from the most simple things. But as the day wears on, he
comes to feel lost in the complex universe of the town, which is
strange and foreign to him after his years in labor camps and
exile. The savor of his new-found life is gone. He goes to a zoo,
where he is struck by the sign in the empty cage of a rhesus
monkey: the monkey had been blinded because an evil man had
thrown tobacco in its eye. "Why?" he asks himself. For no reason
at all—just like that. The question recurs to him as he gazes with
hatred upon the tiger, which reminds him of Stalin. "Just like
that, just like that . . . but why?" (p. 507). Other animals remind
him of other kinds of human beings—the monkeys of his fellow
prisoners in the camps, the predatory beasts of the criminals who
preyed on the political prisoners, the antelope, "a miracle of
spirituality," of Vera.

But Kostoglotov does not go to Vera although this would have
been the one great happiness for him. He would continue to
feel sexual desire for some time, he had been told, but would be
powerless to fulfill that desire. His physical desire now teaches
him that seeing Vera would only end in torture and deceit. "It
would mean his demanding more from her than he could ask
from himself. They had come to a high-minded agreement that
spiritual communion was more valuable than anything else; yet,
having built this tall bridge by hand together, he saw now that
his own hands were weakening" (p. 522). Love is more than
physical gratification, but even spiritual love cannot avoid being
compounded with the physical. Instead of going to Vera, he
writes her a letter declaring his love and telling her that he is
now sure that she will come to bless the day that she did not
commit herself to share his life. He fights his way to the crowded
train going to his distant place of exile, finds a place to lie down
on the baggage rack, and lies there in profound anguish.

The ravages of Stalinism that Kostoglotov had suffered—and that multitudes of others had suffered—cannot simply be wiped away; nothing can restore the Kostoglotovs to wholeness. Yet the indomitable spirit that enabled Kostoglotov—as it did Solzhenitsyn himself—to endure the camps, exile, and cancer remains. He will endure this anguish too and find solace in the place of exile that he has come to love even though there are indications that all exiles are going to be revoked. Moreover, happiness, said Shulubin, is a mirage (and indeed Kostoglotov's happiness on leaving the hospital soon evaporated): all that counts in life is making sacrifices for love. Kostoglotov had made his great renunciation for love of Vera.

And what of the country that lived through Stalinism? Great changes are in the offing, but the final issue is left uncertain—as indeed it was still uncertain when Solzhenitsyn wrote *Cancer Ward* in the 1960s, not knowing whether it would be published. How long will the modified Stalinism of the Rusanovs and their superiors prevail? Even after there is retribution for them, can a new Stalin arise? Kostoglotov's seeing the animals in the zoo as types of humanity recalls Shulubin's "Man is a biological type. It takes thousands of years to change him" (p. 440). Yet if evil, mysteriously present in human nature (why do human beings wilfully hurt defenseless creatures?), persists, so does humanity's inquiring mind and aspiring spirit. We have seen this with Kostoglotov. But it is not only he. When young Dyomka tells Kostoglotov early in the novel that he is interested in history and literature and has "a passion for social problems," Kostoglotov with prison-camp cynicism replies, "Social problems? . . . Oh, Dyomka, you'd better learn to assemble radio sets. Life's more peaceful if you're an engineer" (p. 22). However, at the conclusion, at the same time that he writes to Vera, he writes a letter to Dyomka in which he says, "Get better and live up to your ideals. I'm relying on you" (p. 527). And Dyomka, at the cost of a leg, survives. It is in this representative of Soviet youth—not Asya, Vadim, or Aviette—that the hope of the future lies.

Cancer Ward, we may say, paraphrasing what Lenin wrote about the literary genius of Tolstoy, enables us to understand better the Russian bureaucracy and the society it rules by the depth of its portrait of Rusanov and the breadth of its presentation of the characters of various classes and nationalities, by its moral indignation and its powerful irony, although the doctrine of "ethical socialism" that lies behind it is a muddle. It poses, as Lenin said Tolstoy posed, "the concrete problems of democracy and socialism"[11]—and in this consists its great virtue; but it gives confused answers.

"Ethical socialism" speaks of the need for love. Revolutionists have been hesitant to talk about love because it is a word that has been so abused by the moralists and because love of humanity is not proven by rhetoric but by deeds requiring self-sacrifice. However, Che Guevara, who proved if any man did his readiness to sacrifice himself for humanity, wrote in "Man and Socialism in Cuba":

> At the risk of seeming ridiculous, let me say that the true revolutionary is guided by a great feeling of love. It is impossible to think of a genuine revolutionary lacking this quality. . . . Our vanguard revolutionaries . . . cannot descend, with small doses of daily affection, to the level where ordinary men put their love into practice. The leaders of the revolution have children just beginning to talk, who are not learning to call their fathers by name; wives from whom they have to be separated as part of the general sacrifice of their lives to bring the revolution to its fulfillment.[12]

Rusanov's love for his family is an extension of his selfishness. His wife and he form a partnership in selfishness. He loves his daughter Aviette because he is proud of her accomplishments, which reflect credit upon him. He is disturbed by his son Yuri, who lacks "the Rusanovs' proper grip on life." "He was such a naive boy, he might be led up the garden path by some ordinary weaver girl from the textile factory," a step that "would ruin not only the young man's life, but his family's too, the many years of effort they spent on his behalf" (p. 179). And his softness as a member of a legal inspection team could get himself and his father into trouble. Che's love for his wife and children, however, expressed in his letters to them, is an extension of his selflessness.

But love for humanity can only mean hatred for those who do not permit humanity to realize itself. The prisoners in Kostoglotov's camp cheer when they hear the news of Stalin's death, and Kostoglotov gazes with hatred upon the tiger who reminds him of Stalin. Shulubin, despite his doctrine, does not seem to have any love for Rusanov, nor does Solzhenitsyn himself. There is no expression of forgiveness in the stern retribution he holds threateningly over the terrified bureaucrat. As Trotsky wrote of Tolstoy, "this last apostle of Christian all-forgiving" expresses "the wrath of Biblical prophets"[13]—and, it may be added, of Christ driving the moneychangers out of the temple.

Revolutionists share the hatred of the oppressed masses for their oppressors; however, it is not revolutionary doctrine which promotes class hatred but the social system. The revolutionist seeks to guide that hatred into effective political action against the system of oppression so that it does not dissipate itself in mere personal rage and vindictiveness. This is far different from the Stalinist artificial drumming up of hatred and a lynch spirit against scapegoats for the regime's failures. The Stalinist terror came not because people were "used to hating," as Shulubin says, but because the bureaucracy was intent on consolidating its special privileges.

But what caused the growth of these special privileges? What caused the reaction from the revolution? This is the question which Shulubin raises but for which he has no satisfactory answer. It received such an answer in Leon Trotsky's *The Revolution Betrayed*, written in 1936 just before the major purge trials. The Russian revolution, Trotsky pointed out, has followed the path of all previous revolutions in being succeeded by a reaction that did not throw the nation back to the starting point but took away from the people the lion's share of their conquests. "It is for the very reason that a proletariat still backward in many respects achieved in the space of a few months the unprecedented leap from a semifeudal monarchy to a socialist dictatorship, that the reaction in its ranks was inevitable."[14]

Imperialist intervention on many fronts, a devastating civil war, the failure of revolution in the West which would have brought aid to the beleaguered country, resulted in the utmost suffering and destitution.

And thus after an unexampled tension of forces, hopes and illusions, there came a long period of weariness, decline and sheer disappointment in the results of the revolution. The ebb of the "plebeian pride" made room for a flood of pusillanimity and careerism. The new commanding caste rose to its place upon this wave. The demobilization of the Red Army of five million played no small role in the formation of the bureaucracy. The victorious commanders assumed leading posts . . . and . . . introduced everywhere that regime which had ensured success in the civil war. . . . The reaction within the proletariat caused an extraordinary flush of hope and confidence in the petty bourgeois strata of town and country . . . The young bureaucracy, which had arisen at first as an agent of the proletariat, began now to feel itself a court of arbitration between the classes. . . . The Soviet bureaucracy became more self-confident, the heavier the blows dealt to the world working class. . . . The Opposition was isolated. The bureaucracy [exploited] the bewilderment and passivity of the workers. . . . In the course of a few years, the bureaucracy thus shattered the revolutionary vanguard of the proletariat.[15]

Such, briefly, is a Marxist analysis of the process under which reaction triumphed. To Shulubin's bewildered question "What happened to us? How could we have given in?" (p. 439), Trotsky, writing before the question was asked, replies:

> The revolutionary vanguard of the proletariat was in part devoured by the administrative apparatus and gradually demoralized, in part annihilated in the civil war, and in part thrown out and crushed. The tired and disappointed masses were indifferent to what was happening on the summits.[16]

The social basis for this process was the triumph of the revolution in a backward country without the world revolution coming to its aid, for, although the new social system could bring a remarkable growth of the economy, it could not by itself produce the abundance on which socialism is predicated. This Marxist concept is denied by Shulubin.

> You can't build socialism on the abundance of material goods [he says] because people sometimes behave like buffaloes, they stampede and trample the goods into the ground. . . . When we have enough loaves of white bread to crush them under our heels, when we have enough milk to choke us, we still won't be in the least happy. But if we share things we don't have enough of, we can be happy today! [P. 443]

But how is a country whose people have been formed under capitalism to learn to find happiness in sharing—a happiness which would seem, incidentally, to contradict Shulubin's earlier assertion that "happiness is a mirage"? (p. 443). Undoubtedly, the leadership must set an example—"We have maintained," Che said, "That our children must have, or go without, what the children of the average man have or go without, and that our families should understand this and strive to uphold this standard"[17]—and use moral incentives rather than material incentives as much as possible. Yet the heroic measures of the period of "military communism" in the Soviet Union (1918-1921), equal sharing in a besieged fortress, could not be maintained. The country cried out for an end to the general destitution, and Lenin had to introduce the "New Economic Policy" of stimulating personal interest in agricultural production by the peasants by granting them a controlled capitalist market and giving their upper strata, who had most of the surplus grain, the opportunity to enrich themselves beyond the rest of the population. Want only sharpens the "struggle for individual existence" and the growth of special privilege.

When there is enough goods in a store [says Trotsky], the purchasers can come whenever they want to. When there is little goods, the purchasers are compelled to stand in line. When the lines are very long, it is necessary to appoint a policeman to keep order. Such is the starting point of the power of the Soviet bureaucracy. It "knows" who is to get something and who has to wait.[18]

Even the Bible speaks of the promised land as a land flowing with milk and honey.

It is true that the growth of production in the Soviet Union has, as Trotsky said, given "significant privileges to a minority" and converted "inequality into a whip for spurring on of the majority."[19] But that is because there is still very far from enough for everybody in a society dominated by the bureaucracy and its values. Kostoglotov is swept along by the crowd in the department store after his release from the hospital because the crowd is so hungry for goods that only fitfully appear. To deduce from this stampede that the achievement of socialism is doubtful is to draw an unwarranted conclusion. Nor, on the other hand, will there be a fundamental change in human nature under the urgings of the adherents of "ethical socialism." Human nature is like iron, exceedingly difficult to bend under the hammerings of moral exhortation, and yet, as the study of anthropology has shown, with enough time in the furnace of different social conditions it is infinitely malleable. The gentle Tasaday stone-age people in the Phillipine rain forest are as much a part of the human race as we are ourselves.

Since the writing of *Cancer Ward*, Solzhenitsyn's political and social views have continued to evolve. In his letter nominating Sakharov for the 1973 Nobel Peace Prize, published in the *New York Times*, September 15, 1973, he no longer spoke of "ethical socialism" but only of the need for states to have a "built-in ethical foundation," which he evidently now regarded as possible under capitalism. In publishing abroad in 1974, after his expulsion from the Soviet Union, his 1973 letter to the rulers of the Kremlin appealing to them to be guided by his moral and political precepts while retaining their authoritarian system—like

Tolstoy in his letters to Alexander III and Nicholas II, he actually hoped to convert them to his gospel!—he omitted those portions dealing with the materialism and moral bankruptcy of the West.[20] Again in deference to bourgeois public opinion, he was also silent on the theme of Western moral bankruptcy during his tour of the United States. In fact, the tour, of which an aide said, "he simply stays in his room and works," was said to have "impressed [him] with the freedom and vitality of American life."[21] In his Harvard address, however, he returned to the subject of Western moral bankruptcy, citing as an example of it the American antiwar movement which caused the United States to withdraw its troops from what he evidently felt was a war it should have continued to wage. This from a man who had only a few years before referred to "the dubious classification of wars into 'just' and 'unjust'"![22] Of the CIA's subversion of duly elected governments in Iran, Guatemala, and Chile and of its intervention in the politics of countries throughout the world, notably Italy, through direct subsidies to political parties he has had nothing to say. All seems to be justified in the holy war against Communism. Indeed, he sounds like a Russian Orthodox reincarnation of the Protestant John Foster Dulles.

The magnificent inner strength that enabled Solzhenitsyn to survive the concentration camps unbroken has become a raging egomania that causes him to speak as a prophet about that of which he is ignorant. "Could, say, the Republic of South Africa, without being penalized, ever be expected," he has asked, "to detain and torture a black leader for four years as General Grigorenko has been? The storm of worldwide rage would have long ago swept the roof from that prison!"[23] He has apparently never heard of the many Blacks, of whom Steve Biko was only the most well known, who were tortured and killed in South African prisons. He has also apparently never heard of George Jackson and Martin Sostre, Black leaders not in the Republic of South Africa but the United States, who were brutally mistreated for years in solitary confinement, with George Jackson finally being killed and Martin Sostre being released only after Amnesty International, declaring him a "prisoner of conscience," conducted a worldwide campaign, in which Sakharov joined.

Solzhenitsyn changed his world outlook out of bitter disappointment with the neo-Stalinism which has prevented him from publishing his work in the Soviet Union, and in response to the Western cold-war propaganda of the Voice of America. In this connection he has extolled Arthur Koestler's *Darkness At Noon,* with its fraudulent thesis that Bolshevik "amoralism" brought about Stalinism and its falsification of Bolshevik beliefs and history, and George Orwell's *1984*, which he apparently regards as concerned only with Soviet society.

Now that he has been cut off from Soviet society and has isolated himself from political reality in his Vermont retreat, Solzhenitsyn is serving an utterly reactionary role. That which he wrote in the Soviet Union for the Russian people, however—although only *One Day in the Life of Ivan Denisovich* was published, the rest appearing only in *samizdat*—had, in its presentation of the truth about Stalinism, a great progressive effect, as had his fight for civil rights. Preeminent among these works is *Cancer Ward*, which will have a life of its own, independent of its author's.

Conclusion

The difficult struggle for a social revolution against ruling classes with immense resources for both repression and indoctrination is the history of the twentieth century reflected in the ten novels we have examined. Studied in their chronological order, they provide a profound illumination of our time, a time of worldwide transition from capitalism to socialism, during which the revolutionary struggle has had its ups and downs, its periods of quiescence and intensity.

But these ten novels did more than reflect the thinking of the times. They were themselves a force acting upon that thinking. *Darkness at Noon,* for instance, played an important part, as Arthur Koestler boasted, in defeating the Communist Party in a crucial French election. But more important than their immediate effect is the continuing effect of the best of them. *Fontamara* enables us to experience what it means to be a peasant in an underdeveloped country, *Native Son* enables us to experience what it means to be a ghetto Black in the United States, and so forth, as no sociological or political tract can do.

Moreover, it is not merely a matter of re-creating what it means to exist in a given sphere of life. The best of these novels provide us with an aesthetic experience that, to a greater or lesser degree, goes beyond surface phenomena to the evolving social reality of which they are a part. It is my hope that my analysis will have enabled the reader to go back to the novels better able to partake of the richness of the experience they afford.

NOTES

Preface

1. Ian Watt, *The Rise of the Novel* (Berkeley: University of California Press, 1957), pp. 35-59; John Wain, *Essays on Literature and Ideas* (New York: St. Martin's Press, 1963), pp. 33-34.
2. Steven Marcus, "The Novel Again," *Partisan Review* 29, (1962), p. 176.
3. Lionel Trilling, *The Liberal Imagination* (New York: Viking Press, 1950), pp. 249-51.
4. Gerald Graff, "Babbitt at the Abyss: The Social Context of Postmodern American Fiction," *Triquarterly* 33 (1975), pp. 305-7.
5. Marcus, "The Novel Again," p. 193.
6. Leon Trotsky, *The History of the Russian Revolution* (New York: Simon and Schuster, 1937), vol. 3, p. 355.
7. Rosa Luxemburg, "Life of Korolenko," *International Socialist Review*, 1969, no. 1, p.13.
8. Lionel Trilling, *Beyond Culture* (New York: Viking Press, 1965), p. 168.
9. Leon Trotsky, *Literature and Revolution* (New York: International Publishers, 1925), p. 178.
10. Ibid., p. 181.
11. Ibid., p. 164.
12. Ibid., p. 168.
13. Marcus, "The Novel Again," p. 174.
14. Raymond Williams, "Dickens and Social Ideas," *Dickens,* ed. Michael Slater (New York: Stein and Day, 1970), p. 78.
15. F. R. Leavis, *The Common Pursuit* (New York: George W. Stewart, 1952), p. 194.
16. Friedrich Engels, "Letter to Margaret Harkness," *Marxism and Art,* ed. Maynard Solomon (New York: Knopf, 1973), p. 68.
17. Irving Howe, *Politics and the Novel* (Greenwich, Conn.: Fawcett Publications, 1967), p. 19.

Introduction to Section I

1. Thomas Henry Buckle, *History of Civilization in England* (New York: D. Appleton, 1890), vol. 1, pp. 207, 162, 137.
2. V. I. Lenin, in Karl Marx, *Selected Works* (New York: International Publishers, n.d.), p. 73.

3. Kodne Zilliacus, *Between Two Wars?* (Harmondsworth, England: Penguin, 1939), p. 45.

Chapter 1: Arnold Bennett's 'The Old Wives' Tale'

1. E. M. Forster, *Aspects of the Novel* (New York: Harcourt Brace, 1954), pp. 62-63.

2. Virginia Woolf, *The Hogarth Essays* (Garden City, N.Y.: Doubleday, Doran, 1928), pp. 3-29.

3. V. S. Pritchett, *The Living Novel and Later Appreciations* (New York: Random House, 1964), p. 175.

4. Arnold Bennett, *The Old Wives' Tale* (New York: Harper & Brothers, 1950), p. xvi.

5. Walter Allen, *Arnold Bennett* (London: Home & Van Thal, 1948), p. 28. Bennett called himself a socialist in a letter to H. G. Wells dated September 16, 1906. See *Arnold Bennett and H. G. Wells,* Harris Wilson, ed. (Urbana: University of Illinois Press, 1960), pp. 136-37.

6. G. B. Shaw, ed., *Fabian Essays in Socialism* (London: W. Scott, 1889), p. 48.

7. *The Journal of Arnold Bennett, 1896-1910* (New York: The Literary Guild, 1933), p. 392 (September 15, 1910).

8. Beatrice Webb, *My Apprenticeship* (New York: Longmans, Green, 1926), p. 37.

9. Webb specifically gives credit to Spencer for these ideas. Cf. *Fabian Essays,* pp. 31, 35, 46, 64.

10. Bennett, "Running Away from Life," *T. P.'s Weekly,* August 17, 1906, p. 210. Quoted by James G. Kennedy, "Voynich, Bennett, and Tressall: Two Alternatives for Realism in the Transition Age," *English Literature in Transition, 1880-1923* 13 (1970), p. 266, n. 50. Cf. Herbert Spencer, *First Principles* (New York: D. Appleton, 1912), p. 361.

11. Herbert Spencer, *The Study of Sociology* (Ann Arbor: University of Michigan Press, 1961), p. 361.

12. Spencer, *First Principles,* p. 260.

13. Spencer, *The Study of Sociology,* pp. 360-61.

14. Ibid., p. 356.

15. Karl Kautsky, *The Social Revolution* (Chicago: Charles H. Kerr, 1908), p. 14. Cf. Spencer, *The Study of Sociology,* pp. 366-67: "There is no way from the lowest forms of social life to the highest, but one passing through small successive modifications. If we contemplate the order of nature, we see that everywhere vast results are brought about by accumulations of minute actions."

16. Kautsky, *The Social Revolution,* pp. 15-16.

17. Marx, *Selected Works,* p. 28.

18. Leon Trotsky, *In Defense of Marxism* (New York: Pioneer Publishers, 1942), p. 54.

19. George Gaylord Simpson, *The Meaning of Evolution* (New Haven: Yale University Press, 1950), pp. 238-39.

20. Ibid., p. 189.

21. Arnold Gesell and Frances L. Ilg, *The Child from Five to Ten* (New York: Harper, 1946), pp. 57-59.

22. Marx, *Selected Works*, p. 28.

23. Frank Jellinek, *The Paris Commune of 1871* (New York: Grosset & Dunlap, 1965), p. 411.

24. Spencer, *The Study of Sociology*, p. 187.

25. Jellinek, *The Paris Commune*, p. 419.

Chapter 2: Jack London's 'The Iron Heel'

1. Quoted by Philip S. Foner, ed., *Jack London, American Rebel* (New York: Citadel, 1947), p. 96.

2. Northrop Frye, *Anatomy of Criticism* (New York: Atheneum, 1969), pp. 308-12.

3. Foner, *Jack London*, p. 90.

4. Jack London, *The Iron Heel* (New York: Hill & Wang, 1957), p. 73.

5. Jack London, *Martin Eden* (New York: Review of Reviews, 1915), p. 327.

6. Joan London, *Jack London and His Times* (Seattle: University of Washington Press, 1968), p. 214.

7. Charmion London, *The Book of Jack London* (New York: Century, 1921), vol. 2, p. 43.

8. Ibid., vol. 1, p. viii.

9. Ibid., vol. 2, p. 43.

10. Anton Pannekoek, *Marxism and Darwinism* (Chicago: Charles H. Kerr, 1912), pp. 37-39.

11. Ibid., pp. 50-54.

12. Frederick Engels, *The Origin of the Family, Private Property, and the State* (Chicago: Charles H. Kerr, 1902), p. 215.

13. Bronislaw Malinowski, "War—Past, Present, and Future," *War as a Social Institution*, Jesse D. Clarkson and Thomas Č. Cochran, eds. (New York: AMS Press, 1966), p. 23.

14. M.F. Ashley Montagu, "The New Litany of 'Innate Depravity,' or Original Sin Revisited," in *Man and Aggression*, M. F. Ashley Montagu, ed. (New York: Oxford University Press, 1968), pp. 15-16.

15. Quoted in Morton Mintz and Jerry S. Cohen, *America, Inc.* (New York: Dial, 1971), p. 16.

16. Quoted in *American Society, Inc.*, Maurice Zeitlin, ed. (Chicago: Markham, 1970), p. 18.

17. Ferdinand Lundberg, *The Rich and the Super-Rich* (New York: Lyle Stuart, 1968), p. 19.

18. Richard Parker, *The Myth of the Middle Class* (New York: Liveright, 1972), p. 123.

19. Ibid., pp. 130-31.

20. Paul A. Samuelson, *Economics: An Introductory Analysis*, 7th ed. (New York: McGraw-Hill, 1967), p. 112. Quoted by Parker, p. 6.

21. Karl Marx and Friedrich Engels, "Manifesto of the Communist Party," *Basic Writings on Politics and Philosophy*, Lewis S. Feuer, ed. (New York: Doubleday, 1959), p. 31.

22. George Novack, "Can American Workers Make a Socialist Revolution?" *International Socialist Review* 30, no. 1, (1960), p. 45.

23. Quoted by Zeitlin, p. 511.

24. Abraham Ribicoff, *Congressional Record*, April 2, 1973, p. 10521.

25. *New York Times,* March 14, 1973, p. 43.

26. Paul Sweezy and Harry Magdoff, "Economic Stagnation and Stagnation of Economics," *Monthly Review*, April 1971, p. 8.

27. V. I. Lenin, *Imperialism: The Highest Stage of Capitalism* (New York: International Publishers, 1939), p. 106.

28. *New York Times*, January 15, 1973, p. 1.

29. *New York Times*, May 22, 1968, p. 95.

30. Kenneth Keniston, "For Him, There Is No Exit From the Cellar," *New York Times,* February 20, 1976, p. 33.

31. Marx and Engels, *Basic Writings,* p. 19.

32. Marx and Engels, *Basic Writings,* p. 7.

33. Jack London, *The People of the Abyss* (New York: Garrett Press, 1970), pp. 7-8.

34. Marx and Engels, *Basic Writings,* p. 18.

35. Ibid., p. 15.

36. Ibid., p. 16.

37. V. I. Lenin, *The State and Revolution* (Moscow: Foreign Languages Publishing House, n.d.), pp. 65-66.

38. Robert B. Rigg, "Made in USA," *Army,* January 1968, pp. 24-28.

Introduction to Section II

1. Moshe Lewin, *Lenin's Last Struggle* (New York: Pantheon, 1968), p. 4.

2. *Pravda*, April 4, 1923. Quoted by C. L. R. James, *World Revolution, 1917-1936* (London: Martin Secker and Warburg, 1937), p. 132.

3. Leon Trotsky, *Europe and America* (New York: Pathfinder Press, 1971), p. 61.

4. Isaac Deutscher, *Stalin: A Political Biography* (New York: Oxford University Press, 1967), p. 568.

5. *Europe and America*, p. 28.

6. Ibid., p. 15.

7. Ibid., p. 60.

8. Ibid., p. 31.

9. Ibid., p. 32.

10. Ibid., p. 29.

11. Trotsky, *The Revolution Betrayed* (New York: Doubleday, Doran, 1937), pp. 2-3.

Chapter 3: André Malraux's 'Man's Fate'

1. Alfred Kazin, *Starting Out in the Thirties* (Boston: Little, Brown, 1965), pp. 20-21.

2. Quoted by George Novack, ed., *Existentialism versus Marxism* (New York: Dell, 1966), p. 8.

3. Joseph Frank, *The Widening Gyre* (New Brunswick, N.J.: Rutgers University Press, 1963), p. 106.

4. David Wilkinson, *Malraux—An Essay in Political Criticism* (Cambridge: Harvard University Press, 1967), p. 16.

5. Robert Payne, *A Portrait of André Malraux* (Englewood Cliffs, N.J.: Prentice-Hall, 1970), p. 12.

6. Pierre Galante, *Malraux* (New York: Cowles Book Co., 1971), pp. 48-49.

7. André Malraux, *Man's Fate* (New York: Random House, 1961), p. 267.

8. Harold R. Isaacs, *The Tragedy of the Chinese Revolution* (Stanford: Stanford University Press, 1951), pp. 160-61.

9. Ibid., p. 161.

10. Ibid., p. 160.

11. Ibid., p. 162.

12. André Malraux, *The Walnut Trees of Altenburg* (London: John Lehmann, 1952), p. 222.

13. H. A. Mason, "André Malraux and His Critics," *Scrutiny* 14 (1947), p. 168.

14. Burning alive is scarcely more horrible than such other forms of execution as disembowlment actually used by the Chiang Kai-shek who was blessed by the Christian missionaries and other apologists for imperialism and who, it has been estimated, killed at least one million persons in five years of rounding up victims. Cf. Harold R. Isaacs, ed., *Five Years of Kuomintang Reaction* (Shanghai, 1932).

15. André Malraux, *The Conquerors* (Boston: Beacon Press, 1956), p. 61.

16. Novack, *Existentialism versus Marxism*, p. 318.

17. Ibid., pp. 519-20.

18. Isaac Deutscher, *The Prophet Armed* (New York: Oxford University Press, 1954), p. 54.

19. Novack, *Existentialism versus Marxism*, p. 328.

20. Ernest Mandel and George Novack, *The Marxist Theory of Alienation: Three Essays* (New York: Pathfinder, 1973), p. 28.

21. Ibid., p. 29.

22. Ibid.

23. Ibid., p. 30.

24. Ibid., pp. 38-39.

25. George Novack, "Marxism and Existentialism: Are the Two Compatible?" *International Socialist Review* 26 (1965), p. 60.

Chapter 4: Ignazio Silone's 'Fontamara'

1. Ignazio Silone, *Emergency Exit* (New York: Harper & Row, 1968), p. 147.

2. Ibid., p. 64.

3. Ignazio Silone, *Fontamara* (New York: Dell, 1961), p. 7.

4. Ibid., pp. 7-8.

5. Isaac Deutscher, *Ironies of History: Essays on Contemporary Communism* (Oxford University Press, 1976), p. 108.

6. *Emergency Exit,* p. 1.

7. The story, with a Jewish worker protagonist, is also told by I. L. Peretz in "Bontsha the Silent," which is based on a Yiddish folk tale. The Jews of Eastern Europe and the peasants of southern Italy received solace from the same wry fable.

8. Edward C. Banfield, *The Moral Basis of a Backward Society* (Glencoe, Ill.: Free Press, 1958), p. 10.

9. Ibid., p. 164.

10. Joel S. Migdal, *Peasants, Politics, and Revolution: Pressures Toward Political and Social Change in the Third World* (Princeton: Princeton University Press, 1974), p. 4.

11. Ibid., pp. 229-230.

12. Ibid., p. 232.

13. Deutscher, *The Prophet Outcast* (New York: Oxford University Press, 1963), p. 520.

14. Leon Trotsky, *The Transitional Program for Socialist Revolution,* 3rd ed. (New York: Pathfinder Press, 1977), p. 135.

15. Geoffrey Barraclough, "The Great World Crisis I," *New York Review of Books,* January 23, 1975, pp. 26-27. Cf. the statements by the leading experts on global food problems of sixteen countries at a conference sponsored by the New York Academy of Sciences. According to the *New York Times* (October 13, 1976, p. 1) "economic and political constraints rather than a lack of farming know-how were cited by many speakers as the major factors causing malnutrition and famines." Cf. also the report of an international team of economists led by the Nobel Prize winner Wassily Leontief, which asserted that a three-year study showed that "world resources will be sufficient to support a growing population and higher living standards, without inevitable environmental damage" and that "the limits to growth are not physical, . . . but rather political and institutional deficiencies in the developing countries" (*New York Times,* December 3, 1976).

Chapter 5: Richard Wright's 'Native Son'

1. Quoted by Dan McCall, *The Example of Richard Wright* (New York: Harcourt, Brace & World, 1969), p. 191.

2. *Sunday Worker,* New York, April 14, 1940.

3. Richard Wright, *Native Son* (New York: Harper & Brothers, 1940), pp. 97-98.

4. Irving Howe, *A World More Attractive* (New York: Horizon, 1963), p. 104.

5. Ibid., p. 104.

6. Alfred Kazin, *On Native Grounds* (New York: Harcourt, 1942), p. 387.

7. *Sunday Worker,* April 14, 1940.

8. Edwin Berry Burgum, *The Novel and the World's Dilemma* (New York: Russell, 1963), p. 238; James Baldwin, *Notes of a Native Son* (New York: Dial Press, 1963), p. 42; McCall, *The Example of Richard Wright,* p. 93; Edward Margolies, *The Art of Richard Wright* (Carbondale: Southern Illinois University Press, 1969), p. 112.

9. Baldwin, *Notes of a Native Son,* p. 47.

10. Robert Bone, *The Negro Novel in America* (New Haven: Yale University Press, 1966), p. 151.

11. *A World More Attractive,* p. 104.

12. The theme of blindness was mentioned in Bone, *Negro Novel in America,* p. 147; James A. Emanuel, "Fever and Feeling: Notes on the Imagery in *Native Son,*" *Negro Digest,* 18 Dec. 1968, pp. 20-21; and Russel Carl Brignano, *Richard Wright: An Introduction to the Man and His Works* (Pittsburgh: University of Pittsburgh Press, 1969), p. 117; the theme of the white world as a great natural force, in Bone, p. 147 and Brignano, p. 117; the image of the wall or curtain behind which Bigger withdraws, in Emanuel, pp. 22-24; the theme of Bigger's killing as a means of liberation, in Bone, p. 146, McCall, pp. 87, 100, Margolies, pp. 116-17, Brignano, p. 147. None of these takes note, however, of how these themes and images are gathered up in Max's speech.

13. Bone, p. 150.

14. Introduction to Frantz Fanon, *The Wretched of the Earth* (New York: Grove, 1966), pp. 16-18.

Introduction to Section III

1. Dick Roberts, *Capitalism in Crisis* (New York: Pathfinder Press, 1975), p. 29.

2. Deutscher, *The Prophet Outcast,* p. 518.

3. Ibid.

4. Milovan Djilas, *Conversations with Stalin* (New York: Harcourt, Brace & World, 1962), pp. 8, 74, 82.

5. *United States Relations with China,* pp. 136-40. Quoted by Nahuel Moreno, "The Chinese and Indochinese Revolutions," *Fifty Years of World Revolution (1917-1967),* ed. Ernest Mandel (New York: Merit, 1968), p. 164.

6. Ibid.

7. See the eyewitness account of Jack Belden, *China Shakes the World* (New York: Monthy Review Press, 1970), pp. 169-70.

8. Deutscher, *Ironies of History,* p. 118.

9. Ibid., p. 120.

10. Trotsky's words, cited above, p. 56.

11. Rosa Luxemburg, *The Accumulation of Capital* (New York: Monthly Review Press, 1964), p. 466.

Chapter 6: Arthur Koestler's 'Darkness at Noon'

1. Roy Medvedev, *Let History Judge* (New York: Knopf, 1971), p. 180.

2. *Times Literary Supplement* (London), December 21, 1940, p. 641.

3. Arthur Koestler, *The Invisible Writing* (Boston: Beacon, 1954), p. 394.

4. Ibid., p. 155.

5. Warren Lerner, *Karl Radek, The Last Internationalist* (Stanford: Stanford University Press, 1970), pp. 18, 19, 20, 168, 174, 175.

6. Alexander Orlov, *the Secret History of Stalin's Crimes* (New York: Random House, 1953), p. 197.

7. Lerner, *Karl Radek*, p. 167.

8. *The Invisible Writing*, p. 348.

9. *Darkness At Noon* (New York: Bantam, 1968), p. 46.

10. *The Invisible Writing*, p. 349.

11. Ibid., p. 359.

12. Ibid., p. 360.

13. Ibid., p. 361.

14. Ibid., p. 103.

15. Ibid., p. 360.

16. Ibid., p. 358.

17. Ibid.

18. Leon Trotsky, *Their Morals and Ours* (New York: Merit Publishers, 1969), p. 38.

19. Ibid., p. 37.

20. Medvedev, *Let History Judge*, pp. 183-84.

21. Trotsky, *Their Morals and Ours*, p. 16.

22. Charles E. Mee, Jr., *Meeting at Potsdam* (New York: M. Evans, 1975), p. 22.

23. Grigori Zinoviev, "In Defense of Party Democracy," *International Socialist Review* 33, no. 4 (1972), 43.

24. Medvedev, *Let History Judge*, pp. 183-84.

25. "The Eighteenth Brumaire of Louis Bonaparte," *Basic Writings on Politics and Philosophy*, p. 320.

26. George Katkov, *The Trial of Bukharin* (New York: Stein and Day, 1969), p. 94.

27. *Speech of Nikita Khrushchev Before a Closed Session of the XXth Congress of the Communist Party of the Soviet Union on February 25, 1956* (Washington: U. S. Government Printing Office, 1957), p. 33.

28. Robert C. Tucker and Stephen F. Cohen, eds., *The Great Purge Trial* (New York: Grosset & Dunlap, 1965), p. xxix.

29. Léon Blum, *The Moscow Trial and the Labour & Socialist International* (London, 1931), p. 31.

30. Medvedev, *Let History Judge*, p. 177.

31. Stephen F. Cohen, *Bukharin and the Bolshevik Revolution* (New York: Knopf, 1973), pp. 377-80; Tucker in his introduction to *The Great Purge Trial*, p. xli and n. and pp. xlii-xlviii; Medvedev, p. 187; Orlov, pp. 280-81.

32. *The Invisible Writing*, p. 27.

33. Trotsky, *Their Morals and Ours*, pp. 24-25.

34. Richard Wright, "Introduction: How 'Bigger' Was Born," *Native Son*, (Harper & Row, 1940), p. xxviii.

35. In order to explain the porter's attachment to Rubashov, Koestler has him recall his former commander as one who "knew how to swear in such a pleasant way that it was a joy" (pp. 197-98). Such earthiness, however, is entirely foreign to the Rubashov he has drawn. But Koestler did not wish to show Rubashov inspiring his men, as Trotsky did in his speeches at the front, by giving them a vision of the historic significance of their fight.

Chapter 7: Norman Mailer's 'The Naked and the Dead'

1. Norman Mailer, *Advertisements for Myself* (New York: G. P. Putnam's Sons, 1959), p. 339.

2. Alfred Vagts, *A History of Militarism* (New York: Norton, 1959), p. 35.

3. *The Naked and the Dead* (New York: New American Library, n.d.), pp. 338-39.

4. Norman Podhoretz, "Norman Mailer: The Embattled Vision," *Partisan Review* 26 (1959), p. 376.

5. Ibid.

6. Tony Tanner, *The City of Words* (London: Jonathan Cape, 1971), p. 351.

7. Trotsky, *In Defense of Marxism*, p. 175.

8. Leon Trotsky, *The Struggle Against Fascism in Germany* (New York: Pathfinder Press, 1971), pp. 121-22.

9. *International Press Correspondence*, October 9, 1924. Quoted by C. L. R. James, *World Revolution*, p. 310. This continued to be the slogan of the German Communist Party until Hitler came to power. Cf. James, p. 353.

10. James, *World Revolution*, pp. 334-35.

Chapter 8: George Orwell's '1984'

1. George Orwell, *Homage to Catalonia* (New York: Harcourt, Brace, 1952), pp. 104-5.

2. Orwell, *Collected Essays, Journalism, and Letters* (New York: Harcourt, 1968), vol. 1, p. 269.

3. *Collected Essays, Journalism, and Letters*, vol. 4, p. 502.

4. Notably William Steinhoff, *George Orwell and the Origins of 1984* (Ann Arbor: University of Michigan, 1974), which is the most complete

examination of the sources of *1984.*

5. *Collected Essays, Journalism, and Letters,* vol. 4, p. 165.
6. Ibid., 165-80.
7. Ibid., 321, 322.
8. *1984* (New York: New American Library, 1961), pp. 222, 223.
9. *Collected Essays, Journalism, and Letters,* vol. 2, p. 25.
10. Ibid., 137.
11. *Collected Essays, Journalism, and Letters,* vol. 4, p. 370.
12. Ibid., 318.
13. Howe, *Politics and the Novel,* pp. 246-47.
14. James Burnham, *The Managerial Revolution* (Bloomington: Indiana University Press, 1960), p. 8.
15. Trotsky, *The Revolution Betrayed,* p. 3.
16. *Collected Essays, Journalism, and Letters,* vol. 3, p. 235.
17. *Collected Essays, Journalism, and Letters,* vol. 4, pp. 169, 178.
18. Ibid., 177-78.
19. Ibid., 322.
20. Trotsky, *In Defense of Marxism,* p. 180.
21. *Collected Essays, Journalism, and Letters,* vol. 4, p. 165.
22. Ibid., 24-25.
23. Stephen Spender, *The Creative Element* (London: Hamish Hamilton, 1953), p. 132.
24. Raymond Williams, *George Orwell* (New York: Viking Press, 1971), pp. 78-80.
25. Orwell, *The Road to Wigan Pier* (New York: Harcourt, Brace & World, 1958), p. 157.
26. Ibid., p. 188.
27. Ibid., p. 158.
28. Ibid., pp. 148-49.
29. *Collected Essays, Journalism, and Letters,* vol. 4, p. 325.
30. Deutscher, *Stalin,* pp. 580-85.
31. G. William Domhoff, *Who Rules America?* (Englewood Cliffs, N.J.: Prentice-Hall, 1967), pp. 49-50.
32. Erich Fromm, *The Sane Society* (New York: Holt, Rinehart and Winston, 1960), p. 5.
33. Paul A. Baran and Paul M. Sweezy, *Monopoly Capital* (New York: Monthly Review Press, 1966), pp. 336-67.
34. George Woodcock, *The Crystal Spirit: A Study of George Orwell* (Boston: Little, Brown, 1966), p. 9.

Introduction to Section IV

1. See Deutscher's review of his prognostications in various periodical articles and in *Russia after Stalin,* written immediately after Stalin's death; see also his response to objections made to those prognostications at the time: "A Reply to My Critics," *Heretics and Renegades and Other Essays* (London: Hamish Hamilton, 1955), pp. 191-209. It seems clear,

however, that the liberalization to the point of a restoration of Soviet democracy that Deutscher thought might occur through a combination of reforms from above and pressure from below will not occur without the political revolution for which Trotsky had called.

2. Ernest Mandel, *Marxist Economic Theory* (New York: Monthly Review Press, 1970), vol. 2, p. 532: "The dilemma confronting the state in declining capitalism is *the choice between crisis and inflation.* The former cannot be avoided without intensifying the latter. At first sight, the 'moderate' inflation caused in the capitalist countries of the West by the increase in unproductive expenditure does not appear to threaten the future of capitalist economy. . . . This is, however, a short-sighted view." To combat recession, Mandel predicted, capitalist regimes would employ various kinds of "anti-cyclical" techniques, but, caught on the horns of their dilemma, "hesitatingly, with many misgivings."

Chapter 9: Boris Pasternak's 'Doctor Zhivago'

1. Edmund Wilson, *The Bit Between My Teeth* (New York: Farrar, Straus and Giroux, 1965), p. 446. Cf. Frank Kermode, *Puzzles and Epiphanies* (London: Routledge & Kegan Paul, 1962), p. 108: "an accession to that small group of novels by which all others are, ultimately, judged" and V. S. Pritchett, "In the Great Tradition," *New Statesman,* September 13, 1958, p. 354: "the first work of genius to come out of Russia since the revolution, or at any rate since the Stalinist repression."

2. Ralph E. Matlow, "A Visit with Pasternak," *Nation,* September 12, 1959, p. 135.

3. Boris Pasternak, *Doctor Zhivago* (New York: New American Library, n.d.), p. 60.

4. John Herman Randall, Jr., *The Making of the Modern Mind* (New York: Houghton Mifflin, 1968), p. 423. For an excellent synoptic description of romantic idealism that speaks of all of the above-mentioned themes, see Randall, pp. 415-24. Cf. also René Wellek, "Romanticism in Literary History," *Comparative Literature,* I (1949), 1-23, 147-72, esp. 150-64.

5. Ernst Fischer, *The Necessity of Art: A Marxist Approach* (Harmondsworth, England: Penguin Books, 1971), pp. 58-59.

6. William Hazlitt, *Lectures on the English Poets, and the English Comic Writers* (London: Bell & Daldy, 1869), p. 214.

7. *The Prelude,* Book VII, 11. 512-43.

8. "Preface to *Lyrical Ballads,*" *Literary Criticism,* ed. Lionel Trilling (New York: Holt, Rinehart and Winston, 1970), p. 148.

9. "The Tables Turned."

10. "Lines Written in Early Spring."

11. "Tintern Abbey."

12. William Weidle, "The Poetry and Prose of Boris Pasternak," *Pasternak: Modern Judgements,* ed. Donald Davie and Angela Livingstone (New York: Macmillan, 1969), p. 120.

13. Nils Äke Nillson, "Pasternak: 'We Are the Guests of Existence,'" *The Reporter,* November 27, 1958, p. 34.

14. Pasternak, "Three Letters," *Encounter,* August 1960, pp. 4-5. Pasternak apologized for his English. His diction is sometimes imprecise or unidiomatic, but his meaning is clear.

15. Arnold Kettle, *An Introduction to the English Novel* (London: Hutchinson House, 1953), vol. 2, p. 87.

16. *Pasternak: Modern Judgements,* p. 194.

17. Matlow, "Visit with Pasternak," p. 135.

18. *Pasternak: Modern Judgements,* pp. 251-52.

19. Ibid., pp. 253-54.

20. Robert Payne, *The Three Worlds of Boris Pasternak* (London: Robert Hale, 1961), p. 104.

21. *Pasternak: Modern Judgements,* p. 323.

22. Quoted by Payne, p. 105.

23. Robert Conquest, *The Pasternak Affair: Courage of Genius* (Philadelphia: J. B. Lippincott, 1962), p. 34.

24. *Pasternak: Modern Judgements,* pp. 104-7.

25. Ibid., p. 107.

26. Pasternak, "Translating Shakespeare," *The Twentieth Century* 164 (1958), p. 216.

27. Larissa Reisner, "Svyazhsk," *Leon Trotsky: The Man and His Work* (New York: Merit Publishers, 1969), p. 114.

Chapter 10: Alexander Solzhenitsyn's 'Cancer Ward'

1. *A Lenten Letter to Pimen, Patriarch of all Russia,* ed. Theofanis G. Staurou (Minneapolis: Burgess, 1972); *The Nobel Lecture on Literature* (New York: Harper and Row, 1972); "Letter Proposing Andrei D. Sakharov for the 1973 Nobel Peace Prize," *New York Times,* September 15, 1973, p. 31; *Letter to the Soviet Leaders* (New York: Harper and Row, 1974).

2. Cf., e.g., Paul Avrich, "Solzhenitsyn's Political Philosophy," *Nation,* October 19, 1974, pp. 373-77.

3. Ibid., p. 373.

4. Leopold Labedz, ed., *Solzhenitsyn: A Documentary Record* (London: Penguin, 1970), p. 97.

5. Ibid., pp. 97-98.

6. *Cancer Ward* (New York: Bantam, 1969), p. 520.

7. Labedz, p. 38.

8. Ibid., p. 156.

9. *Times Literary Supplement* (London), October 4, 1974.

10. David Burg and George Peifer, *Solzhenitsyn* (New York: Stein and Day, 1972), p. 239.

11. Lenin, *On Literature and Art* (Moscow: Progress Publishers, 1970), p. 52.

12. *Che Guevara Speaks: Selected Speeches and Writings,* ed. George

Lavan, (Pathfinder Press, 1967), p. 136.
13. Paul N. Siegel, ed., *Leon Trotsky on Literature and Art,* New York: Pathfinder Press, 1972).
14. Trotsky, *The Revolution Betrayed,* p. 89.
15. Ibid., pp. 89-92.
16. Ibid., p. 105.
17. *Che Guevara Speaks,* p. 137.
18. Trotsky, *The Revolution Betrayed,* p. 112.
19. Ibid., pp. 112-13.
20. *New York Times,* March 5, 1974, p. 9.
21. Ibid., July 10, 1975, p. 31.
22. Ibid., September 15, 1973, p. 31.
23. Ibid.

Index